Henry Mintzberg
McGill University

Structure in Fives

DESIGNING EFFECTIVE ORGANIZATIONS

Prentice Hal

Library of Congress Cataloging in Publication Data

MINTZBERG, HENRY.
    Structure in fives.

    Bibliography: p.
    Includes index.
    1. Organization. I. ⌐ ...
HD31.M4572 1983   6: ⌐'02   82–12329
ISBN 0-13-855479-X

To Tutyi

. . . beyond Adhocracy
(but still in the studio)

Editorial/production supervision and interior design: Esther S. Koehn
Cover design: 20/20 Services Inc., Mark Berghash
Manufacturing buyer: Robert Anderson

Printed in the United States of America

10 9 8 7 6 5 4

ISBN 0-13-855479-X

Prentice-Hall International (UK) Limited, London
Prentice-Hall of Australia Pty. Limited, Sydney
Prentice-Hall Canada Inc., Toronto
Prentice-Hall Hispanoamericana, S.A., Mexico
Prentice-Hall of India Private Limited, New Delhi
Prentice-Hall of Japan, Inc., Tokyo
Simon & Schuster Asia Pte. Ltd., Singapore
Editora Prentice-Hall do Brasil, Ltda., Rio de Janeiro

CONTENTS

A NOTE TO THE READER

What could be more important to the effective functioning of our organizations—from repair shops to automobile companies, police forces to national governments—than the design of their structures? Yet what do we really know about such design?

Ironically, we know a great deal, but not in a form accessible to those people who must create such designs—managers, staff specialists, and consultants. The vast literature on organizational structuring, much of it based on systematic empirical research, has largely escaped the practitioner, for two reasons. First, it is mostly contained in articles and books written in an academic style, for other researchers. Those practitioners willing to work through the jargon found that the orientation of such writings was more on what is than what should be; in other words, on what takes place in organizations rather than on how to design an effective organization. Second, despite the vastness of the literature and its many available insights, what it lacked was synthesis. The practioner could find these insights in no one place; he or she virtually had to wade through the entire range of literature to find out what it had to say. And even then, the synthesis was left to the reader. Contradictions abound in the research findings, with little real reconciliation even attempted. So whoever had the patience to go through all this literature was apt to emerge more confused than before he or she began.

In the mid-1970s, I set out to try to order this literature, to extract its key messages and—above all—to synthesize them into an integrated picture of the structuring of organizations. The result of almost three full years of effort was a book by that title, published by Prentice-Hall in 1979. That book containted 512 pages of very small type, but it satisfied my intentions: to synthesize the research literature on organizational structuring (it was subtitled, "A Synthesis of the Research") and to address the issues of what makes an organizational design effective. Since I had in mind as readers not only students and practitioners but also my academic colleagues, the book contained a thorough referencing of the evidence for each of the findings, sprinkled generously with quotations from the literature. The arguments were, in other words, supported as much as possible, so that the reader could also use the book as a reference text. Hence the 512 pages. Despite that length, the book has had a good deal of success, both from critics and in the marketplace, especially in university course adoptions.

In 1981, Ted Jursek of Prentice-Hall's Professional Book Program suggested that I redo the book to make it more convenient for practitioners. Essentially, this meant reducing its length considerably by removing most of the references and quotations while maintaining the basic line of argument, and tilting its orientation more toward the issue of designing an effective organization. This suggestion I took up enthusiastically, because I felt that the time I invested in the original book would be in good part wasted if the messages did not get directly to practitioners on a large scale. I was further encouraged by the reactions I had received from those practitioners who did read through the 512 pages, and by comments I received on my *Harvard Business Review* article, "Organization Design: Fashion or Fit?" a summary of the main points of the book, which appeared in the January–February 1981 issue. Clearly, if the full message was to get through to many busy practitioners, then something was needed between a 14-page summary article and a 512-page fully referenced book.

Hence *Structure in Fives: Designing Effective Organizations*. I trust that I have accomplished the objective: to present and, more important, to synthesize the messages from the research on what it takes to design an effective organization, presented in a form that will be read by managers, staff specialists, and consultants who are concerned with the structuring of organizations. The one thing I had to sacrifice was the referencing that supports each of the arguments. But the reader who requires this information, or who wishes to probe into the research that underlies any of the arguments, can easily find what he needs in *The Structuring of Organizations: A Synthesis of the Research* (Prentice-Hall, 1979). The general outline of that book (if not the specific chapters) follows this one, and it contains a very thorough index as well as a bibliography that numbers over 300 entries. That volume can be considered a companion to this one by those readers who wish to probe more deeply. (The only important addition to this book is some material at the end of the last chapter, on pages 294–96.)

In terms of how this book should be read, I like to think of it as a kind of banquet. I do not mean to comment on the quality of its offerings, only on the manner and order in which they must be taken. They cannot be consumed on the run, as a snack, nor can they be sampled at random, as at a buffet table. They are meant to be taken in the specific order presented.

Chapter 1 is designed to whet the reader's appetite, and also to prepare the palate for the offerings that follow—a kind of hors d'oeuvre, if you like. Two important concepts are introduced in Chapter 1 that serve as the foundation for all that follows.

In Chapters 2, 3, 4, and 5, the reader is given a taste of the main flavors of organization design, what we call the design parameters. This part of the book is largely in the form of analysis, not synthesis; that is, we are concerned here with delineating the basic elements of structural design, not with combining them. But by the end of Chapter 5, the reader should find these flavors beginning to blend. Chapter 6 also represents analysis, putting these design parameters into the context of various situational factors. In effect, a different set of flavors is introduced in this chapter, flavors that themselves will be seen to blend with the others.

Chapters 7–12 are the pièces de résistance of this banquet. Here, all the flavors of the earlier chapters are fully blended into five main dishes, called configurations, forming our synthesis. They are labeled Simple Structure, Machine Bureaucracy, Professional Bureaucracy, Divisionalized Form, and Adhocracy. In a sense, the first six chapters prepare the palate for the next six, which are the real reasons for this banquet. Chapter 7 introduces our configurations, each of which is then discussed in one of the subsequent chapters. A final chapter, entitled "Beyond Five"—a kind of *digestif*—considers some important relationships among our five configurations and looks beyond them.

Note that the main points of the book have been highlighted in boldface type (like this); taken together, these serve to summarize the central line of argument. This has not been done to encourage scanning—the meat between these bones is required for a full appreciation of these offerings—but simply to emphasize and summarize the key conclusions for the reader.

So there you have it. Bon appètit!

Henry Mintzberg

FOUNDATIONS OF ORGANIZATION DESIGN

Ms. Raku made pottery in her basement. That involved a number of distinct tasks—wedging clay, forming pots, tooling them when semidry, preparing and then applying the glazes, and firing the pots in the kiln. But the coordination of all these tasks presented no problem; she did them all herself.

The problem was her ambition and the attractiveness of her pots: the orders exceeded her production capacity. So she hired Miss Bisque, who was eager to learn pottery making. But this meant Ms. Raku had to divide up the work. Since the craft shops wanted pottery made by Ms. Raku, it was decided that Miss Bisque would wedge the clay and prepare the glazes, and Ms. Raku would do the rest. And this required coordination of the work—a small problem, in fact, with two people in a pottery studio: they simply communicated informally.

The arrangement worked well, so well that before long, Ms. Raku was again swamped with orders. More assistants were needed. But this time, foreseeing the day when they would be forming pots themselves, Ms. Raku decided to hire them right out of the local pottery school. So whereas it had taken some time to train Miss Bisque, the three new assistants knew exactly what to do at the outset and blended right in; even with five people, coordination presented no problem.

As two more assistants were added, however, coordination problems did arise. One day Miss Bisque tripped over a pail of glaze and broke five pots; another day, Ms. Raku opened the kiln to find that the hanging planters had all been glazed fuchsia by mistake. At this point, she realized that seven people in a small pottery studio could not coordinate all their work through the simple mechanism of informal communication. Making matters worse was the fact that Ms. Raku, now calling herself president of Ceramics Inc., was forced to spend more and more time with customers; indeed, these days she was more apt to be found in a Marimekko dress than a pair of jeans. So she named Miss Bisque studio manager; she was to occupy herself full-time with supervising and coordinating the work of the five producers of the pottery.

The firm continued to grow. Major changes again took place when a work-study analyst was hired. He recommended changes whereby each person performed only one task for one of the product lines (pots, ashtrays, hanging planters, and ceramic animals)—the first wedged, the second formed, the third tooled, and so on. Thus, production took the form of four assembly lines. Each person followed a set of standard instructions, worked out in advance to ensure the coordination of all their work. Of course, Ceramics Inc. no longer sold to craft shops; Ms. Raku would only accept orders by the gross, most of which came from chains of discount stores.

Ms. Raku's ambition was limitless, and when the chance came to diversify, she did. First ceramic tiles, then bathroom fixtures, finally clay bricks. The firm was subsequently partitioned into three divisions—consumer products, building products, and industrial products. From her office on the fifty-fifth story of the Pottery Tower, she coordinated the activities of the divisions by reviewing their performance each quarter of the year and taking personal action when their profit and growth figures dipped below those budgeted. It was while sitting at her desk one day going over these budgets that Ms. Raku gazed out at the surrounding skyscrapers and decided to rename her company "Ceramico."

Every organized human activity—from the making of pots to the placing of a man on the moon—gives rise to two fundamental and opposing requirements: the *division of labor* into various tasks to be performed, and the *coordination* of these tasks to accomplish the activity. **The structure of an organization can be defined simply as the sum total of the ways in which its labor is divided into distinct tasks and then its coordination is achieved among these tasks.**

How should that structure be designed? Is there one best way to design it? Or should its various elements—the several means to divide its labor and coordinate its tasks—be picked and chosen independently, the way a shopper selects vegetables at the market or a diner dishes at a buffet table?

For years the literature of management favored an affirmative answer to the first question. A good structure was one based on rules and a rigid hierarchy of authority with spans of control no greater than six. More recently, that literature has implicitly come to favor an affirmative answer to the second question. The organization designer has been expected to mix good doses of long-range planning, job enrichment, and matrix structure, among many other things.

This book rejects both these approaches in favor of a third. **The ele-**

ments of structure should be selected to achieve an internal consistency or harmony, as well as a basic consistency with the organization's situation—its size, its age, the kind of environment in which it functions, the technical systems it uses, and so on. Indeed, these situational factors are often "chosen" no less than are the elements of structure themselves. The organization's niche in its environment, how large it grows, the methods it uses to produce its products or services—all these are selected too. This leads us to the conclusion that both the design parameters and the situational factors should be clustered to create what we shall call *configurations*.

Depending on how the various choices are made, different configurations can, of course, be designed—in principle, a great number of them. But in practice, as we shall see, the number of them that are effective for most organizations may be far smaller. **The central theme of this book is that a limited number of these configurations explain most of the tendencies that drive effective organizations to structure themselves as they do. In other words, the design of an effective organizational structure—in fact, even the diagnosis of problems in many ineffective ones—seems to involve the consideration of only a few basic configurations.**

This is a book in fives. In this first chapter, we introduce a set of basic mechanisms used to achieve coordination among divided tasks. They number five. Later in this chapter, we develop a visual representation of the organization to help guide us through the book. This has five parts. As we move into the body of the book, we describe the various parameters of structural design. Among the most important of these is decentralization. We shall see that this can take five basic forms. Then, after discussing the situational factors, we introduce our basic configurations of structure and situation. These too number five. In fact, we shall discover that all these fives are not independent at all. They exist in fundamental interrelationships. Specifically, each of the configurations favors one of the forms of decentralization, and in each, one of the coordinating mechanisms and one of the parts of the organization tend to dominate. Does that mean that five is the magic number in the design of effective organizations?

Let us set aside the most interesting questions and get on with the more pragmatic ones. To set the underlying framework for this book, we need to introduce two concepts in this chapter. The first describes the basic mechanisms by which organizations achieve coordination. The second describes the organization itself, in terms of a set of interrelated parts.

Coordination in Fives

Recall that structure involves two fundamental requirements—the division of labor into distinct tasks, and the achievement of coordination among these tasks. In Ms. Raku's Ceramico, the division of labor—wedging, forming, tooling, glazing, firing—was dictated largely by the job to be done and the technical system available to do it. Coordination, however, proved to be a more complicated affair, involving various means. These can be referred to as *coordinating mechanisms*, although it should be noted that they are as much concerned with control and communication as with coordination.

Five coordinating mechanisms seem to explain the fundamental ways in which organizations coordinate their work: mutual adjustment, direct supervision, standardization of work processes, standardization of work outputs, and standardization of worker skills. These should be considered the most basic elements of structure, the glue that holds organizations together. Let us look at each of them briefly.

■   *Mutual adjustment* achieves the coordination of work by the simple process of informal communication. Under mutual adjustment, control of the work rests in the hands of the doers, as shown in Figure 1–1(a). Because it is such a simple coordinating mechanism, mutual adjustment is naturally used in the very simplest of organizations—for example, by two people in a canoe or a few in a pottery studio. Paradoxically, it is also used in the most complicated. Consider the organization charged with putting a man on the moon for the first time. Such an activity requires an incredibly elaborate division of labor, with thousands of specialists doing all kinds of specific jobs. But at the outset, no one can be sure exactly what needs to be done. That knowledge develops as the work unfolds. So in the final analysis, despite the use of other coordinating mechanisms, the success of the undertaking depends primarily on the ability of the specialists to adapt to each other along their uncharted route, not altogether unlike the two people in the canoe.

■   As an organization outgrows its simplest state—more than five or six people at work in a pottery studio, fifteen people paddling a war canoe—it tends to turn to a second coordinating mechanism. *Direct supervision* achieves coordination by having one person take responsibility for the work of others, issuing instructions to them and monitoring their actions, as indicated in Figure 1–1(b). In effect, one brain coordinates several hands, as in the case of the supervisor of the pottery studio or the caller of the stroke in the war canoe. Consider the structure of an American football team. Here the division of labor is quite sharp: eleven players are distinguished by the work they do, its location on the field, and even its physical requirements. The slim halfback stands behind the line of scrimmage and carries the ball; the squat tackle stands on the line and blocks. Mutual adjustments do not suffice to coordinate their work, so a field leader, called the quarterback, is named, and he coordinates their work by calling the plays.

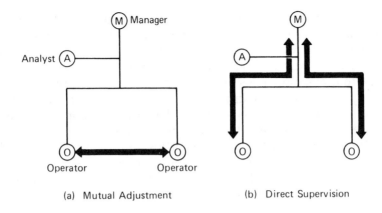

(a) Mutual Adjustment (b) Direct Supervision

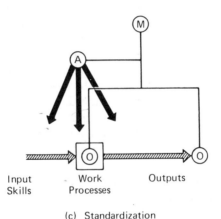

(c) Standardization

Figure 1-1. *The five coordinating mechanisms*

Work can also be coordinated without mutual adjustment or direct supervision. It can be *standardized*. Coordination is achieved on the drawing board, so to speak, before the work is undertaken. The workers on the automobile assembly line and the surgeons in the hospital operating room need not worry about coordinating with their colleagues under ordinary circumstances—they know exactly what to expect of them and proceed accordingly. Figure 1–1(c) shows three basic ways to achieve standardization in organizations. The work processes themselves, the outputs of the work, or the inputs to the work—the skills (and knowledge) of the people who do the work—can be designed to meet predetermined standards.

■ *Work processes* are *standardized* when the contents of the work are specified, or programmed. An example that comes to mind involves the assembly instructions provided with a child's toy. Here, the manufacturer

5

in effect standardizes the work process of the parent. ("Take the two-inch round-head Phillips screw and insert it into hole BX, attaching this to part XB with the lock washer and hexagonal nut, at the same time holding. . . .") Standardization can be carried to great lengths in organizations, as in the four assembly lines in Ceramics Limited, or the pie filler I once observed in a bakery who dipped a ladle into a vat of pie filling literally thousands of times every day—cherry, blueberry, or apple, it made no difference to him—and emptied the contents into a pie crust that came around on a turntable. Coordination of his work was accomplished by whoever designed that turntable. Of course, other work standards leave more room to maneuver: the purchasing agent may be required to get at least three bids on all orders over $10,000 but is otherwise left free to do his work as he sees fit.

- *Outputs* are *standardized* when the results of the work—for example, the dimensions of the product or the performance—are specified. Taxi drivers are not told how to drive or what route to take; they are merely informed where to deliver their fares. The wedger is not told how to prepare the clay, only to do so in four-pound lumps; the thrower on the wheel knows that those lumps will produce pots of a certain size (his own output standard). With outputs standardized, the coordination among tasks is predetermined, as in the book bindery that knows that the pages it receives from one place will fit perfectly into the covers it receives from another. Similarly, all the chiefs of the Ceramico divisions coordinated with headquarters in terms of performance standards. They were expected to produce certain profit and growth levels every quarter; how they did this was their own business.

- Sometimes neither the work nor its outputs can be standardized, yet coordination by standardization may still be required. The solution—used by Ms. Raku to hire assistants in the pottery studio—is to standardize the worker who comes to the work, if not the work itself or its outputs. *Skills (and knowledge)* are *standardized* when the kind of training required to perform the work is specified. Commonly, the worker is trained even before joining the organization. Ms. Raku hired potters from school, just as hospitals engage doctors. These institutions build right into the workers-to-be the work programs, as well as the bases of coordination. On the job, the workers appear to be acting autonomously, just as the good actor on the stage seems to be speaking extemporaneously. But in fact both have learned their lines well. So standardization of skills achieves indirectly what standardization of work processes or of work outputs does directly: it controls and coordinates the work. When an anesthesiologist and a surgeon meet in the operating room to remove an appendix, they need hardly communicate; by virtue of their training, they know exactly what to expect of each other. Their standardized skills take care of most of the coordination.[1]

These are our five coordinating mechanisms, and they seem to fall into a rough order. **As organizational work becomes more complicated, the favored means of coordination seems to shift from mutual adjustment to direct supervision to standardization, preferably of work processes, otherwise of outputs, or else of skills, finally reverting back to mutual adjustment.**

A person working alone has no great need for any of the mechanisms—coordination takes place simply, in one brain. Add a second person, however, and the situation changes significantly. Now coordination must be achieved across brains. Generally, people working side by side in small groups adapt to each other informally; mutual adjustment becomes the favored means of coordination. As the group gets larger, however, it becomes less able to coordinate informally. A need for leadership arises. Control of the work of the group passes to a single individual—in effect, back to a single brain that now regulates others; direct supervision becomes the favored coordinating mechanism.

As the work becomes more involved, another major transition tends to occur—toward standardization. When the tasks are simple and routine, the organization is tempted to rely on the standardization of the work processes themselves. But more complex work may preclude this, forcing the organization to turn to standardization of the outputs—specifying the results of the work but leaving the choice of process to the worker. In very complex work, on the other hand, the outputs often cannot be standardized either, and so the organization must settle for standardizing the skills of the worker, if possible. Should, however, the divided tasks of the organization prove impossible to standardize, it may be forced to return full cycle, to favor the simplest yet most adaptable coordinating mechanism— mutual adjustment. As noted earlier, sophisticated problem solvers facing extremely complicated situations must communicate informally if they are to accomplish their work.

Our discussion up to this point implies that under specific conditions, an organization will favor one coordinating mechanism over the others. It also suggests that the five are somewhat substitutable; the organization can replace one with another. These suggestions should not, however, be taken to mean that any organization can rely on a single coordinating mechanism. Most, in fact, mix all five. At the very least, a certain amount of direct supervision and mutual adjustment is always required, no matter

[1]The same can apparently be said about much more complex operations. Observation of one five-hour open-heart surgical procedure indicated that there was almost no informal communication between the cardiovascular surgeons and the anesthesiologist (Gosselin, 1978).

what the reliance on standardization. Contemporary organizations simply cannot exist without leadership and informal communication, even if only to override the rigidities of standardization. In the most automated (that is, fully standardized) factory, machines break down, employees fail to show up for work, schedules must be changed at the last minute. Supervisors must intervene, and workers must be free to deal with unexpected problems.

This favoring and mixing of the coordinating mechanisms is also reflected in the literature of management across this century. The early literature focused on *formal structure*, the documented, official relationship among members of the organization. Two schools of thought dominated the literature until the 1950s, one preoccupied with direct supervision, the other with standardization.

The "principles of management" school, fathered by Henri Fayol, who first recorded his ideas in 1916, and popularized in the English-speaking world by Luther Gulick and Lyndall Urwick, was concerned primarily with formal authority—in effect, with the role of direct supervision in the organization. These writers popularized such terms as *unity of command* (the notion that a "subordinate" should have only a single "superior"), *scalar chain* (the direct line of this command from chief executive through successive superiors and subordinates to the workers), and *span of control* (the number of subordinates reporting to a single superior).

The second school really includes two groups that, from our point of view, promoted the same issue—the standardization of work throughout the organization. Both groups were established at the turn of the century by outstanding researchers, one on either side of the Atlantic Ocean. In America, Frederick Taylor led the "Scientific Management" movement, whose main preoccupation was the programming of the contents of operating work—that of pig-iron handlers, coal shovelers, and the like. In Germany, Max Weber wrote of machinelike, or "bureaucratic" structures where activities were formalized by rules, job descriptions, and training.

And so for about half this century, organization structure meant a set of official, standardized work relationships built around a tight system of formal authority.

With the publication in 1939 of Roethlisberger and Dickson's interpretation of a series of experiments carried out on workers at the Western Electric Hawthorne plant came the realization that other things were going on in organizational structures. Specifically, their observations about the presence of *informal structure*—unofficial relationships within the work group—constituted the simple realization that mutual adjustment serves as an important coordinating mechanism in all organizations. This led to the establishment of a third school of thought in the 1950s and 1960s, originally called "human relations," whose proponents sought to demonstrate by empirical research that reliance on formal structure—specifically, on the mechanisms of direct supervision and standardization—was at best misguided, at worst dangerous to the psychological health of the worker.

More recent research has shifted away from these two extreme positions. In the last decade, there has been a tendency to look at structure more comprehensively; to study, for example, the relationships between the formal and informal, between direct supervision and standardization on the one hand and mutual adjustment on the other. These studies have demonstrated that **formal and informal structures are intertwined and often indistinguishable.** Some have shown, for example, how direct supervision and standardization have sometimes been used as *informal* devices to gain power, and conversely, how devices to enhance mutual adjustment have been designed into the *formal* structure. They have also conveyed the important message that formal structure often reflects official recognition of naturally occurring behavior patterns. Formal structures evolve in organizations much as roads do in forests—along well-trodden paths.

The Organization in Five Parts

Organizations are structured to capture and direct systems of flows and to define interrelationships among different parts. These flows and interrelationships are hardly linear in form, with one element following neatly after another. Yet words must take such a linear form. Hence, it sometimes becomes very difficult to describe the structuring of organizations exclusively in words. These must be supplemented with images. Thus we rely heavily on diagrams in this book. In fact, we require a basic diagram to represent the organization itself, a diagram that can be played with in various ways to show the different things that can happen in organizations and the different forms that organizations themselves can take.

We can develop such a diagram by considering the different component parts of the organization and the people contained in each. At the base of the organization can be found its *operators,* those people who perform the basic work of producing the products and rendering the services. They form the *operating core.* As we noted earlier, in the simplest of organizations, the operators are largely self-sufficient, coordinating through mutual adjustment. The organization needs little more than an operating core.

But as the organization grows and adopts a more complex division of labor among its operators, the need for direct supervision increases. It becomes mandatory to have a full-time manager who sits at what we shall call the *strategic apex.* And as the organization is further elaborated, more managers are needed—not only managers of operators but also managers of managers. A *middle line* is created, a hierarchy of authority between operating core and strategic apex. Note that the introduction of managers gives rise to a new form of division of labor, of the *administrative* type—between those who do the basic work and those who administer it in one form or another.

As the process of elaboration continues, the organization may turn increasingly to standardization as a means of coordinating its work. The responsibility for much of this standardization falls on another group of people, whom we shall call the analysts. They too perform administrative duties, but of a different nature—often called "staff." These analysts form what we shall call the *technostructure*, outside the hierarchy of line authority. Here, then we have a second administrative division of labor—between those who do (or supervise) the work and those who standardize it. In fact, by substituting standardization for direct supervision—a process known as the "institutionalization" of the manager's job—the analysts weaken the control that managers are able to exercise over the operators' work, much as the earlier substitution of direct supervision for mutual adjustment weakened the operators' control over their own work.

Finally, as it grows, the organization tends to add staff units of a different nature, not to effect standardization but to provide indirect services to itself, anything from a cafeteria or mailroom to a legal counsel or public relations department. We call these people and the part of the organization they form the *support staff*.

This gives us five parts of the organization. As shown in Figure 1–2, we have the operating core at the base joined to the strategic apex on top by the middle line, with the technostructure and support staff off to either side. This figure will serve as the theme diagram of this book, its "logo," if you like. We shall use this figure repeatedly to make our points about structure, sometimes overlaying flows on it, sometimes distorting it to show distinctive characteristics of particular kinds of organizations.

Our logo shows a small strategic apex connected by a flaring middle line to a large, flat operating core. These three parts of the organization are shown in one uninterrupted sequence to indicate that they are typically connected through a single line of formal authority. The technostructure and the support staff are shown off to either side to indicate that they are separate from this main line of authority and influence the operating core only indirectly.

It might be useful at this point to relate this scheme to some terms commonly used in organizations. The term *middle management*, although seldom carefully defined, generally seems to include all members of the organization not at the strategic apex or in the operating core. In our scheme, therefore, "middle management" would comprise three distinct groups—the middle-line managers, the analysts, and the support staff. To avoid confusion, however, the term *middle level* will be used here to describe these three groups together, the term *management* being reserved for the managers of the strategic apex and the middle line.

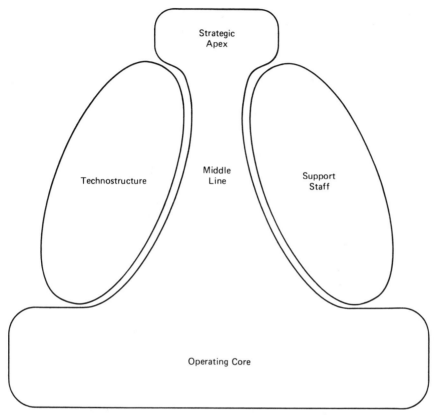

Figure 1-2. *The five basic parts of the organization*

The word *staff* should also be put into this context. In the early literature, the term was used in contrast to *line;* in principle, line positions had
formal authority to make decisions, staff positions did not; they merely
advised those who did. As we shall see later, this distinction between line
and staff holds up in some kinds of structures (at least for the analytic staff,
not the support staff) and breaks down in others. Nevertheless, the distinction between line and staff is of some use to us, and we shall retain the
terms here though in somewhat modified form. *Staff* will be used to refer to
the technostructure *and* the support staff, those groups shown on either
side of our theme diagram. *Line* will refer to the central part of the diagram,
those managers in the flow of formal authority from the strategic apex to
the operating core. Note that this definition does not mention the power to
decide or advise. As we shall see, the support staff does not primarily
advise; it has distinct functions to perform and decisions to make, although
these relate only indirectly to the functions of the operating core. The chef
in the plant cafeteria may be engaged in a production process, but it has

nothing to do with the basic manufacturing process. Similarly, the technostructure's power to advice sometimes amounts to the power to decide, but that is outside the flow of formal authority that oversees the operating core.[2]

Let us now take a closer look at each of the five parts of the organization.

The operating core

The operating core of the organization encompasses those members—the operators—who perform the basic work related directly to the production of products and services. The operators perform four prime functions: (1) They *secure the inputs* for production. For example, in a manufacturing firm, the purchasing department buys the raw materials, and the receiving department takes them in the door. (2) They *transform the inputs into outputs.* Some organizations transform raw materials—for example, by chopping down trees and converting them to pulp and then paper. Others transform individual parts into complete units—for example, by assembling typewriters—and still others transform information or people, by writing consulting reports, educating students, cutting hair, or curing illness. (3) They *distribute the outputs*—for example, by selling and physically distributing what comes out of the transformation process. (4) They *provide direct support* to the input, transformation, and output functions—for example, by performing maintenance on the operating machines and inventorying the raw materials.

Standardization is generally carried the furthest in the operating core, in order to protect the operations from external disturbance. How far, of course, depends on the work being done. Assemblers in automobile factories and professors in universities are both operators, although the work of the former is far more standardized than that of the latter.

The operating core is the heart of every organization, the part that produces the essential outputs that keep it alive. But except for the very smallest ones, organizations need *administrative* components too. The ad-

---

[2]There are other, completely different uses of the term *staff* that we are avoiding here. The military "chiefs of staff" are really managers of the strategic apex; the hospital "staff" physicians are really operators. Also, the introduction of the line/staff distinction here is not meant to sweep all its problems under the rug, only to distinguish those involved directly from those involved peripherally with the operating work of organizations. By our definition, the production and sales functions in the typical manufacturing firm are clearly line activities, marketing research and public relations clearly staff. To debate whether engineering is line or staff—does it serve the operating core indirectly, or is it an integral part of it?—depends on the importance one imputes to engineering in a particular firm. There is a gray area between line and staff: Where it is narrow, for many organizations, we retain the distinction; where it is wide, later we shall explicitly discard it.

ministrative component comprises the strategic apex, middle line, and technostructure.

The strategic apex

At the other end of the organization lies the strategic apex. Here are found those people charged with *overall* responsibility for the organization—the chief executive officer (whether called president, superintendent, or pope), and any other top-level managers whose concerns are global. Included here as well are those who provide direct support to the top managers—their secretaries, assistants, and so on.[3] In some organizations, the strategic apex includes the executive committee (because its mandate is global even if its members represent specific interests); in others, it includes what is known as the chief executive office—two or three people who share the job of chief executive. **The strategic apex is charged with ensuring that the organization serve its mission in an effective way, and also that it serve the needs of those who control or otherwise have power over the organization** (such as its owners, government agencies, unions of the employees, pressure groups).

This entails three sets of duties. One already discussed is that of direct supervision. To the extent that the organization relies on this mechanism of coordination, it is the managers of the strategic apex (as well as the middle line) who effect it. They allocate resources, issue work orders, authorize major decisions, resolve conflicts, design and staff the organization, monitor employee performance, and motivate and reward employees.

Second is the management of the organization's boundary conditions—its relations with its environment. The managers of the strategic apex must spend a good deal of their time informing influential people in the environment about the organization's activities, developing high-level contacts for the organization and tapping these for information, negotiating major agreements with outside parties, and sometimes serving as figureheads as well, carrying out ceremonial duties such as greeting important customers. (Someone once defined the manager, only half in jest, as that person who sees the visitors so that everyone else can get their work done.)

The third set of duties relates to the development of the organization's strategy. Strategy may be viewed as a mediating force between the organization and its environment. Strategy formulation therefore involves the interpretation of the environment and the development of consistent patterns in streams of organizational decisions ("strategies") to deal with

---

[3]Our subsequent discussion will focus only on the managers of the strategic apex, the work of the latter group being considered an integral part of their own.

it. Thus, in managing the boundary conditions of the organization, the managers of the strategic apex develop an understanding of its environment; and in carrying out the duties of direct supervision, they seek to tailor strategy to its strengths and its needs, trying to maintain a pace of change that is responsive to the environment without being disruptive to the organization. Of course, as we shall see later, the process of strategy formulation is not as cut and dried as all that. For one thing, the other parts of the organization—in certain cases, even the operating core—can play an active role in formulating strategy. For another, strategies sometimes form themselves, almost inadvertently, as managers respond to the pressures of the environment, decision by decision. But one point should be stressed— the *strategic* apex, among the five parts of the organization, typically plays the most important role in the formulation of its strategies.

In general, the strategic apex takes the widest, and as a result the most abstract, perspective of the organization. Work at this level is generally characterized by a minimum of repetition and standardization, considerable discretion, and relatively long decision-making cycles. Mutual adjustment is the favored mechanism for coordination among the managers of the strategic apex itself.

The middle line

The strategic apex is joined to the operating core by the chain of middle-line managers with formal authority. This chain runs from the senior managers to the *first-line supervisors* (such as shop foremen), who have direct authority over the operators, and embodies the coordinating mechanism that we have called direct supervision. Most such chains are scalar— that is, run in a single line from top to bottom. But as we shall see later, not all: some divide and rejoin, a "subordinate" having more than one "superior."

The organization needs this whole chain of middle-line managers to the extent that it is large and reliant on direct supervision for coordination. In theory, one manager—the chief executive at the strategic apex—can supervise all the operators. In practice, direct supervision requires close personal contact between manager and operator, with the result that there is some limit to the number of operators any one manager can supervise— his so-called span of control. Small organizations can get along with one manager (at the strategic apex); bigger ones require more (in the middle line). Thus, an organizational *hierarchy* is built, as a first-line supervisor is put in charge of a number of operators to form a basic organizational unit, another manager is put in charge of a number of these units to form a higher level unit, and so on until all the remaining units can come under a single manager at the strategic apex—designated the "chief executive officer"—to form the whole organization.

In this hierarchy, the middle-line manager performs a number of tasks in the flow of direct supervision above and below him. He collects "feedback" information on the performance of his own unit and passes some of this up to the managers above him, often aggregating it in the process. He also intervenes in the flow of decisions. Flowing up are disturbances in the unit, proposals for change, decisions requiring authorization. Some the middle-line manager handles himself, others he passes up for action at a higher level in the hierarchy. Flowing down are resources that he must allocate in his unit, rules and plans that he must elaborate, and projects that he must implement there. But like the top manager, the middle manager is required to do more than simply engage in direct supervision. He, too, has boundary conditions to manage. Each middle-line manager must maintain liaison contacts with other managers, analysts, support staffers, and outsiders whose work is interdependent with that of his own unit. Furthermore, the middle-line manager, like the top manager, is concerned with formulating the strategy for his unit, although this strategy is, of course, significantly affected by the strategy of the overall organization. But managerial jobs shift in orientation as they descend in the chain of authority. They become more detailed and elaborated, less abstract and aggregated, more focused on the work flow itself.

The technostructure

In the technostructure we find the analysts (and their supporting clerical staff) who serve the organization by affecting the work of others. These analysts are removed from the operating work flow—they may design it, plan it, change, it, or train the people who do it, but they do not do it themselves. Thus, the technostructure is effective only when it can use its analytical techniques to make the work of others more effective.

Who makes up the technostructure? There are the analysts concerned with adaptation, with changing the organization to meet environmental change, and those concerned with control, with stabilizing and standardizing patterns of activity in the organization. In this book we are concerned largely with the control analysts, those who focus their attention directly on the design and functioning of structure. **The control analysts of the technostructure serve to effect certain forms of standardization in the organization.** This is not to say that operators cannot standardize their own work—just as everyone establishes his or her own procedure for getting dressed in the morning—or that managers cannot do it for them. But in general, the more standardization an organization uses, the more it relies on its technostructure. Such standardization reduces the need for direct supervision, sometimes enabling clerks to do what managers once did.

We can distinguish three types of control analysts, to correspond to the three forms of standardization: work-study analysts (such as industrial engineers), who standardize work processes; planning and control analysts (such as long-range planners, quality control engineers, production schedulers, and accountants), who standardize outputs; and personnel analysts (including trainers and recruiters), who standardize skills (although most of this standardization takes place outside the organization, before the workers are hired).

In a fully developed organization, the technostructure may perform at all levels of the hierarchy. At the lowest levels of the manufacturing firm, analysts standardize the operating work flow by scheduling production, carrying out time-and-method studies of the operators' work, and instituting systems of quality control. At middle levels, they seek to standardize the intellectual work of the organization (for instance, by training middle managers) and carry out operations research studies of informational tasks. And on behalf of the strategic apex, they design strategic planning systems and develop financial systems to control the goals of major units.

Although the analysts exist to standardize the work of others, their own work would appear to be coordinated with others largely through mutual adjustment. (Standardization of skills does play a part in this coordination, however, because analysts are typically highly trained specialists.) Thus, analysts spend a good deal of their time in informal communication.

The support staff

A glance at the chart of almost any large contemporary organization reveals a great number of units, all specialized, that exist to provide support to the organization outside its operating work flow. Those make up the *support staff.* For example, in a university, we find the alma mater fund, university press, bookstore, printing service, payroll department, janitorial service, mailroom, security department, switchboard, athletics department, student residence, faculty club, and so on. None is a part of the operating core; that is, none engages in teaching or research, or even supports it directly (as does, say, the computing center or the library). Yet each exists to provide indirect support to these basic missions. In the manufacturing firm, these units run the gamut from legal counsel to plant cafeteria.

The surprising thing is that these support units have been all but totally ignored in the literature on organizational structuring. Most often they are lumped together with the technostructure and labeled the "staff" that provides advice to management. But these support units are most decidedly different from the technostructure—they are not preoccupied with standardization and they cannot be looked upon primarily as advice givers (although they may do some of that, too). Rather, they have distinct functions to perform. The university press publishes books, the faculty club provides a social setting for the professors, the alma mater fund brings in money.

Why do large organizations provide so many of their own support services, instead of purchasing them from outside suppliers? The answer seems to lie in control, the large organization wishing to exercise close control over these services, perhaps to reduce the uncertainty of having to buy them on the open market. By publishing its own books, the university avoids some of the uncertainties associated with the commercial houses; by fighting its own court cases, the manufacturing corporation maintains close control over the lawyers it uses; and by feeding its own employees in the plant cafeteria, it shortens the lunch period and, perhaps, even helps to determine the nutritiousness of the food.

Many support units are self-contained; they are mini-organizations, many with their own equivalent of an operating core, as in the case of the printing service in a university. These units take resources from the larger organization and, in turn, provide specific services to it. But they function independently of the main operating core. Compare, for example, the maintenance department with the cafeteria in a factory, the first a *direct* service and an integral part of the operating core, the second quite separate from it.

The support units can be found at various levels of the hierarchy, depending on the receivers of their service. In most manufacturing firms, public relations and legal counsel are located near the top, since they tend to serve the strategic apex directly. At middle levels are found the units that support the decisions made there, such as industrial relations, pricing, and research and development. And at the lower levels are found the units with more standardized work, akin to the work of the operating core—cafeteria, mailroom, reception, payroll. Figure 1–3 shows all these support groups overlaid on our logo, together with typical groups from the other four parts of the organization, again using the manufacturing firm as our example.

Because of the wide variations in the types of support units, we cannot draw a single definitive conclusion about the favored coordinating mechanism for all of them. Each unit relies on whatever mechanism is most appropriate for itself—standardization of skills in the office of legal council, mutual adjustment in the research laboratory, standardization of work processes in the cafeteria. However, because many of the support units are highly specialized and rely on professional staff, standardization of skills may be the single most important coordinating mechanism.

Do the staff groups of the organization—technocratic as well as support—tend to cluster at any special level of the hierarchy? One study of twenty-five organizations (Kaufman and Seidman, 1970) suggested that whereas the middle lines of organizations tend to form into pyramids, the staff does not. Its form is "extremely irregular"—if anything, inversely

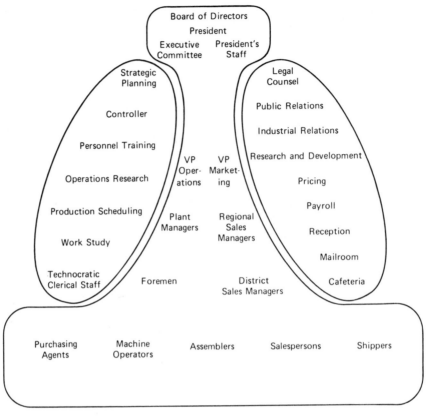

Figure 1-3. *Some members and units of the parts of the manufacturing firm*

pyramidal (p. 446). Hence, while our logo shows the middle line as flaring out toward the bottom, it depicts both the technostructure and the support staff as forming ellipses. Later we shall see that, in fact, the specific shape varies according to the type of structure used by the organization.

Organizations have always had operators and top managers, people to do the basic work and people to hold the whole system together. As they grew, typically they first elaborated their middle-line component, to effect coordination by direct supervision. But as standardization became an accepted coordinating mechanism, the technostructure began to emerge. The work of Frederick Taylor gave rise to the "scientific management" movement of the 1920s, which saw the hiring of many work-study analysts. Just after World War II, the establishment of operations research and the advent of the computer pushed the influence of the technostructure well into the middle levels of many organizations, and with the more recent popularity of techniques such as strategic planning and sophisticated financial controls, the technostructure has entrenched itself firmly at the highest levels of organizations as well. And the more recent growth of the support staff has perhaps been even more dramatic, as all kinds of specialization developed—scientific research in a wide number of fields, industrial relations, public relations, and many more. Organizations have sought increasingly to bring these as well as the more traditional support functions such as maintenance and cafeteria within their boundaries. Thus, the ellipses to the left and right in our logo have become great bulges in many organizations. Indeed, one researcher found that firms in the modern process industries (such as oil refining) averaged one staff member for fewer than three operators, and in some cases, the staff people actually outnumbered the operators by wide margins (Woodward, 1965:60).

The Functioning of the Organization

Here then we have our representation of the organization in five parts. As noted, we can and shall use this diagram in various ways. One way is to overlay the diagram with various types of flows to depict how the organization functions, at least as has been characterized in the literature of management. Figure 1–4 shows five of these flows. Each represents, in a sense, a distinct theory of organizational functioning.

Figure 1–4a represents the organization as a system of *formal authority*—the flow of formal power down the hierarchy. What we have here is an organization chart (I prefer the term *organigram*, borrowed from the French) overlaid on our logo. The organigram is a controversial picture of the structure, for although most organizations continue to find it indispensable (the organigram is inevitably the first thing handed to anyone inquiring about structure), many organizational theorists reject it as an inadequate description of what really takes place inside the organization. Clearly, every organization has important power and communication relationships that are not put down on paper.

However, the organigram should not be rejected, but rather placed in context. It is somewhat like a map. A map is invaluable for finding towns and their connecting roads, but it tells us nothing about the economic or social relationships of the regions. Similarly, **even though the organigram does not show informal relationships, it can represent an accurate picture of the division of labor, showing at a glance (1) what positions exist in the organization, (2) how these are grouped into units, and (3) how formal authority flows among them** (in effect, describing the use of direct supervision).

Figure 1–4b depicts the organization as a network of *regulated flows*— of production work through the operating core, of commands and instructions down the administrative hierarchy to control the operating core, of

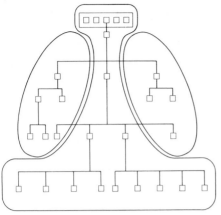

(a): the flow of formal authority

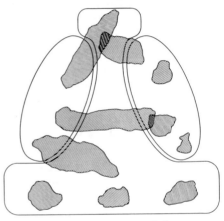

(b): the flow of regulated activity

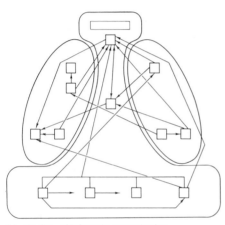

(c): the flow of informal communication
(adapted from Pfeffner and Sherwood, 1960: 291)

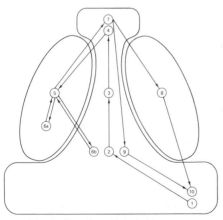

(d): the set of work constellations

(e): the flow of an ad hoc decision process

Figure 1-4. *Five views (or theories) of how the organization functions*

feedback information on results (in a management information system, or MIS) back up, and of staff information and advice feeding into decision making from the sides. This is a view of the organization consistent with traditional notions of authority and hierarchy, but, unlike the first view, one that places greater emphasis on standardization than on direct supervision.

Figure 1–4c describes the organization as a system of *informal communication*, emphasizing the role of mutual adjustment in coordination. What we have here, in fact, is a "sociogram"—a map of who actually communicated with whom in a study of one municipal government (drawn from the work of Pfiffner and Sherwood, 1960). What this view of the organization indicates is that unofficial centers of power exist in organizations and that rich networks of informal communication supplement and sometimes circumvent the channels of authority and regulation. The neatness of the first two views disappears in this third one.

Figure 1–4d depicts the organization as a system of *work constellations*. The underlying view here is that people in the organization cluster into peer groups (not related to the hierarchy or even necessarily to our five parts) to get their work done. Each cluster or constellation deals with distinct decisions appropriate to its own level in the hierarchy, and is only loosely coupled to the others. Here, then, in contrast to the organization as a kind of orderly spiral spring of the first two views, and as a confusing marble cake of the third, we see it as a kind of semiorderly layer cake. In Figure 1–4d, in terms of a typical manufacturing firm, we have three work constellations in the operating core—one concerned with fabrication, a second with assembly, a third with distribution. Above them is an administrative production constellation, comprising analysts and first-line supervisors, concerned with production scheduling and general plant administration. Above that is a new-product constellation, including analysts, line managers, and support staffers (such as researchers). Exclusively within the support staff are three constellations, concerned with the plant cafeteria, research and development (overlapping the new-product constellation), and public relations. Finally, at the top, the finance constellation connects senior managers with the financial support staff, and the long-range-planning constellation joins senior managers with senior analysts of the technostructure.

Last is Figure 1–4e, which depicts the organization as a system of *ad hoc decision processes*. What we have in this overlay is the flow of one strategic decision, from beginning to end (but, like all the other overlays, vastly simplified). At point 1, a salesman meets a customer, who suggests a modification in a product. The suggestion is taken up at successively higher levels in the hierarchy (2, 3, 4), until a decision is made at the top (4) to create a task force of analysts and line managers to investigate it and make recommendations (5, 6). Senior management approves the subsequent rec-

ommendations to introduce a new product (7), and implementation proceeds (8, 9). The salesman eventually returns to the customer with the new
product (10).

We now have five views or theories of how the organization functions. Which is correct? Clearly, by itself, none is. Each is a gross simplification of organizational reality. Yet each contains a grain of truth. Only by
combining them, as we have done in Figure 1–5, do we begin to get a sense
of the true complexity of the functioning of the organization. It is this
complexity with which we must now deal.

With this foundation laid—our five coordination mechanisms as the
glue of structure, our five parts making up our logo or theme diagram, and
our point just made about the complexity of the functioning of the organization—we can begin our story of the structuring of organizations. We
start with the design parameters, those levers that can be pulled and knobs
that can be turned to affect the division of labor and the coordination of

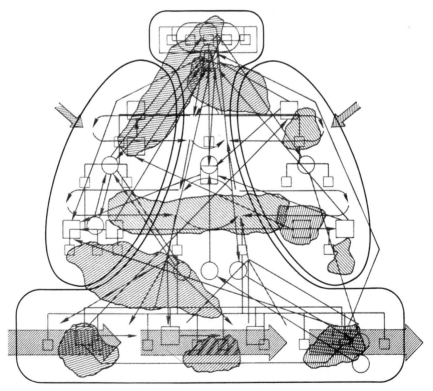

Figure 1-5. *A combined overlay: the functioning of the*
organization

tasks in the organization. We discuss these in four chapters, the first on parameters that can be used to design individual positions in the organization, the second on parameters to design the organization's whole superstructure, the third on parameters used to flesh out that superstructure, and the fourth on parameters used to design the decision-making system of the organization (that is, related to its "decentralization").

Then we devote a chapter to the situational factors, in an attempt to put the parameters of design into context. Here we consider how the various design parameters should be influenced by the age and size of the organization, the technical system it uses, the environment in which it operates, and the power relationships that surround and infuse it.

This brings us to the meat of the book, our synthesis of the preceding materials—the configurations. In Chapter 7, we introduce our basic five:

- *Simple Structure*, based on direct supervision, in which the strategic apex is the key part
- *Machine Bureaucracy*, based on standardization of work processes, in which the technostructure is the key part
- *Professional Bureaucracy*, based on standardization of skills, in which the operating core is the key part
- *Divisionalized Form*, based on standardization of outputs, in which the middle line is the key part
- *Adhocracy*, based on mutual adjustment, in which the support staff (sometimes with the operating core) is the key part

Five subsequent chapters discuss each of these configurations at length—its basic combination of design parameters, how it functions, the conditions under which it is appropriately found, and various issues, social as well as managerial, associated with its functioning. The final chapter of the book, titled "Beyond Five," takes up the one unanswered question of this chapter: Is five the magic number in the design of effective organizations?

2

DESIGNING INDIVIDUAL POSITIONS

As Herbert Simon (1969) has pointed out, the essence of the man-made sciences—whether engineering, medicine, or management—is *design*. Design assumes discretion, an ability to alter a system. In the case of organizational structure, design means turning those knobs that influence the division of labor and the coordinating mechanisms, thereby affecting how the organization functions. The next four chapters discuss these knobs—the essential parameters of organizational structure—and the ways in which each can be turned.

Consider the following questions:

- How many tasks should a given position in the organization contain, and how specialized should each task be?
- To what extent should the work content of each position be standardized?
- What skills and knowledge should be required for each position?
- On what basis should positions be grouped into units and units into larger units?
- How large should each unit be; how many people should report to a given manager?
- To what extent should the output of each position or unit be standardized?
- What mechanisms should be established to facilitate mutual adjustment among positions and units?
- How much decision-making power should be delegated to the managers of line units down the chain of authority?
- How much decision-making power should pass from the line managers to the staff specialists and operators?

These are the basic issues of structural design we shall be discussing. They suggest a set of nine *design parameters*—the basic components of organizational structure—that fall into four broad groupings, the subjects of these four chapters. They are listed in Table 2–1 together with the most closely related concepts from Chapter 1.

We begin with the design of individual positions. Three design parameters come into play here: the specialization of the job, the formalization of behavior in carrying the job out, and the training and indoctrination required by the job.

Job Specialization

Jobs can be specialized in two dimensions. The first is "breadth" or "scope"—how many different tasks are contained in each and how broad or narrow is each of these tasks. At one extreme, the worker is a jack-of-all-trades, forever jumping from one broad task to another; at the other extreme, he focuses his efforts on the same highly specialized task, repeated day in and day out, even minute in and minute out. The second dimension of specialization relates to "depth," to the control over the work. At one extreme, the worker merely does the work without any thought as to how or why; at the other, he controls every aspect of the work in addition to doing it. The first dimension may be called *horizontal job specialization* (in that it deals with parallel activities) and its opposite, *horizontal job enlargement*; the second, *vertical job specialization* and *vertical job enlargement*.

Horizontal job specialization

Job specialization in the horizontal dimension—the predominant form of division of labor—is an inherent part of every organization, indeed every human activity. On a seal hunt, for example, the Gilyak eskimos divide their labor within the boat among harpooner, oarsman, and helmsman (Udy, 1959:91). In fact, the term "division of labor" dates back to the eighteenth century, when Adam Smith wrote *The Wealth of Nations*. There he presented his famous example in which, even by 1776, "the division of labor has been very often taken notice of, the trade of the pin maker":

> One man draws out the wire, another straights it, a third cuts it, a fourth points it, a fifth grinds it at the top for receiving the head; to make the head requires two or three distinct operations; to put it on is a peculiar business, to whiten the pins is another; it is even a trade by itself to put them into the papers. . . (Smith, 1910:5)

Organizations so divide their labor—specialize their jobs—to increase productivity. Adam Smith noted that in one pin factory, ten men spe-

TABLE 2–1. Design Parameters

Group	Design Parameter	Related Concepts
Design of positions	Job specialization	Basic division of labor
	Behavior formalization	Standardization of work content
		System of regulated flows
	Training and indoctrination	Standardization of skills
Design of superstructure	Unit grouping	Direct supervision
		Administrative division of labor
		Systems of formal authority, regulated flows, informal communication, and work constellations
		Organigram
	Unit size	System of informal communication
		Direct supervision
		Span of control
Design of lateral linkages	Planning and control systems	Standardization of outputs
		System of regulated flows
	Liaison devices	Mutual adjustment
		Systems of informal communication, work constellations, and ad hoc decision processes
Design of decision-making system	Vertical decentralization	Administrative division of labor
		Systems of formal authority, regulated flows, work constellations, and ad hoc decision processes
	Horizontal decentralization	Administrative division of labor
		Systems of informal communication, work constellations, and ad hoc decision processes

cialized in their work were each able to turn out about 4,800 pins per day. "But if they had all wrought separately and independently, and without any of them having been educated to this peculiar business, they certainly could not each of them have made twenty, perhaps not one pin in a day . . ." (p. 5).

What are the reasons for such productivity increases? Smith notes three: the improved dexterity of the workman from specializing in one task, the saving in time lost in switching tasks, and the development of new methods and machines that come from specialization. All three reasons point to the key factor that links specialization to productivity: repetition. Horizontal specialization increases the repetition in the work, thereby facilitating its standardization. The outputs can be produced more uniformly and more efficiently. Horizontal specialization also focuses the attention of the worker, which facilitates learning. A final reason for specialization is that it allows the individual to be matched to the task. In Chapter 1 we noted that football teams put their slim players in the backfield, their squat players on the line. Likewise, Udy notes that the Gilyak eskimos put their best oarsmen toward the stern, their best shots in the bow.

Vertical job specialization

Vertical job specialization separates the performance of the work from the administration of it. Teaching offers a good example. Students who use workbooks or copy their lectures word for word have rather vertically specialized work—they simply carry out the activity. In contrast, when the students do projects, they assume control of much of the decision making in their work—their "jobs" become vertically enlarged, and they shift from passive responders to active participants. In the case of the pie filler, discussed in Chapter 1, his job was highly specialized in the vertical (as well as the horizontal) dimension. Alternatively, were he told to bake a pie to sell for $1.50 or, better still, had he owned a bakery and decided for himself what to bake and at what price, he could have been described as having a vertically enlarged job.

Organizations specialize jobs in the vertical dimension in the belief that a different perspective is required to determine how the work should be done. In particular, when a job is highly specialized in the horizontal dimension, the worker's perspective is narrowed, making it difficult for him to relate his work to that of others. So control of the work is often passed to a manager with the overview necessary to coordinate the work by direct supervision or to an analyst who can do so by standardization. Thus, jobs must often be specialized vertically because they are specialized horizontally. But not always, as we shall soon see.

Job enlargement

Job specialization is hardly a panacea for the problems of position design; quite the contrary, **job specialization creates a number of its own problems, notably of communication and coordination.** Consider a simple example, the way in which orders are taken in French and American restaurants. In this respect, the work in many French restaurants is more specialized: the maître d'hôtel takes the order and writes it on a slip of paper, and the waiter serves it. In the American restaurant, the waiter generally does both tasks. Thus, if the customer in the French restaurant has a special request—for example, to have his coffee with his dessert instead of after it as is the norm in France—a communication problem arises. The maître d'hôtel must go to the trouble of telling the waiter or making a note on the slip of paper. (In fact, it is unlikely that he will do either, and it is left to the customer to try, often in vain, to get his message across to the waiter directly.) In effect, specialization creates problems of coordination. In more complex work, such as medicine, specialization has also been a mixed blessing. The great advances—for example, open-heart surgery, control of tuberculosis, transplants of various kinds—have been brought about by specialization in research and clinical work, but so too has specialization placed all kinds of artificial barriers across the practice of medicine. Few doctors treat the body as an integrated system; rather, they treat clogged arteries, or emotional stress, or unhealthy diets.

High task specialization in the horizontal dimension also creates balancing problems for the organization. If a barbershop designates one person to cut only children's hair, it may face a situation in which adult customers are forced to wait while the children's barber stands idle. Clearly, size is an important factor here: A high volume of work facilitates high horizontal specialization. Only the large barbershops can afford children's specialists.

Another serious problem, especially in the operating core, is what high specialization in both dimensions can do to the worker—to his feelings about his work and his motivation to do it well. With the rise of Taylor's Scientific Management movement after World War I, American industry (and, for that matter, Russian industry, too) became virtually obsessed with job specialization. "One has the feeling of division of labor having gone wild, far beyond any degree necessary for efficient production," wrote James Worthy, an executive of Sears, Roebuck, in 1950 (p. 174). The belief that "all possible brain work should be removed from the shop floor and centered in the planning and laying out department" led to the most machinelike of jobs, as engineers sought to "minimize the characteristics of workers that most significantly differentiate them from machines" (p. 67). All this, Worthy argues, "has been fantastically wasteful for industry and society," failing to make proper use of "management's most valuable resource: the complex and multiple capacities of people." Because "the meaning of work itself" was destroyed, people could only be treated as means; they could no longer exercise initiative. In place of intrinsic motivation, workers had "to be enticed by rewards and threatened by punishments" (pp. 69, 70, 71).

Charlie Chaplin popularized the plight of the human robot in his pre–World War II film, *Modern Times*. But the problem has persisted to the present day. Only recently, however, with increasing worker alienation posing a direct threat to productivity itself, has there been a real thrust to change the situation. This has proceeded under the terms "job enlargement," for horizontal enlargement, and "job enrichment," for vertical coupled with horizontal enlargement (Herzberg, 1968);[1] more recently, all this has been subsumed under the broader title, "quality of working life," now sufficiently in vogue to merit the acronym QWL. Here, for simplicity's sake and to contrast with job specialization, we shall stay with the term "job enlargement," whether horizontal or vertical.

In horizontal job enlargement, the worker engages in a wide variety of the tasks associated with producing products and services. He may either do more tasks in sequence, or do them one at a time, as before, but interchange tasks with his colleagues periodically so that his work becomes more varied. For example, in the assembly of the parts of a small motor, the assembly line may be eliminated and each worker may assemble the whole motor himself, or the workers may interchange positions on the assembly line periodically. **When a job is enlarged vertically, or "enriched," not only does the worker carry out more tasks, but he also gains more control over them.** For example, a group of workers may be given responsibility for the assembly of the motor, a natural unit of work, including the power to decide how the work will be shared and carried out.

Does job enlargement pay? The proponents say yes, and back up their conclusion with enthusiastic anecdotal reports. But more detached observers report failures as well as successes, and reviews of the research suggest that although the successes probably predominate, the overall results of job enlargement are mixed.

The results of job enlargement clearly depend on the job in question. To take two extreme examples, the enlargement of the job of a secretary who must type the same letter all day every day cannot help but improve things; in contrast, to enlarge the job of the general practitioner (one wonders how—perhaps by including nursing or pharmacological tasks) could only frustrate the doctor and harm the patient. In other words, jobs can be too large as well as too narrow. So the success of any job redesign clearly depends on the job in question and how specialized it is in the first place. The natural tendency has, of course, been to select for redesign the narrowest, most monotonous of jobs, some specialized to almost pathological degrees, of which there has been no shortage in this industrialized world left to us by the followers of Frederick Taylor. Hence, we should not be surprised to find more successes than failures reported in this research.

---

[1]In these types of jobs, it is unlikely that vertical job enlargement could proceed without some horizontal job enlargement.

That, however, should not lead to the conclusion that job enlargement is good per se.

There is also the question of tradeoffs inherent in any attempt to redesign a job. What the writings of people like Worthy have done is to introduce the human factor into the performance equation, alongside the purely technical concerns of the time-and-motion-study analysts. That has changed the equation: **job enlargement pays to the extent that the gains from better-motivated workers in a particular job offset the losses from less than optimal technical specialization.** Thus, like job specialization, job enlargement is hardly a panacea for the problems of position design; it is one design parameter among many, to be considered alongside the others.

So far, the question of whether job enlargement pays has been addressed solely from the point of view of the organization. But the worker counts, too, as a human being who often deserves something better than a monotonous job. But here the research throws a curve, with its evidence that **some workers prefer narrowly specialized, repetitive jobs.** Nowhere is this point made clearer than in Stud Terkel's fascinating book, *Working* (1972), in which all kinds of workers talk candidly about the work they do and their feelings about it. A clear message comes through: "One man's meat is another man's poison." Occasionally, Terkel juxtaposes the comments of two workers in the same job, one who relishes it and another who detests it.

Why should the same routine job motivate one person and alienate another? Some researchers believe the answer relates to the age of the workers, others to where they live—older and urban workers having been shown in some studies to be more tolerant of narrow jobs. Others describe the differences in terms of Maslow's (1954) "Needs Hierarchy Theory," which orders human needs into a hierarchy of five groups—physiological, safety or security, love and belongingness, esteem or status, and self-actualization (to create, to fulfill oneself). The theory postulates that one group of needs becomes fully operative only when the next lower group is largely satisfied. In job design, the argument goes, people functioning at the lower end of the Maslow scale, most concerned with security needs and the like, prefer the specialized jobs, whereas those at the upper end, notably at the level of self-actualization, respond more favorably to enlarged jobs. Perhaps this explains why QWL has recently become such a big issue: with growing affluence and rising educational levels, the citizens of the more industrialized societies have been climbing up Maslow's hierarchy. Their growing need for self-actualization can be met only in enlarged jobs. The equation continues to change.

Job specialization by part of the organization

We would expect to find some relation between the specialization of jobs and their location in the organization. Productivity is more important in the operating core, where the basic products and services get produced; also, this is where the work is most repetitive. Hence, we would expect to find the most specialized jobs there, especially in the horizontal dimension. In the vertical dimension, however, we would expect to find more variation. Many operators—such as those on assembly lines—perform the narrowest of jobs in both breadth and depth. These are the *unskilled* workers, on whom the job-enlargement programs have been concentrated. But other operators, because their specialized tasks are more complex, retain considerably control over them. In other words, their jobs are specialized horizontally but not vertically. Performing open-heart surgery, putting out fires in oil wells, and teaching retarded children all require considerable specialization, to master the skills and knowledge of the jobs. But the jobs are complex, requiring years of training, and that complexity precludes close managerial and technocratic control, thereby precluding vertical specialization. **Complex jobs, specialized horizontally but not vertically, are generally referred to as professional.** And job enlargement is not an issue in these jobs, at least not from the perspective of the worker. Society tends to look very favorably on this kind of specialization; indeed, unskilled operators frequently try to have their jobs labeled "professional" to increase their status and reduce the controls imposed on them by the administrators.

Many of the same conclusions can be drawn for the staff units, both support and technocratic. Each support staff unit has a specialized function to perform—producing food in the plant cafeteria, fighting legal battles in the corporate legal office, and so on—with the result that support-staff jobs tend to be highly specialized in the horizontal dimension. How specialized they are in the vertical dimension depends, as it does for the operator's jobs, on how complex or professional they are. In general, we would expect the support staffers of the lower echelons, such as those in the cafeterias, to have narrow, unskilled jobs subject to close control, and those at the high levels, such as in the legal office, to have more professional jobs, specialized horizontally but not vertically. As for the analysts of the technostructure, they are professionals, in that their work requires considerable knowledge and skill. Hence, we would also expect their jobs to be specialized horizontally but not vertically. However, the technocratic clerks—those who apply the systems of standardization routinely—would tend to be less skilled and therefore have jobs specialized in both dimensions.

Managers at all levels appear to perform a basic set of interpersonal, informational, and decisional roles; in that sense, their work is specialized horizontally. But in a more fundamental sense, no true managerial job is specialized in the horizontal dimension. The roles managers perform are so varied, and so much switching is required among them in the course of any given day, that managerial jobs are typically the least specialized in the

TABLE 2–2. Job Specialization by Part of the Organization

		Horizontal Specialization	
		High	Low
Vertical Specialization	High	Unskilled jobs (operating core and staff units)	Certain lowest-level managerial jobs
	Low	Professional jobs (operating core and staff units)	All other managerial jobs

organization. Managers do not complain about repetition or boredom in their work, but rather about the lack of opportunity to concentrate on specific issues. This seems to be as true for foremen as it is for presidents. That is why attempts to redesign the job of chief executive generally move in the direction of job specialization, not enlargement—for example, by creating a chief executive office in which different people split up the top job of the organization. That such efforts have been successful is far from clear (see Mintzberg, 1973a:179–80, for possible reasons why), and the job of CEO seems to remain as enlarged as ever.

Managerial jobs can differ in vertical specialization by level in the hierarchy. Whereas top managers generally have great discretion in their work, some first-line supervisors—notably assembly-line foremen, and supervisors of clerks and other unskilled workers—have highly circumscribed jobs. Indeed, some of them are so subjected to the weight of authority and the standards of the technostructure that their jobs can hardly be called managerial at all.

Our conclusions about vertical and horizontal job specialization as a function of the part of the organization are summarized in Table 2–2.

Behavior Formalization

A second parameter of organizational design, related to individual positions, has, in the opinion of David Hickson (1966–67), been a virtual obsession of organization theorists. In fact, Hickson's list of who has focused on this parameter reads like a veritable Who's Who of writers in management—Taylor, Fayol, McGregor, Argyris, Simon, Crozier, and so on. Often referred to as the *formalization of behavior*, this parameter represents the organization's way of proscribing the discretion of its members, essentially of standardizing their work processes. Behavior may be formalized in three basic ways:

- *By the position,* specifications being attached to the job itself, as in a job description
- *By the work flow,* specifications being attached to the work, as in the case of a printing-order docket
- *By rules,* specifications being issued in general, as in the various regulations—everything from dress to the use of forms—contained in so-called policy manuals

No matter what the means of formalization—by job, work flow, or rules—the effect on the person doing the work is the same: His behavior is regulated. Power over how that work is to be done passes from him to the person who designs the specifications, often an analyst in the technostructure. Thus, formalization of behavior leads to vertical specialization of jobs. Also, it stands to reason that formalization is related to horizontal specialization: the narrowest of the unskilled jobs are the simplest, the most repetitive, and the ones most amenable to high degrees of formalization.

Why formalize behavior?

Organizations formalize behavior to reduce its variability, ultimately to predict and control it. One prime motive for doing so is to coordinate activities. As noted earlier, standardization of work content is a very tight coordinating mechanism. Its corresponding design parameter, behavior formalization, is used therefore when tasks require precise, carefully predetermined coordination. Firemen cannot stop each time they arrive at a new fire to figure out who will attach the hose to the hydrant and who will go up the ladder; similarly, airline pilots must be very sure about their landing procedures well in advance of descent.

Formalization of behavior is also used to ensure the machinelike consistency that leads to efficient production. Tasks are specialized in the horizontal dimension to achieve repetition; formalization is then used to impose the most efficient procedures on them.

Formalization is also used to ensure fairness to clients. The national tax office must treat everyone equally; that is why it tends to emphasize formalization of behavior. Government organizations are particularly sensitive to accusations of favoritism; hence, they tend to proliferate rules and specifications. Sometimes rules are instituted to protect the clients, at other times the employees. For example, promotion by seniority is used to preclude arbitrary decisions by managers.

Organizations formalize behavior for other reasons as well, of more questionable validity. Formalization may, for example, reflect an arbitrary desire for order. Some tennis courts require all players to wear white, yet it is difficult to understand what difference it would make if some appeared in mauve. The highly formalized structure is above all the neat one; it warms the hearts of people who like to see things orderly—everyone in his proper box on the organigram, all work processes predetermined, all contingencies accounted for, everyone in white.

Bureaucratic and organic forms of structure

Organizations that rely primarily on the formalization of behavior to achieve coordination are generally referred to as *bureaucracies.* It is appropriate at this point to take a close look at this important concept, since it lies at the very heart of a great deal of discussion about organizational structure.

The word *bureaucracy* had an innocent-enough beginning—it derived from the French word *bureau,* meaning "desk" or "office." But since Max Weber, the great German sociologist, used it at the turn of the century to describe a particular type of organizational structure, it has had a rather tumultuous existence. Weber intended the term as a purely technical one, and it retains that sense today in the literature of organizational theory and sociology. But elsewhere, the word has taken on a decidedly pejorative meaning—it has become a dirty word. Here the reader is asked to put aside this pejorative meaning and accept the word in its technical sense.

Weber described bureaucracy as an "ideal type" of structure, "ideal" meaning not perfect but pure. He delineated the characteristics of this pure structural type as follows:

    I. There is the principle of fixed and official jurisdictional areas, which are generally ordered by rules, that is, by laws or administrative regulations.

      1. The regular activities required for the purposes of the bureaucratically governed structure are distributed in a fixed way as official duties.

      2. The authority to give the commands required for the discharge of these duties is distributed in a stable way and is strictly delimited by rules concerning the coercive means, physical, sacerdotal, or otherwise which may be placed at the disposal of officials.

      3. Methodical provision is made for the regular and continuous fulfillment of these duties and for the execution of the corresponding rights; only persons who have the generally regulated qualification to serve are employed.

    II. The principles of office hierarchy and of levels of graded authority mean a firmly ordered system of super- and subordinate in which there is a supervision of the lower offices by the higher ones.

    III. The management of the modern office is based upon written documents ("the files"), which are preserved in their original or draught form.

    IV. Office management, at least all specialized office management—and such management is distinctly modern—usually presupposes thorough and expert training.

    V. The management of the office follows general rules, which are more or less stable, more or less exhaustive, and which can be learned. Knowledge of these rules represents a special technical learning which the officials possess. It involves jurisprudence, or administrative or business management. (Gerth and Mills, 1958: 196–98)

Weber's description brings together a number of the concepts we have already discussed—division of labor, specialization, formalization of behavior, hierarchy of authority, chain of command, regulated communication, and standardization of work processes and of skills. But how well do all these defining characteristics hold together in real organizations? In other words, does Weber's "ideal type" really exist, or are there, in fact, different types of bureaucratic structures, each exhibiting some but not all of these characteristics?

We shall investigate this question more fully later. It is sufficient at this point to note that the research has been inconsistent, some studies finding, for example, that although measures of specialization and formalization intercorrelated, ones related to decentralization did not. The implication was that there may be some bureaucracies where decision-making power is centralized and others where it is not. With this finding in mind, **we can define a structure as bureaucratic to the extent that its behavior is predetermined or predictable, in effect standardized** (whether by work processes, outputs, or skills, and whether or not centralized). This seems to be the main thread running through Weber's description.

So far, we have talked only of bureaucratic structure. But if some organizations emphasize standardization, others presumably do not. They are characterized by flexible working arrangements, basing their coordination on mutual adjustment or direct supervision. **We shall define organic structure by the absence of standardization in the organization.** In effect, we put bureaucratic and organic structure at the two ends of the continuum of standardization.

Some dysfunctions of highly formalized structures

Perhaps no topic in management has generated more heat than the consequences of extensive formalization of behavior in organizations. Early in this century, before the Hawthorne studies of the 1930s, mentioned earlier, industrial psychologists were concerned primarily with the physiological fatigue caused by monotonous work. This was, in fact, the original focus of the Hawthorne studies themselves. But there it became apparent that fatigue was only the tip of the iceberg, that such work—highly repetitive, formalized, and specialized horizontally and vertically—created psychological as well as physiological problems for many workers. Subsequently, people like Argyris, Bennis, Likert, and McGregor build their careers on the analysis of the psychological dysfunctions of highly formalized structures. They pointed out man's inherent propensity to resist formalization and impersonalization, and they showed the organizational "pathologies" that result from excesses in this direction. The dysfunctional consequences take various forms: the ossification of behavior, with the automatic rejection of all innovative ideas, the mistreatment of clients, increases in absenteeism, high turnover, strikes, and sometimes the subversion of the operations of the organization.

Michael Crozier (1964) looked into these issues too, in the context of two French government bureaucracies, but he came up with some very different results. For one thing, he found that many of the rules were favored by the operators, because, even though these rules may have limited their own discretion, they also reduced the arbitrary power their managers could exercise over them. The rules in effect protected the operators, giving rise to a kind of perverse democracy at lower levels in the hierarchy: everyone was treated more or less equally because everyone was controlled by the same overwhelming set of rules. As a result, however, the decisions not covered by the rules (including those to determine the rules themselves) had to be made elsewhere, at distant headquarters, which often lacked the local information needed to make such decisions.

Crozier also found that rules and central authority could not regulate quite everything. A few areas of uncertainty had to remain, and it was around these that informal power relationships developed. People who could deal with uncertainties achieved great influence. This was the case for the maintenance men in the government tobacco factories Crozier studied; these men were the only ones able to deal with machine breakdown, the one major uncertainty in these highly regulated plants.

Behavior formalization by part of the organization

One key relationship should be evident by now: **the more stable and repetitive the work, the more programmed it is and the more bureaucratic that part of the organization that contains it.** Thus, there can be considerable differences in formalization of behavior and bureaucratization across the various parts of a single organization. Although we can (and will) characterize certain organizations as bureaucratic or organic overall, none is uniformly so across its entire range of activities.

In the operating core, the part of the organization that the other parts seek to insulate and protect, we would generally expect to find the most stable conditions and the most repetitive tasks, leading to the most bureaucratic structure. This should not be taken to mean that the work of the operating core is always formalized or bureaucratized. Some organizations, such as creative research centers and small entrepreneurial firms, tend to be rather organically structured even in their operating cores. Nevertheless, relatively speaking, **behavior formalization is most common in the operating core of the organization.**

As we leave the operating core and climb the hierarchy of authority, we would expect the work to become increasingly less repetitive and so less formalized. The middle-line manager closest to the operating core would tend to be most influenced by the conditions there, and those farthest away would operate in the most organic conditions. Of course, there can be variations in formalization at a given level of the hierarchy, depending on the work in the unit supervised and the boundary conditions it faces. Thus we might expect to find the work of a production manager more formalized than that of a corresponding sales manager, although the two may be peers in terms of their positions in the hierarchy. One is concerned primarily with stabilizing the work of the operating core; the other must remain flexible to deal with the variability of customer demands.

At the strategic apex, which typically comes face to face with the most fluid boundary—the environment at large—the work is the least programmed, and so we should expect to find highly organic conditions. This conclusion became apparent in over fifty studies of different organizations carried out by student groups of ours at McGill University. Time and again, the organigrams were put on the blackboard and the students proceeded to explain why they were not accurate at upper levels of the hierarchy. The charts specified formal authority, but they did not describe the communication patterns and power relationships that really existed there. These relationships were simply too fluid to formalize; the structure had to evolve naturally and to shift continually. In a word, it had to be organic.

In the support staff, we would expect to find a range of structures, according to the work done and the boundary conditions faced. Support units that face little uncertainty and do repetitive work, such as the plant cafeteria, would tend to be highly formalized. In contrast, in a research laboratory, where the need for creativity is high, or in a public relations department, where there are significant work variations from day to day, little of the work can be formalized and so we would expect the structure to remain relatively organic, at least if the units are to be effective.

Similarly, in the technostructure, we would expect that those units closest to the operating core, such as production scheduling, would have many rules and rather formalized work procedures. Others with more variable work, such as operations research, would probably adopt relatively organic structures. (It should be noted here that whatever its *own* structure, it is the technostructure that takes primary responsibility for the formalization of everyone else's work in the organization.)

Finally, it should be noted that organizations with strong orientations toward either bureaucratic or organic structure sometimes set up independent work constellations with the opposite kinds of structure to do special tasks. For example, in highly bureaucratic manufacturing firms, the new product or "venture" team is created as a pocket of organic structure isolated from the rest of the organization administratively, financially, spatially, and sometimes even legally. In this way, it is able to innovate, free of the restraints of bureaucracy.

Training and Indoctrination

The third aspect of position design entails the specifications of the requirements for holding a position in the first place. In particular, the organization can specify what knowledge and skills jobholders must have and what norms they must exhibit. It can then establish recruiting and selection procedures to screen applicants in terms of those position requirements; alternatively, it can establish its own programs to develop them in the candidates it hires. In either case, the intention is the same—to ensure that the jobholder develops the necessary behaviors before beginning work. Furthermore, the organization may later reinforce these behaviors with a host of personnel devices—job rotation, attendance at conferences, organizational development programs, and so on. **Training refers to the process by which job-related skills and knowledge are taught,** whereas **indoctrination is the process by which organizational norms are acquired.** Both amount to the "internalization" of accepted (that is, standardized) patterns of behavior in the workers.

Training

When a body of knowledge and a set of work skills are highly rationalized, the organization factors them into simple, easily learned jobs—that is, unskilled ones—and then relies on the formalization of behavior to achieve coordination. An automobile is a complex machine, its assembly an involved procedure. But over the years, that procedure has been reduced to thousands of simple tasks, so that today, workers with minimal skills and knowledge can assemble automobiles. Training is, therefore, an insignificant design parameter in the automobile assembly plant—it takes place in the first few hours on many jobs.

Where, however, a job entails a body of knowledge and a set of skills that are both complex and nonrationalized, the worker must spend a great deal of time learning them. For some jobs, of course, these requirements are not recorded as formal knowledge, and so they must be learned on the job: the worker assumes the role of "apprentice" under a "master," who earlier learned the job in the same way. Such work is generally referred to as *craft*. But where a body of knowledge has been recorded and the required skills have—in part at least—been specified, the individual can be trained before beginning work. This kind of work—complex and nonrationalized, yet in part recorded and specified—is referred to as *professional.* Thus, **training is a key design parameter in all work we call professional.**

The "specification" of knowledge and skill is, of course, synonomous with the "standardization" of it. Thus, training is the design parameter for the exercise of the coordinating mechanism that we have called the standardization of skills. Lest anyone doubt the relation between professionalism and standardization, we need only quote the words of a reputed professional about his most complex of professions. Writing about cardiovascular surgery, Frank Spencer discusses his "surgical cookbooks" as follows:

> The jargon term "cookbook" evolved from my loyal office staff, as this essentially describes "How I do this operation," somewhat analogous to "How I bake a cake." . . .
>
> The components of a complex operation, such as repair of tetralogy of Fallot, may be divided into 10 to 15 sequential steps, with two to five essential features in each step. If each feature is symbolized by a single word, essential steps of an operation can be readily reduced to a series of chains of symbols, varying from six to ten chains containing 30 to 40 symbols. These are committed to memory, with review frequently enough so the essential 30 to 40 symbols representing key features of an operation can be reviewed mentally in 60 to 120 seconds at some time during the day preceding the operation. (1976:1182)

Professionals are trained over long periods of time, before they ever assume their positions. Generally, this training takes place outside the organization, often in a university. (There are, of course, exceptions. For example, police forces generally train their own personnel.) In effect, the training itself usually requires a particular and extensive expertise, beyond the capacity of the organization to provide. So the responsibility for it falls away from the technostructure, to some kind of professional association, which may use the university as its training ground. In the process, of course, the organization surrenders some control not only over the selection of its workers but also over the methods they use in their work.

Once the trainees have demonstrated the required behavior—that is, have internalized the standard skills and associated body of knowledge—they are duly certified by the professional association as appropriate for the job, and are subsequently hired by the organization to perform it.

Of course, the professional training program can seldom impart all the necessary skills and knowledge; some must always remain beyond specification and standardization. So professional training must generally be followed by some kind of on-the-job apprenticeship before the person is considered fully trained. For example, as Spencer notes, after perhaps four years of postgraduate university training, the medical doctor must spend five years or more in on-the-job training, first as an intern and then as a resident, before being allowed to practice as a surgeon.

Indoctrination

Socialization "refers to the process by which a new member learns the value system, the norms, and the required behavior patterns of the society, organization, or group which he is entering" (Schein, 1968: 3). A good deal of socialization takes place informally in the organization; indeed, some of it is carried out by the informal group in contradiction to the system of formal authority. **Indoctrination is the label used for the design parameter by which the organization formally socializes its members for its own benefit.**

Organizations allow some indoctrination to take place outside their own boundaries, as part of professional training. Law students, for example, learn more at the university than just legal precedent; they are expressly given clues about how a lawyer should behave. But much socialization is related to the "culture" of the specific organization, and so indoctrination is largely a responsibility of the organization itself.

Again, a good deal of this "in-house" indoctrination activity takes place before the person starts the job, to ensure that he or she is sufficiently socialized to exhibit the desired behavior. Apprenticeship programs generally contain a good dose of indoctrination along with the training. Some organizations design programs solely for the purposes of indoctrination. Freshly minted MBAs, for example, are often put through a "training" (read "indoctrination") program on first joining a large organization. They rotate through various departments for periods too brief for them to learn the work but not to sense the culture.

Often such indoctrination is supplemented by later programs designed to reinforce the employees' allegiance to the organization. For example, they are brought together for social events or inspiring speeches by the top managers, or they are rotated in their jobs so that they develop their allegiances to the whole organization rather than to any one of its parts.

In-house indoctrination programs are particularly important where jobs are sensitive or remote—managers of the foreign subsidiary, agents of the CIA, ambassadors of the nation, mounties of the R.C.M.P. In these cases, the need for coordination is paramount, particularly for the assurance that individuals working autonomously will act in the best interests of the organization. The nature and location of the work preclude the formalization of behavior and the use of direct supervision. So the organization must rely on training, and especially on indoctrination. The Catholic Church and the Communist Party are examples of organizations that rely heavily on indoctrination as a design parameter. Antony Jay, in his book *Management and Machiavelli*, provides us with an excellent illustration of one branch of the former's use of indoctrination:

> St. Augustine once gave as the only rule for Christian conduct, "Love God and do what you like." The implication is, of course, that if you truly love God, then you will only ever want to do things which are acceptable to Him. Equally, Jesuit priests are not constantly being rung up, or sent memos, by the head office of the Society. The long, intensive training over many years in Rome is a guarantee that wherever they go afterwards, and however long it may be before they even see another Jesuit, they will be able to do their work in accordance with the standards of the Society. (1970:70)

Training and indoctrination by part of the organization

No matter what the part of the organization, training is most important where jobs are complex, involving difficult, yet specified skills and sophisticated recorded bodies of knowledge—jobs essentially professional in nature. And indoctrination is most important where jobs are sensitive or remote, and where the culture and ideology of the organization demand a strong loyalty to it.

In some organizations—known as professional—a great deal of the work of the operating core involves complex skills and sophisticated knowledge. Examples are hospitals, law firms, social-work agencies, and school systems. In each case, the organization relies extensively on training as a design parameter. Some organizations—sometimes the same professional ones—also make extensive use of indoctrination in the operating core because their operators do sensitive jobs or work in remote places. The R.C.M.P. and the Jesuits were both cited above as examples.

Training and indoctrination are also used extensively in many of the staff units. Much of the technocratic work of the organization—for example, operations research and industrial engineering—is professional in nature. That is, it involves complex skills and knowledge that can be learned formally. So training is an important parameter in the design of their positions. Where the analysts have sensitive control responsibilities—for example, in the case of accountants who are sent out to divisions to keep watch over expenditures—indoctrination may be important as well. To ensure that their allegiances remain with the head office, job rotation from factory to factory is often used. Similarly, many of the jobs in the support staff—legal council, researcher, industrial relations specialist—are professional in nature, requiring extensive training.

In the managerial ranks—the middle line and the strategic apex—the work is certainly complex, but it is not well understood, and so formal training is not paramount. True, there are skills and knowledge to be learned, and management schools to teach them, but so much of what managers do remains beyond recorded knowledge that management can hardly be called a profession. This is exemplified by the fact that the leaders of a great many of society's most important institutions—especially government—have had no management training whatsoever. Their work is craft; they learn it by observation and by working with masters. Thus, **training is not yet considered a major design parameter at the strategic apex or in the middle line,** although organizations do try to use brief "executive development" programs where specific managerial skills or knowledge can be taught.

Indoctrination plays perhaps a more important role in the managerial ranks, since the managers are, after all, the guardians of the organization's ideology. Thus, the newly hired MBA is put through the indoctrination program, and many large organizations rotate their managers frequently. Again, where managerial jobs are also sensitive or remote—ambassador, manager of a foreign subsidiary—these indoctrination programs take on special importance.

Relating the Position Design Parameters

It has been evident throughout our discussion that specialization, formalization, and training and indoctrination are not completely independent design parameters. In essence, we have been describing two fundamentally different kinds of positions. One we have called *unskilled:* because the work is highly rationalized, it involves extensive specialization in both the horizontal and vertical dimensions, and it is often coordinated and controlled by the direct formalization of behavior. The other we have called *professional:* because the work is complex, it cannot easily be specialized in the vertical dimension or formalized by the organization's technostructure. It is, however, horizontally specialized—professionals are experts in well-defined fields—and the coordination is often achieved by the standardization of skills in extensive training programs, generally given outside the organization. (There are, of course, other kinds of work that are coordinated neither by formalization nor by training.)

This suggests that **formalization and training are basically substitutes.** Depending on the work in question, the organization can either control it directly through its own procedures and rules, or else achieve indirect control by hiring duly trained professionals. That is not to say that the one cannot supplement the other; hospitals rely on professional training to coordinate much of their operating work, yet they also have rules. But in general, most positions seem to stress one coordinating mechanism or the other, not both equally.

In the case of formalization, it is quite clear where the control of the work lies—with the designers of the work standards, notably the organization's analysts. But the issue is less clear in the case of training. Control ostensibly rests with the professional. But although they have a good deal of discretion and appear to be autonomous, professionals are in fact products of their development, much like the actor who has learned his lines well. So some control lies too with those outside agencies that do the training and set the professional standards—universities and professional associations. Thus, **the professional organization surrenders a good deal of control over its choice of workers as well as their methods of work to the outside institutions that train and certify them and thereafter set standards that guide them in the conduct of their work.** With control passes allegiance; professionals tend to identify more with their profession than with the organization wherein they happen to practice it.

It may be recalled that Weber included training in his definition of bureaucracy: "Office management . . . usually presupposes thorough and expert training," and "only persons who have the generally regulated qualifications to serve are employed." But we have just seen that training and formalization—the latter central to the Weber definition—are to some extent mutually exclusive. Might this explain the finding that bureaucracy may be centralized or decentralized? Perhaps in one kind of organization, because the operating work is unskilled, day-to-day control of it passes to the technostructure and the structure becomes centralized; in the other, because the work is professional, control of it remains with the operators themselves, and beyond them, with their associations.

This is not the place to answer that question. Suffice it at this point to note that by our definitions, **professionalism and bureaucracy can coexist in the same structure.** Remember that we defined bureaucracy as the extent to which organizational "behavior is predetermined or predictable, in effect standardized." We did not specify *how* it is standardized.

3

DESIGNING THE SUPERSTRUCTURE

Given a set of positions, designed in terms of specialization, formalization, and training and indoctrination, two obvious questions face the designer of organizational structure: How should these positions be grouped into units? And how large should each unit be? Both questions—which pertain to the design of the *superstructure* of the organization—have received extensive consideration in the literature. In this chapter we take them up.

It is through the process of grouping into units that the system of formal authority is established and the hierarchy of the organization is built. The organigram is the pictorial representation of this hierarchy—that is, of the results of the grouping process. Grouping can be viewed as a process of successive clustering. Individual positions are grouped into first-order clusters, or units; these are, in turn, grouped into larger clusters or units; and so on, until the entire organization is contained in the final cluster. For example, soldiers are grouped into squads, squads into platoons, platoons into companies, companies into battalions, and so on through regiments, brigades, and divisions, until the final grouping into armies.

Combining this process with those described in the preceding chapter, organizational design can proceed as follows, at least in principle. Given overall organizational needs—goals to be achieved, missions to be accomplished, as well as a technical system to accomplish them—the designer delineates all the tasks that must be done. This is essentially a "top-down" procedure, from general needs to specific tasks. He or she then combines these tasks into positions according to the degree of specialization desired, and determines how formalized each should be as well as what kind of training and indoctrination it should require. The next step is to build the superstructure, first by determining what types and how many positions should be grouped into the first-order units, and then what types and how many units should be grouped into ever-more-comprehensive units, until the hierarchy is complete. This last step is, of course, a "bot-

45

tom-up" procedure, from specific tasks to the overall hierarchy. Finally, the superstructure is fleshed out and decision-making powers allocated, as we shall see in the next two chapters.

As noted, this is the procedure *in principle*. In practice, the organizational designer takes many shortcuts, reversing the top-down or bottom-up procedure. For example, he typically starts with a knowledge of specific structures and so can often move from missions to units directly. The designer of army structure need not work down to the level of soldier and then back up to the level of army. Instead, he shuffles divisions or armies around directly, as fixed blocks on the organigram. Likewise, he sometimes forms units from the top down, as when soldiers who were grouped into platoons for general training are later divided into squads for battlefield training. In other words, organization design is seldom carried out in a vacuum; in general, it proceeds with knowledge of past structures. In fact, organizational design is much less common than organizational redesign—incremental shifts from existing structures. In practice, **as goals and missions change, structural redesign is initiated from the top down; as the technical system of the operating core changes, it proceeds from the bottom up.**

Unit Grouping

The grouping of positions and units is not simply a convenience for the sake of creating an organigram, a handy way of keeping track of who works in the organization. Rather, **grouping is a fundamental means to coordinate work in the organization.** Grouping can have at least four important effects:

1 Perhaps most important, **grouping establishes a system of common supervision among positions and units.** A manager is named for each unit, a single individual responsible for all its actions. And it is the linking of all these managers into a superstructure that creates the system of formal authority. Thus, **unit grouping is the design parameter by which the coordinating mechanism of direct supervision is built into the structure.**

2 **Grouping typically requires positions and units to share common resources.** The members or subunits of a unit share, at the very least, a common budget, and often are expected to share common facilities and equipment as well.

3 **Grouping typically creates common measures of performance.** To the extent that the members or subunits of a unit share common resources, the costs of their activities can be measured jointly. Moreover, to the extent that they contribute to the production of the same products or services, their outputs can also be measured jointly. Joint performance measures further encourage them to coordinate their activities.

4 Finally, **grouping encourages mutual adjustment.** In order to share resources and to facilitate their direct supervision, the members of a unit are often forced to share common facilities, thereby being brought into close physical proximity. This, in turn, encourages frequent informal contacts among them, which in turn encourages coordination by mutual adjustment.

Thus, **grouping can stimulate to an important degree two important coordinating mechanisms—direct supervision and mutual adjustment— and can form the basis for a third—standardization of outputs—by providing common measures of performance.** Unit grouping is, as a result, one of the most powerful of the design parameters. (A prime characteristic of the two other coordinating mechanisms—standardization of work processes and of skills—is that they provide for the automatic coordination of the work of individuals; as a result, they can be used independently of the ways in which positions are grouped.)

But for the same reason that grouping encourages strong coordination *within* a unit, it creates problems of coordination *between* units. As we have seen, the communication is focused within the unit, thereby isolating the members of different units from each other. In the terms of Lawrence and Lorsch (1967), units become *differentiated* in their various orientations— in their goals, time perspectives, interpersonal styles of interaction, and degrees of formalization of their structures. For example, a production department might be oriented toward the goal of efficiency as opposed to that of creativity, have a short time perspective, exhibit an orientation to getting the job done rather than to the feelings of those who do it, and have a highly bureaucratic structure. In contrast, a research department may exhibit exactly the opposite characteristics on all four dimensions. Sometimes this differentiation is reinforced by special languages used in the different departments; there are times when personnel in production and in research simply cannot understand each other.

The result of all this is that each unit develops a propensity to focus ever more narrowly on its own problems while separating itself ever more sharply from the problems of the rest of the organization. **Unit grouping encourages intragroup coordination at the expense of intergroup coordination.** The management school that adopts a departmental structure soon finds that its finance professors are interacting more closely with each other but are seeing less of the policy and marketing professors, and all become more parochial in their outlook. Of course, this can also work to the advantage of the organization, allowing each unit to give particular attention to its own special problems. Earlier, we saw the example of the new venture team isolated from the rest of a bureaucratic structure so that it can function organically and therefore be more creative.

Bases for grouping

On what basis does the organization group positions into units and units into large ones? Six bases are perhaps most commonly considered:

1 **Grouping by Knowledge and Skill.** Positions may be grouped according to the specialized knowledge and skills that members bring to the job. Hospitals, for example, group surgeons in one department, anesthetists in another, psychiatrists in a third. Figure 3–1 shows the organigram for the medical component of a Quebec teaching hospital, with the physicians grouped by knowledge and skill in two tiers. Grouping may also be based on *level* of knowledge or skill; for example, different units may be created to house craftsmen, journeymen, and apprentices, or simply skilled and unskilled workers.

2 **Grouping by Work Process and Function.** Units may be based on the process or activity used by the worker. For example, a manufacturing firm may distinguish casting, welding, and machining shops, and a football team may divide into a line unit and a backfield unit for practice. Often, the technical system is the basis for process grouping, as in a printing shop that sets up separate letterpress and offset departments, two different processes to produce the same outputs. Work may also be grouped according to its basic function in the organization—to purchase supplies, raise capital, generate research, produce food in the cafeteria, or whatever. Perhaps the most common example of this is grouping by "business function"—manufacturing, marketing, engineering, finance, and so on, some of these groups being line and others staff. (Indeed, the grouping of line units into one cluster and staff units into another—a common practice—is another example of grouping by work function.) Figure 3–2 shows the organigram for a cultural center, where the grouping is based on work process and function.

3 **Grouping by Time.** Groups may also be formed according to *when* the work is done. Different units do the same work in the same way but at different times, as in the case of different shifts in a factory.

4 **Grouping by Output.** Here, the units are formed on the basis of the products they make or the services they render. A large manufacturing company may have separate divisions for each of its product lines—one for chinaware, another for bulldozers, and so on. A restaurant may separate organizationally as well as spatially its bar from its dining facilities. Figure 3–3 shows the product grouping by divisions in Imasco, a Canadian con-

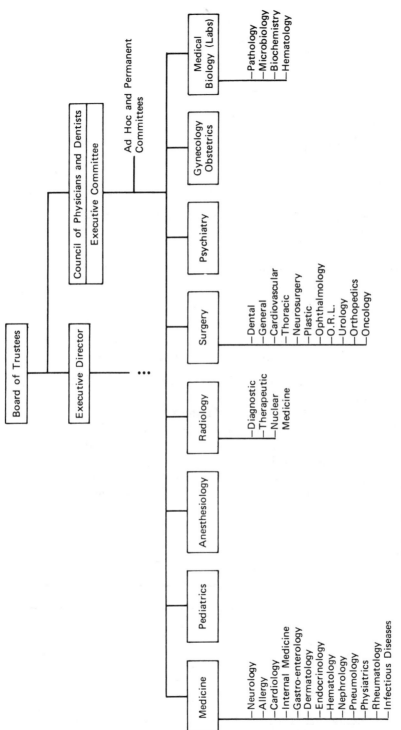

Figure 3-1. *Grouping by knowledge and skill: medical departments of the teaching hospital*

49

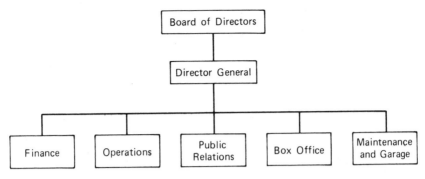

Figure 3-2. *Grouping by work process and function: a cultural center*

glomerate firm (with two units—public relations and finance—based on function).

5   Grouping by Client. Groups may also be formed to deal with different types of clients. An insurance firm may have separate sales departments for individual and group policies; similarly, hospitals in some countries have different wards for public and private patients.

6   Grouping by Place. Groups may be formed according to the geographical regions in which the organization operates. In May 1942, the U.S. War Department was organized in terms of seven "theaters"—North American, African Middle Eastern, European, Asiatic, Pacific, Southwest Pacific, and Latin American. On a less global scale, a bread company may have the same baking facility duplicated in twenty different population areas to ensure fresh daily delivery in each. Figure 3–4 shows another example of geographical grouping—in this case two-tier—in the superstructure of the Canadian Post Office. A very different basis for grouping

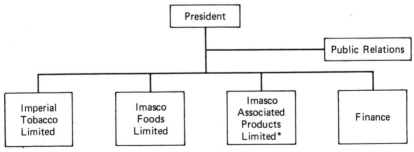

* Retail chain stores, etc.

Figure 3-3. *Grouping by output: Imasco Limited (circa 1975). Used by permission.*

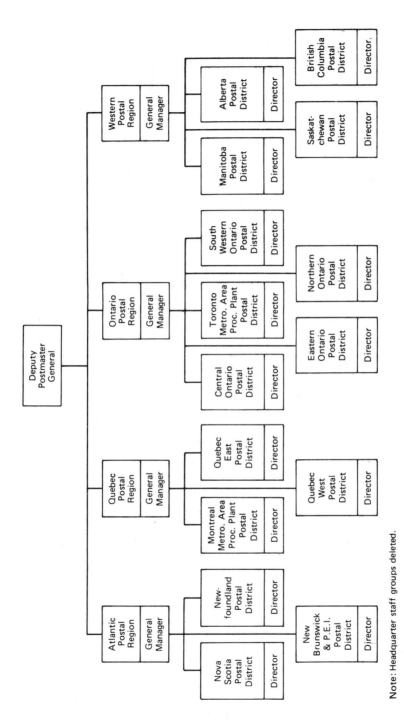

Note: Headquarter staff groups deleted.

Figure 3-4. *Grouping by place: the Canadian Post Office (circa 1978). Used with permission.*

by place relates to the specific location (within a geographic area) where the work is actually carried out. Football players are differentiated according to where they stand on the field relative to the ball (linemen, backfielders, ends); aircraft construction crews are distinguished by the part of the airplane on which they work (wing, tail); and some medical specialists are grouped according to the part of the body on which they work (the head in psychiatry, the heart in cardiology).

Of course, like all nice, neat categorization schemes, this one has its own gray areas. Psychiatry was purposely included in two examples—one in grouping by place, the other in grouping by knowledge and skill—to illustrate this point. Consider, for example, the medical specialties of surgery and obstetrics. These are defined in the *Random House Dictionary* as follows:

- *Surgery:* the act, practice, or work of treating diseases, injuries, or deformities by manual operation or instrumental appliances.
- *Obstetrics:* the branch of medical science concerned with childbirth and caring for and treating women in or in connection with childbirth.

These definitions are not consistent in our terms. Obstetrics is defined according to client; surgery is defined according to work processes. A closer look indicates that even within a medical specialty, the basis for specialization can be ambiguous. Obstetricians may deal with particular clients, but they also use particular work processes, and their outputs are also unique to their grouping (namely, delivered babies); surgeons treat special kinds of patients and they also have their own distinct outputs (removed or replaced organs). In the same vein, so to speak, Herbert Simon points out that "an education department may be viewed as a purpose (to educate) organization, or a clientele (children) organization; the Forest Service as a purpose (forest conservation), process (forest management), clientele (lumbermen and cattlemen utilizing public forests), or area (publicly owned forest lands) organization" (1957:30, 31).

The notion of grouping by process, people, place, or purpose (output) is, in fact, one of the pillars of the classical literature on organization design, and Simon devotes some of his sharpest criticism of the classical principles to it (pp. 28–35). He is especially severe on the "ambiguities" of the terms, arguing, as in the quotation above, that the same group can often be perceived in different ways.

A typist moves her fingers in order to type; types in order to reproduce a letter; reproduces a letter in order that an inquiry may be answered. Writing a letter is then the purpose for which the typing is performed; while writing a letter is also the process whereby the purpose of replying to an inquiry is achieved. It follows that the same activity may be described as purpose or process. (p. 30)

Simon's basic point is that process and purpose are linked in a hierarchy of organizational means and ends, each activity being a process for a higher-order goal (typing a letter to answer an inquiry, manufacturing products to satisfy customers), and a purpose for a lower-order one (moving fingers to type a letter, buying machines to manufacture a product). In the same sense, the *whole* organization can be viewed as a process in society—police departments for protection so that the citizens can live in peace, food companies to supply nourishment so that people can sustain themselves.

It is interesting to note that Simon's illustrations of ambiguities between process and purpose in specific departments all come from organizations in which the operators are professionals. So, too, does our example of surgery and obstetrics. In fact, it so happens that their training differentiates the professionals by their knowledge and skills as well as by the work processes they use, which leads them to be grouped on these two bases concurrently. In professional organizations, clients select the professionals on these bases as well. One does not visit a cardiologist for an ingrown toenail; students interested in becoming chemists do not register in the business school. In other words, in professional organizations such as hospitals, accounting firms, and school systems, where professional operators serve their own clients directly, grouping the operators by knowledge, skill, work process, and client all amount to the same thing.

But is that true in other organizations? The purchasing department in a manufacturing firm is far removed from the clients; it merely performs one of the functions that eventually leads to the products' sale to the clients. Thus, it cannot be considered to be a client-based or output-based group. Of course, in Simon's sense, it does have its own outputs and its own clients—purchased items supplied to the manufacturing department. But this example shows how we can clarify the ambiguity Simon raises: simply by making the context clear. Specifically, we can define output, client, and place only in terms of the *entire* organization. In other words, in our context, purpose is defined in terms of the purpose of the organization vis-à-vis *its* clients or markets, not in terms of intermediate steps to get it to the point of servicing clients and markets, nor in terms of the needs of the larger society in which the organization is embedded.

In fact, we shall compress all the bases for grouping discussed above to two essential ones: *market* grouping, comprising the bases of output, client, and place,[1] and *functional* grouping, comprising the bases of knowl-

---

[1]The term *market* is used expressly to refer to business as well as nonbusiness organizations. Every organization exists to serve some market, whether that consist of the citizens for a police force, the students for a school system, or the customers for a manufacturing firm.

edge, skill, work process, and function. (Grouping by time can be considered to fall into either category.) In effect, **we have the fundamental distinction between grouping activities by ends, by the characteristics of the ultimate markets served by the organization—the products and services it markets, the customers it supplies, the places where it supplies them—or by the means, the functions (including work processes, skills, and knowledge) it uses to produce its products and services.**

Each of these two bases for grouping merits detailed attention. But to better understand them, we must first consider some of the criteria organizations can use to group positions and units.

Criteria for grouping

We can isolate four basic criteria that organizations are able to use to select the bases for grouping positions and units: interdependencies related to the work flow, the work process, the scale of the work, and the social relationships around the work.

1   **Work-Flow Interdependencies.** A number of studies that have focused on the relationships among specific operating tasks stress one conclusion: grouping of operating tasks should reflect natural work-flow interdependencies. In Figure 3–5, for example, we have one writer's view of "natural" and "unnatural" grouping in a sequential manufacturing process in an Indian weaving mill. Grouping on the basis of work-flow interdependencies creates what some researchers call a "psychologically complete task." **In the market-based grouping, the members of a single unit have a sense of territorial integrity; they control a well-defined organizational process; most of the problems that arise in the course of their work can be solved simply, through their mutual adjustment; and many of the rest, which must be referred up the hierarchy, can still be handled within the unit, by that single manager in charge of the work flow.** In contrast, when well-defined work flows, such as mining a coal face or producing a purchase order, are divided among different units, coordination becomes much more difficult. Workers and managers with different allegiances are called upon to cooperate. Since they often cannot, problems must be handled higher up in the hierarchy, by managers removed from the work flow.

James Thompson puts some nice flesh on the bones of these concepts, describing how organizations account for various kinds of interdependencies between tasks. Thompson discusses three basic kinds of interdependence: pooled, involving only the sharing of resources; sequential, where the work is fed from one task to the next; and reciprocal, where the work is passed back and forth between tasks. Thompson claims that organizations try to group tasks so as to minimize coordination and commu-

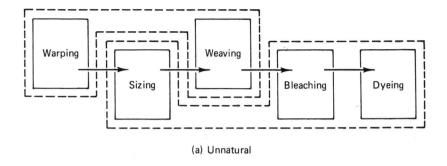

(a) Unnatural

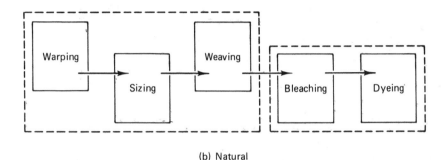

(b) Natural

Figure 3-5. *"Natural" and "unnatural" grouping in a weaving mill according to work flow (from Miller, 1959:257)*

nication costs. Since reciprocal interdependence is the most complex and hence the most costly, followed by sequential, Thompson concludes:

> The basic units are formed to handle reciprocal interdependence, if any. If there is none, then the basic units are shaped according to sequential interdependence, if any. If neither of the more complicated types of interdependence exists, the basic units are shaped according to common processes [to facilitate the handling of pooled interdependence]. (1967: 59)'

The question of grouping does not, however, end there, because "residual" interdependencies typically remain: one grouping cannot contain all the interdependency. This must be picked up in higher-order groupings, thus necessitating the construction of a hierarchy. And so, "The question is not which criterion to use for grouping, but rather in which *priority* are the several criteria to be exercised" (p. 51). Thompson's answer is, of course, that the organization designs the lowest-level groups to contain the major reciprocal interdependencies; higher-order groups are then formed to handle the remaining sequential interdependencies, and the final groups, if necessary, are formed to handle any remaining pooled interdependencies.

Figure 3–6 illustrates this with a five-tier hierarchy of an apocryphal international manufacturing company. The first and second groupings are by work process, the third by business function, the fourth by output (product), and the top one by place (country). (Staff groups are also shown at each level; these will be discussed later in the chapter.) The tightest interdependencies, reciprocal in nature, would be between the turning, milling, and drilling departments in the factory. The next level contains the sequential interdependencies from fabricating to assembly. Similarly, the level above that, largely concerned with product development, contains important sequential interdependencies. In mass production, typically, the products are first designed in the engineering department, then produced in the manufacturing department, and finally marketed by the marketing department. Above this, the interdependencies are basically pooled: For the most part, the product divisions and the national subsidiaries are independent of each other except that they share common financial resources and certain staff support services.

2 **Process Interdependencies.** Work-flow interdependencies are not, of course, the only ones to be taken into consideration by the designer of organization structure. A second important class of interdependence relates to the *processes* used in the work flow. For example, one lathe operator may have to consult another, working on a different product line (that is, in a different work flow), about what cutting tool to use on a certain job. In effect, **we have interdependencies related to specialization, which favor functional grouping.** Positions may have to be grouped to encourage process interactions, even at the expense of work-flow coordination. When like specialists are grouped together, they learn from each other and become more adept at their specialized work. They also feel more comfortable "among their own," with their work judged by peers and by managers expert in the same field.

3 **Scale Interdependencies.** The third criterion for grouping relates to economies of scale. **Groups may have to be formed to reach sizes large enough to function efficiently.** For example, every department in the factory requires maintenance. But that does not necessarily justify attaching one maintenance man to each department—in effect, grouping him by work flow. There may not be enough work for each maintenance man. So a central maintenance department may be set up for the whole factory.

This, of course, encourages process specialization: whereas the maintenance man in each department would have to be a jack of all trades, the one among many in a maintenance department can specialize, for example, in preventive maintenance. Similarly, it may make economic sense to have only one data-processing department for the entire company, so that it can use a large, efficient computer; data-processing departments in each division might have to use smaller, less efficient ones.

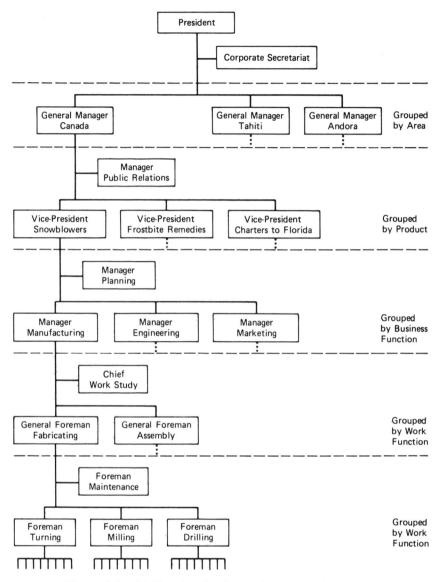

Figure 3-6. *Multiple levels of grouping in a multinational firm*

This issue—essentially of the *concentration* or *dispersal* of services—arises in a great many contexts in the organization. Should secretaries be grouped into typing pools or assigned to individual users; should the university have a central library or a series of satellite ones attached to each faculty; should the corporation have a single strategic planning group at headquarters or one attached to each division (or both); should there be a central telephone switchboard or a centrex system, allowing the public to dial directly inside the organization? The issue lends itself well to mathematical formulation and has been so treated in some of the literature (for example, Kochen and Deutsch, 1973). We shall return to this issue shortly.

4 **Social Interdependencies.** A fourth criterion for grouping relates not to the work done but to the social relationships that accompany it. One study in coal mines (Trist and Bamforth, 1951) showed clearly the importance of these social factors. Workers had to form groups to facilitate mutual support in a dangerous environment. To use a favorite term of the well-known British Tavistock Institute, the system was *sociotechnical.*

Other social factors can enter into the design of units. For example, the Hawthorne studies suggested that when the work is dull, the workers should be close together, to facilitate social interaction and so avoid boredom. Personalities enter the picture as well, often as a major factor in organizational design. People prefer to be grouped on the basis of "getting along." As a result, **the design of every superstructure ends up as a compromise between the "objective" factors of work flow, process, and scale interdependency, and the "subjective" factors of personality and social need.** Organigrams may be conceived on paper, but they must function with flesh-and-blood human beings. "Sure, the sales manager should report to the area superintendent. But the fact is that they're not on speaking terms, so we show him reporting to the head of purchasing instead. It may seem screwy, but we had no choice." How often have we heard such statements? Scratch any structure of real people and you will find it loaded with such compromises.

In many cases, "getting along" encourages process specialization. Specialists get along best with their own kind, in part because their work makes them think alike, but also, perhaps more importantly, because in many cases it was common personality factors that caused them to choose their specialties in the first place. The extroverts seek out marketing or public relations, the analytic types end up in the technostructure. Sometimes it is best to keep them apart, at least on the organigram.

These four criteria—work flow, process, scale, and social interdependencies—constitute the prime criteria organizations use to design units. Now let us see how these apply to the functional and market bases for grouping.

Grouping by function

Grouping by function—by knowledge, skill, work process, or work function—reflects an overriding concern for process and scale interdependencies (and perhaps secondarily for social interdependencies), generally at the expense of those of the work flow. By grouping on a functional basis, the organization can pool human and material resources across different work flows. Functional structure also encourages specialization—for example, by establishing career paths for specialists within their own area of expertise, by enabling them to be supervised by one of their own, and by bringing them together to encourage social interaction. Thus, one researcher found in a detailed study of thirty-eight firms working on U.S. government R&D contracts that "while the existence of project [market-based] teams increased the likelihood of meeting cost and time targets, the presence of a strong functional base was associated with higher technical excellence as rated by both managers and clients" (Knight, 1976:115–16).

But these same characteristics indicate the chief weaknesses of the functional structure. The emphasis on narrow specialty detracts from attention to broader output. Individuals focus on their own means, not the organization's broader ends. Moreover, performance cannot easily be measured in the functional structure. When sales drop, who is at fault: marketing for not pushing hard enough, or manufacturing for shoddy workmanship? One will blame the other, with nobody taking responsibility for the overall result. Someone up above is supposed to take care of all that.

In effect, **the functional structure lacks a built-in mechanism for coordinating the work flow.** Unlike the market structures that contain the work-flow interdependencies within single units, functional structures impede both mutual adjustment among different specialists and direct supervision at the unit level by the management. The structure is incomplete; additional means of coordination must be found.

The natural tendency is to let coordination problems rise to higher-level units in the hierarchy, until they arrive at a level where the different functions in question meet. The trouble with this, however, is that the level may be too far removed from the problem. In our Figure 3–6, for example, a problem involving the functions of both drilling and selling (perhaps a request by a customer to have a special hole drilling on his snowblowers for rear-view mirrors) would have to rise three levels to the vice-president in charge of snowblowers, the first person whose responsibilities involve both functions.

Of course, functional structures need not rely on direct supervision for coordination. These are specialized structures; where their jobs are unskilled, they can rely on formalization to achieve coordination. Thus, we can conclude that **the functional structures—notably, where the operating work is unskilled—tend to be the more bureaucratic ones.** Their work tends to be more formalized, and that requires a more elaborate administrative structure—more analysts to formalize the work, and higher up the hierarchy, more managers to coordinate the work across the functional units. So some of the gains made by the better balancing of human and machine resources are lost in the need for more personnel to achieve coordination.

To put this issue the other way around, bureaucratic structures (with unskilled operators) rely more extensively on the functional bases for grouping. That is, they tend to be organized by the function performed rather than the market served. (And where there are many levels of grouping, they tend to be organized on functional bases at higher levels in the hierarchy.) In seeking, above all, to rationalize their structures, such bureaucracies prefer to group according to the work processes used and then to coordinate by the formalization of work, involving the proliferation of rules. This way, on paper at least, all relationships are rationalized and coherent.

Grouping by market

Lawrence and Lorsch provide us with an interesting illustration of the advantages of market grouping. They reproduce a memo from an advertising agency executive to his staff describing the rationale for a conversion from a functional structure (based on copy, art, and TV departments) to one of the market groups:

> Formation of the "total creative" department completely tears down the walls between art, copy, and television people. Behind this move is the realization that for best results all creative people, regardless of their particular specialty, must work together under the most intimate relationship as total advertising people, trying to solve creative problems together from start to finish.
>
> The new department will be broken into five groups reporting to the senior vice president and creative director, each under the direction of an associate creative director. Each group will be responsible for art, television, and copy in their accounts. (1967:37)

In this case, market-based grouping is used to set up relatively self-contained units to deal with particular work flows. Ideally, these units contain all the important sequential and reciprocal interdependencies, so that only the pooled ones remain: each unit draws its resources and perhaps certain support services from the common structure and in turn contributes its surpluses or profits back to it. And because each unit performs all the functions for a given set of products, services, clients, or places, it tends to identify directly with them, and so its performance can easily be measured in these terms. Markets, not processes, get the employees' undivided attention. And, of course, with the necessary mutual adjustment and direct supervision contained right inside the unit, the organization need rely less on formalization for coordination, and so tends to emerge as less bureaucratic.

But with the focus on coordination across specialties, there is, of course, less process specialization. Compare, for example, these two bases for grouping in a retail company, say, in hardware. The company can build one large downtown store that sells everything imaginable, organizing itself on the basis of specialist departments. In contrast, it can set itself up as a retail chain, a market-based structure with small stores throughout the city. In search of special items for his nail sculptures, the customer in the large, specialized store would simply find the nail department and seek out a salesperson there who could tell him if copper roofing nails with crosshatched heads were available in the five-centimeter size or only in the seven-centimeter size. Should the nail sculptor find himself in the smaller branch store, almost certainly more conveniently located, he would probably find no copper nails of any kind in stock—or any salesperson who could distinguish copper nails from brass-plated ones. But the salesperson in the chain store could better tell him where to find a hammer.

In general, the market structure is a less machinelike structure, less able to do a specialized or repetitive task well. But it can do more tasks and change tasks more easily, its essential flexibility deriving from the fact that its units are relatively independent of each other. New units can easily be added and old ones deleted. Any one store in a retail chain can easily be closed down, usually with little effect on the others. But closing down one specialized department in a large store may bankrupt it. There are chain stores that sell only bread or cheese, but there is no supermarket that can afford to dispense with either.

The market basis for grouping is, however, no panacea for the problems of organizational design. We can see this most clearly in a study by Kover (1963–64). He, too, looked at an advertising agency that reorganized, in virtually the same way as the one cited earlier. But Kover found effects not mentioned above: Specialists had much less communication with colleagues in their own functions and even with the clients (communication with them now being restricted largely to the managers of the market units); their sense of professional worth diminished, in part because their work was judged by general managers instead of their specialist peers. Those who saw themselves as craftsmen became increasingly dissatisfied with their work and alienated from the firm; many, in fact, left within a year of the reorganization. In effect, the market-based structure detracted from an emphasis on specialization, apparently with a resulting decrease in the quality of the specialized work.

The market structure is also more wasteful of resources than the functional one—at the lowest unit level if not in the administrative hierarchy—since it must duplicate personnel and equipment or else lose the advantages of specialization.

> . . . if the organization has two projects, each requiring one half-time electronics engineer and one half-time electromechanical engineer, the pure project [market] organization must either hire two electrical engineers—and reduce specialization—or hire four engineers (two electronics and two electromechanical)—and incur duplication costs. (Galbraith; 1971:30)

Moreover, the market structure, because of less functional specialization, cannot take advantage of economies of scale the way the functional structure can. The large hardware store can perhaps afford a lift truck at its unloading dock, whereas the small one cannot. Also, there may be wasteful competition within the market structure, as, for example, when stores in the same chain compete for the same customers.

What all this comes down to is that **by choosing the market basis for grouping, the organization opts for work-flow coordination at the expense of process and scale specialization. Thus, if the work-flow interdependences are the significant ones and if they cannot easily be contained by standardization, the organization should try to contain them in a market-based grouping to facilitate direct supervision and mutual adjustment. However, if the work flow is irregular (as in a job shop), if standardization can easily contain work-flow interdependences, or if the process and scale interdependences are the significant ones (as in the case of organizations with sophisticated machinery), then the organization should seek the advantages of specialization and choose the functional basis for grouping instead.**

Grouping in different parts of the organization

At this point it is useful to distinguish the first-order grouping—that is, individual positions into units—from higher-order grouping—units into larger units. The former, of course, pertains to the grouping of operators, analysts, and support staffers as individuals into their basic working units, and the latter pertains to the grouping of managers in order to build the formal hierarchy.

A characteristic of the first-order groupings is that **operators, analysts, and support staffers tend to be grouped into their own respective units in the first instance.** That is, operators tend to form units with other operators, analysts with other analysts, and staff support personnel with other staff support personnel. (Obviously, this assumes that the organization is large enough to have a number of positions of each. An important exception to this—to be discussed later—is the case where a staff member is assigned as an individual to a line group, as for example when an accountant reports directly to a factory manager.) It is typically when the higher-order groups are formed that different operators, analysts, and support staffers come together under common supervision. We shall elaborate on this point in our discussion of each of these groups.

The examples cited in this chapter have shown that positions in the operating core can be grouped on a functional or a market basis, depending primarily on the importance of process and scale interdependences as opposed to those of the work flow. Assembly lines are market-based groups, organized according to the work flow, whereas job shops, because of irregular work flows or the need for expensive machinery, group their positions by work process and so represent functional groupings. And as we noted earlier, in operating cores manned by professionals, the functional and market bases for grouping are often achieved concurrently: The professionals are grouped according to their knowledge and skills and the work processes they use, but since their clients select them on these bases, the groups become, in effect, market-based as well.

Which basis for grouping is more common in the operating core? The research provides no definite answer on this question. But ours is a society of specialists, and that is most clearly manifested in our formal organizations, particularly in their operating cores and staff structures. Thus, we should expect to find the functional basis for grouping the most common in the operating core.

There is, by definition, only one level of grouping in the operating core—the operators grouped into units managed by the first-line supervisors. From there on, grouping brings line managers together and so builds the administrative superstructure of the middle line.

In designing this superstructure, we meet squarely the question that Thompson posed: not which basis of grouping, but rather in which order of priority? Much as fires are built by stacking logs first one way and then the other, so organizations are often built by varying the bases for grouping units. For example, in Figure 3–6, the first grouping within the middle line is based on work process (fabricating and assembling), the next above on business function (engineering, manufacturing, and marketing), the one above that on market (snowblowers, and so on), and the last one on place (Canada, and so on). The presence of market-based groups in the upper region of the administrative hierarchy is probably indicative: **anecdotal evidence (published organigrams, and the like) suggests that the market basis for grouping is more common at the higher levels of the middle line than at the lower ones, particularly in large organizations.**

As a final note on the administrative superstructure, it should be pointed out that, by definition, there is only one grouping at the strategic apex, and that encompasses the entire organization—all its functions and markets. From the organization's point of view, this can be thought of as a market group, although from society's point of view, the whole organization can also be considered as performing some particular function (delivering the mail in the case of the post office, or supplying fuel in the case of an oil company).

Staff personnel—both analysts and support staff—seem, like wolves, to move in packs, or homogeneous clusters, according to the function they perform in the organization. To put this another way, staff members are not often found in the structure as individuals reporting with operators or different staffers directly to line managers of market units they serve. Instead, they tend in the first instance to report to managers of their own specialty—the accountant to a controller, the work-study analyst to the manager of industrial engineering, the scientist to the chief of the research laboratory, the chef to the manager of the plant cafeteria. This in large part reflects the need to encourage specialization in their knowledge and skills, as well as to balance their use efficiently across the whole organization. For example, the need for specialization as well as its high cost dictate that there be only one research laboratory in many organizations.

Sometimes, in fact, an individual analyst, such as an accountant, is placed within a market unit, ostensibly reporting to its line manager. But he is there to exercise control over the behavior of the line unit (and its manager), and whether de facto or de jure, his allegiance runs straight back to his specialized unit in the technostructure.

But at some point—for staff units if not for staff individuals—the question arises as to where they should be placed in the superstructure. Should they be dispersed in small units to the departments they are to serve—often market-based units—or should they be concentrated into larger ones at a central location to serve the entire organization? And how high up in the superstructure should they be placed; that is, to line managers at what level should they report?

As for level, the decision depends on the staffers' interactions. A unit of financial experts who work with the chief executive officer would naturally report to him, and one of work-study analysts might report to the manager at the plant level. As for concentration or dispersal, the decision reflects all the factors discussed above, especially the tradeoff between work-flow interdependencies (namely, the interactions with the users) and the need for specialization and economies of scale. For example, in the case of secretaries, the creation of a pool allows for specialization (one secretary can type manuscripts, another letters, and so on) and the better balancing of personnel, whereas individual assignment allows for a closer rapport with the user (I cannot imagine every member of a typing pool learning to read my handwriting!). Thus, in universities, where the professors' needs are varied and the secretarial costs low relative to those of the professors, secretarial services are generally widely dispersed. In contrast, university swimming pools, which are expensive, are concentrated, and libraries may go either way, depending on the location and specific needs of the various users.

Referring back to Figure 3–6, we find staff units at all levels of the hierarchy, some concentrated at the top, others dispersed to the market divisions and functional departments. The corporate secretariat serves the whole organization and links closely with the top management; thus, it reports directly to the strategic apex. The other units are dispersed to serve more or less local needs. One level down, public relations is attached to each of the national general managers so that, for example, each subsidiary can combat political resistance at the national level. Planning is dispersed to the next level, the product divisions, because of their conglomerate nature; each must plan independently for its own distinct product lines. Other staff units, such as work study, are dispersed to the next, functional level, where they can serve their respective factories. (We also find our ubiquitous cafeteria here—one for each plant.) Finally, the maintenance department is dispersed down to the general-foreman level, to serve fabricating or assembly.

Unit Size

The second basic issue in the design of the superstructure concerns how large each unit or work group should be. How many positions should be contained in the first-level grouping, and how many units in each successively higher-order unit? This question of unit size can be rephrased in two important ways: How many people should report to each manager? That is, what should be the manager's *span of control*? And what *shape* should the superstructure be: *tall*, with small units and narrow spans of control, or *wide*, with large units and wide spans of control?

On this point, the traditional literature was firm: "No supervisor can supervise directly the work of more than five or, at the most, six subordinates whose work interlocks," said Colonel Lydal Urwick unequivocally (1956, p. 41). But subsequent investigation has made this statement seem rather quaint. One study (Holden et al., 1968:95) reported an average span of control of ten for corporate chief executive officers, with a range from one to fourteen. Woodward (1965) found an average of six for the chief executives of the industrial firms she studied, but that measure climbed above twelve in five of the "successful" firms. For the first-line supervisors in the firms in mass production, the average span of control was close to fifty, and it ranged into the nineties in some cases. Worthy reported that the merchandising vice-president of Sears, Roebuck and Co. had forty-four senior executives reporting to him; for the typical store manager, the figure was "forty-odd" department managers (1959:109). And Pfiffner and Sherwood (1960) noted the extreme example of "the Bank of America, which has over 600 branches throughout California, each of which reports directly to corporate headquarters at San Francisco. There is no intervening area structure with directive powers over the branch offices" (p. 161). In some of these cases, notably the Bank of America and perhaps also Sears, Roebuck, Urwick's qualification about interlocking work may apply. But certainly not in all.

About the concept of span of control, Pfiffner and Sherwood have commented:

> Much blood has been let to reduce the executive's span with inconsequential results to administrative performance. Yet span of control sails merrily on. There is much written about it. Most consultants tab this as an essential in

reform proposals. Students sweat over its definition, mainly because they assume the concept should be more complicated than it really is. Thus, regardless of what its merits may be, span of control is so entrenched in the administrative culture that it must be accorded a prominent place in any book on organization. (pp. 155–56)

There is no doubt that the concept merits a prominent place in this book. But there is reason to doubt Pfiffner and Sherwood's suggestion that it is a simple one. Who should be counted as a subordinate? For example, what about the assistant to, or those whose work is reviewed by the manager even though they do not formally report to him? What about the nonsupervisory aspects of the manager's job—collecting information, developing liaison contacts, and so on? Does a narrow span of control necessarily mean close "control," as the traditional literature suggested, or might it instead imply that the manager is busy doing these other things? What about the influence of the coordinating mechanisms other than direct supervision on the size of the work unit?

What all this suggests is that the issue is not a simple one and the focus on control is misplaced. Control—that is, direct supervision—is only one factor among many in deciding how many positions to group into one unit, or how many units to group in one larger unit, in both cases under a single manager. Hence, we prefer the term *unit size* to "span of control."

Unit size in relation to the coordinating mechanisms

Much of the confusion in this area seems to stem from considering unit size only with respect to the coordinating mechanism of direct supervision, not of standardization or mutual adjustment. The traditional management theorists set the tone by implying that control and coordination could be achieved only by direct supervision. What else would have prompted Urwick to insist on his "five, or at the most, six" formula?

As has been pointed out repeatedly since the start of our discussion, the five coordinating mechanisms are to some extent substitutable. For example, the manager's job can be "institutionalized" by standardization; and mutual adjustment within the work group can be used in place of direct supervision from above. We would, of course, expect such replacement of direct supervision by another coordinating mechanism to affect significantly the size of a unit. Thus, we should be able to explain variations in unit size largely in terms of the mechanisms used to coordinate work.

We can summarize our conclusions in terms of two basic propositions, one dealing with standardization, the other with mutual adjustment. First, **compared with direct supervision, the greater the use of standardization for coordination, the larger the size of the work unit.** It stands to reason that the more coordination in a unit is achieved through the systems of standardization designed by the technostructure, the less time its manager need spend on the direct supervision of each employee, and so the greater the number of employees that can report to him. With this conclusion, we can rather easily explain Woodward's finding about the very high spans of control encountered in the mass-production firms. Bear in mind two points about her findings. First, the very wide spans of control were found at the first level of supervision—namely, in those units containing the operators themselves. Second, the largest operating units—with an average of almost fifty employees—were found in the mass-production firms. Those in unit (custom) and in process production had units averaging less than twenty-five and fifteen operators, respectively. Indeed, they had virtually no units even as large as the *average* for the mass producers. Now, when we combine this with Woodward's findings that the mass-production firms were the only bureaucratic ones, the other two being structured organically, we see an evident relationship. Unit size was largest where the work was the most standardized—in the operating cores of the most bureaucratic organizations.

So far, we have discussed only the standardization of work processes. However, our first proposition is not restricted to any special kind of standardization. In other words, standardization of skills and of outputs should also lead to larger unit size. In the case of skills, it stands to reason that the more highly trained the employees, the less closely they need be supervised, and so the larger their work units can be. We see this most clearly in general hospitals and universities. At the time of this writing, sixty of my colleagues and I work in a single unit, which runs smoothly under a single dean with no department heads.

Similarly, we would expect that the more standardized the outputs, the larger can be the size of the work unit. Thus, although the Bank of America justified its span of control of 600 on the basis of encouraging the initiative of its branch managers, we would be on safe ground in assuming that this enormous span of control would simply be impossible without a very tight system of performance (output) control, not to mention the use of all kinds of rules and regulations and of training and indoctrination programs for the branch managers. Similarly, those who shop at Sears well know how standardized that operation is. As Moore, referring implicitly to the role of indoctrination, commented, "Sears can decentralize [that is, release the store managers from close supervision]; everyone thinks alike anyway" (quoted in Wilensky, 1967:60). Chains of banks and retail stores frequently exhibit very wide spans of control precisely because each outlet is a carbon copy of all the others, thereby facilitating standardization.

Thus, we cannot conclude that being a member of a large unit automatically frees the individual from close control. Control from the boss, perhaps, but not necessarily from the systems of the technostructure—or even from the person's earlier training and indoctrination. In fact, the most tightly controlled members of organizations are typically those in the largest units—the operators doing unskilled work in highly bureaucratic operating cores. Even their managers feel the same control. I once spoke to eighty branch managers of large Canadian banking firms on the nature of managerial work; the ensuing discussion period was dominated by one issue—their extreme frustration in being unable to act as full-fledged managers, because of the rules imposed on their branches by the corporate technostructures.

Our second proposition is as follows: **Compared with standardization and often even direct supervision, the greater the reliance on mutual adjustment (owing to interdependencies among complex tasks), the smaller the size of the work unit.** A relationship between complex interdependent tasks and small unit size can be explained in two ways. The obvious one is that, all coordinating mechanisms (especially standardization) remaining equal, the more interdependent the tasks (complex or not) in a unit, the greater will be the need for contact between the manager and the employees to coordinate their work. Ostensibly, the manager will have to monitor and supervise the unit's activities more closely and to be more readily available for consultation and advice. Therefore, the manager requires a small span of control. This suggests yet another angle on the Sears and Bank of America stories—namely, the absence of interdependence. Geographically dispersed retail branches, each serving its own customers, are neither reciprocally nor sequentially interdependent; far more of them can, therefore, be supervised than, say, the sequentially interdependent departments of a factory. That is why Urwick qualified his principle of span of control with the word "interlocks."

But there is a second, more subtle explanation for the hypothesized relationship between *complex* interdependent tasks and small unit size. These kinds of tasks are difficult to supervise, so instead of an increase in direct supervision, they give rise to an increase in mutual adjustment. The employees themselves must communicate on a face-to-face basis to coordinate their work. But for such communication to function effectively, the work unit must be small, small enough to encourage convenient, frequent, and informal interaction among all its members. Thus, one study indicated that beyond ten members, groups tend to fragment into cliques—that is, smaller groups—and another found that five to seven members was optimal for consensus. Now, organizations, being what they are, designate a leader—a "manager"—for each of their units, no matter how small, even when that person acts as little more than the unit's official spokesperson. And so, when the span of control of units doing interdependent complex tasks is measured, lo and behold, it turns out to be small.

Let us reflect on this conclusion for a moment. On the surface, it is counterintuitive, since it could be restated as follows: the less the reliance on direct supervision (in favor of mutual adjustment), the *narrower* the manager's span of control. The confusion, of course, lies with the term used, for here, span of control has nothing to do with "control"; it is merely an indication of the need to maintain a small face-to-face work group to encourage mutual adjustment when the work is complex and interdependent. In other words, although the restatement of the proposition may be technically correct, it is misleading to use terms like "direct supervision" and "span of control." We are better off to conclude that, because of the need for "mutual adjustment," "unit size" must be small.

This point suggests two lessons. First, in the area of structure (I am tempted to say management in general), things are not necessarily what they seem. We cannot rely on the pleasant conceptualizations of the armchair; we have to go out and research phenomena directly. Careful observation produces its own share of surprises. Second, we had better choose our terms (like "control") very carefully, and be quite sure of what we are measuring when we do empirical research.

One final point should be mentioned. Much of the evidence showing that complex interdependent tasks lead to small unit size comes from studies of professional groups. But how can we reconcile this finding with that of the first proposition—namely, that professionalism (that is, standardization of skills) leads to a large unit size? The answer lies in interdependence: Professional work is always complex (as we define it), but it is not always interdependent. **There are, in effect, two kinds of professional work—independent and interdependent—requiring two very different structural forms.** In one case, the standardization of skills handles most of the interdependencies, so there is little need for mutual adjustment and the professionals can work independently, in large units. This is the situation we find in most accounting firms and educational systems, where individual professionals serve their own clients. In the other case, interdependencies remain that cannot be handled by the standardization of skills, so there must be considerable mutual adjustment. The professionals must work cooperatively in small, informal units. This happens, for example, in research laboratories and think-tank consulting firms.

Thus, looking at unit size in terms of all the coordinating mechanisms helps to sweep away some of the confusion. Before we conclude this discussion, however, we should mention some of the findings of other research—notably on tall versus flat structures, often carried out in the social psychological laboratory—because that has suggested some other factors that effect unit size. In particular, tall structures (with small units at each level, giving rise to many levels, or a "tall" hierarchy) have been shown to serve better the individual's need for security, since a manager is always readily available, although they can frustrate the needs for autonomy and self-actualization. Indeed, top managers seem to be more satisfied in tall structures—it is they, after all, who do the controlling—whereas lower-level managers have reported themselves in some studies as happier in flat ones (with large units and few levels in the hierarchy), where they have more freedom from their own managers. Thus, both Worthy and Pfiffner and Sherwood explain the large unit sizes in Sears and the Bank of America by this factor. As the latter note about the span of control of over 600:

> When officers of the bank are questioned about this seemingly unorthodox setup, their response is that they do not want to risk setting up an echelon that would take authority away from the branch managers. They want them to be self-reliant local businessmen with a maximum opportunity for making decisions on their own. (p. 161)

Studies of tall versus flat structures have also found that tall structures interrupt the vertically upward flow of information more frequently, which can lead to greater distortion; and flat ones can require more discussion and consultation to get decisions made. Finally, studies have shown that the tall structure (or small-sized units), rather than encouraging closer supervision, may free the manager from the need to spend time on supervision, allowing him to get on with other duties (such as making decisions and interacting with outsiders).

To conclude our general discussion, we have seen that **unit size is driven up by (1) standardization of all three types, (2) similarity in the tasks performed in a given unit, (3) the employees' needs for autonomy and self-actualization, and (4) the need to reduce distortion in the flow of information up the hierarchy; and it is driven down by (1) the need for close direct supervision, (2) the need for mutual adjustment among complex interdependent tasks, (3) the extent to which the manager of a unit has nonsupervisory duties to perform, and (4) the need for members of the unit to have frequent access to the manager for consultation or advice, perhaps because of security needs.**

Unit size by part of the organization

How does unit size vary from one part of the organization to another? Generalizations are somewhat risky here, since, as we have seen, unit size is influenced by many factors. Nevertheless, some general comments are warranted.

It is in the operating core that we would expect to find the largest units, since this part of the organization tends to rely most extensively on standardization for coordination, especially standardization of work processes.

Managerial work is generally complex, so we might expect the size of units in the administrative structure to depend heavily on the interdependence encountered at a given level of the hierarchy. As we saw earlier in this chapter, market grouping is often selected because it contains the work-flow interdependences within each unit (and because the process interdependences are secondary), whereas functional grouping often does not, requiring either that a higher-level manager coordinate the work flow across different units or that the managers or members of each of the units in question do so themselves through mutual adjustment. In either event, the result is the same: **only a few functional units can be grouped into a higher-order unit, whereas, typically, many more market-based units can be so grouped.** A great many autonomous divisions can report to one company president, as can a great many schools to one superintendent; in contrast, the president of an integrated manufacturing firm or the manager of a television station can supervise only a few interdependent functional departments. (It will be recalled that both Sears stores and Bank of America branches are market-based units.) And since organizations vary the bases for grouping used at different levels in the administrative hierarchy, we would not expect the middle line of the large organization to be uniformly tall or flat, but rather to exhibit a wavy shape, flat where grouping is based on markets, tall where it is based on function.

Earlier we noted that as we move up the hierarchy, managerial decision making becomes more complex, less amenable to regulation. Therefore, holding interdependence constant, we would expect a greater need for mutual adjustment at the higher levels, with a resulting decrease in unit size. So **the overall managerial hierarchy should look like a cone—albeit a wavy one—with progressively steepening sides.** Thus, holding all else constant, we should expect the chief executive officer to have the narrowest average span of control in the organization. What may not, however, remain constant is the basis for grouping. As noted earlier, the market basis is often used toward the top of the middle line. Where it is so used, and the people reporting to the chief executive themselves supervise functional units, we would expect his span of control to be wider than theirs.

Another factor that confounds the span of control for the managers of the middle line is their relationship with the staff units. Coordination of line and staff activities typically requires mutual adjustment—that is, flexible communication outside the chain of authority. This, of course, takes a good deal of the line manager's time, leaving less for direct supervision. So we would expect that where there is much line/staff interdependence, spans of control in the middle line should be narrower. **Organizations with great proliferations of technocratic and support staff units should have rather small units in the middle line.**

This leads us to an interesting conclusion about highly bureaucratic organizations, heavily dependent on technocratic staff groups to formalize the operating work: although the spans of control of the first-line supervisors should be high because of the extensive standardization in the operating core, that of the managers higher up should be small because of the need for mutual adjustment with the staff members. In fact, this is exactly what comes out of the Woodward study. Mass-production firms, which she found to have bureaucratic structures, followed this pattern. In contrast, firms in process industries, with organic structures and more extensive staff units, exhibited very narrow spans of control for both first-line supervisors and managers in the center of the middle line.

Finally, what about the size of the staff units themselves? How many staff members can a staff manager supervise? In those support units that do relatively unskilled work—the cafeteria and mailroom, for example—the structure would tend to be bureaucratic and the units therefore large. But what of the other units in the technostructure and support staff? **The factors we discussed earlier indicate small size for most of the professional-type staff units.** The work within these units is complex and, being of a project nature, typically creates interdependences among the professionals. In other words, these staff members are professionals of the second type discussed earlier—namely, those who must function in small interdependent units rather than as independent individuals attached to larger units. Furthermore, the managers of technocratic units must spend a good deal of their time "selling" the proposals of their units in the middle line. Likewise, the support specialists do not work in a vacuum but serve the rest of the organization, and so their managers must spend a good deal of time in liaison with it. In both cases, this reduces the number of people the staff managers can supervise, and so shrinks the average size of staff units.

To conclude, in general we would expect the operating core of the organization to assume a flat shape, the middle line to appear as a cone with progressively steepening sides, and the technostructure and more professional support units to be tall in shape. That is, in fact, the design of our logo, as a quick glance back at Figure 1–2 will illustrate.

4

FLESHING OUT THE SUPERSTRUCTURE

Organizational design is not complete when the positions have been established and the superstructure built. At one time, the literature on organizational design stopped here. But contemporary research has made clear the need to flesh out the bones of the superstructure with linkages that are lateral, as opposed to strictly vertical. Two main groups of these linkages have received extensive treatment in the contemporary literature on organizational design—planning and control systems that standardize outputs, and liaison devices that grease the wheels of mutual adjustment. We discuss these in this chapter.

Planning and Control Systems

The purpose of a plan is to specify a desired output—a standard—at some future time. And the purpose of control is to assess whether or not that standard has been achieved. Thus, planning and control go together like the proverbial horse and carriage: There can be no control without prior planning, and plans lose their influence without follow-up controls. Together plans and controls regulate outputs and, indirectly, behavior as well.

Plans may specify (standardize) the quantity, quality, cost, and timing of outputs, as well as their specific characteristics (such as size and color). *Budgets* are plans that specify the costs of outputs for given periods of time; *schedules* are plans that establish time frames for outputs; *objectives* are plans that detail output quantities for given periods of time; *operating plans* are those that establish a variety of standards, generally the quantities and costs of outputs. Typically, planning systems, as well as the reporting systems that feed back the control information, are designed in the technostructure, by analysts with titles such as Planner, Budget Analyst, Controller, MIS Analyst, Production Scheduler, and Quality Control Analyst.

73

We can distinguish two fundamentally different kinds of planning and control systems, one that focuses on the regulation of overall performance and the other that seeks to regulate specific actions. Since the former is concerned primarily with *after-the-fact* monitoring of results, we shall call it *performance control*. The latter, oriented to specifying activities that *will* take place, is labeled *action planning*. In other words, as shown in Figure 4–1, the organization can regulate outputs in two ways. It can use performance control to measure the results of a whole series of actions, and use this information to make changes: "The profit rate should increase from 7 percent to 10 percent," or, "The drilling of holes should be increased from fifty to sixty per day." Alternatively, it can use action planning to determine in advance what specific decisions or actions are required: "Blue widgets should be sold to customers X, Y, and Z," or, "The hole should be drilled 1.108 centimeters wide." As we shall see, whereas performance control is a pure means of standardizing outputs, action planning—because it specifies particular actions—resembles in some ways the design parameter of formalization of behavior.

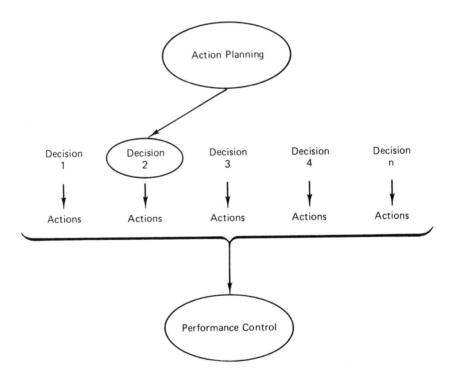

Figure 4-1. *The relationships between decisions and action planning and performance control*

Performance control

The purpose of performance control is to regulate the overall results of a given unit. Objectives, budgets, operating plans, and various other kinds of general standards are established for the unit, and its performance is later measured in terms of these standards and the results fed back up the hierarchy by the MIS. This suggests two important points: First, performance control systems map onto the bases for grouping in the organization. The planning system establishes output standards for each unit, and the control system assesses whether or not these have been met. Second, performance control is concerned with overall results for given periods of time, not with specific decisions or actions at specific points in time. For example, a performance plan may call for the production of 70,000 widgets in June, or the reduction of costs by 3 percent in July; it does not call for the shift from blue widgets to green ones or the achievement of cost reduction by the purchase of a more efficient machine. Thus, performance control influences decision making and action taking only indirectly, by establishing general targets that the decision maker must keep in the back of his mind as he makes specific decisions in the front.

Where is performance control used in the organization? To some extent, everywhere. Because cost control is always crucial and because costs—at least economic ones—are easily measured, virtually every organizational unit is given a budget—that is, a performance plan to standardize its expenditures. And where the unit's production is easily measured, its performance plan will typically specify this as well. The plant is expected to produce 400,000 widgets this month; marketing is expected to sell 375,000 of them.

But **performance control systems are most relied upon where the interdependencies between units are primarily of a pooled nature—namely, where the units are grouped on the basis of market.** Here, the major concern is that the unit perform adequately, that it make an appropriate contribution to the central organization without squandering its resources. In other words, because there is little interdependence between units, coordination requires the regulation of performance, not actions. And this is facilitated in the market-based structure by the fact that each unit has its own distinct outputs. Thus, its overall behavior is regulated by performance controls; otherwise, it is left alone to do its own action planning.

Indeed, such performance controls are typically crucial for market-based units. Because they are self-contained, they are generally given considerable freedom to act. Typically, as noted in the last chapter, a great many such units report to a single manager. Without a performance control system, the manager may be unable to catch serious problems, until it is much too late. A wayward Sears store or Bank of America branch could, for example, get lost for years, too small a part of the organization to be otherwise noticed. And from the perspective of the market unit itself, the performance control system serves to preclude direct supervision and so to grant it the freedom it needs to determine its own decisions and actions. Thus, the conglomerate corporation sets up each of its market units (its "divisions") as a profit or investment center, and holds it responsible for its own financial performance.[1]

Performance control systems can serve two purposes: to measure and to motivate. On the one hand, they can be used simply to signal when the performance of a unit has deteriorated. Higher-level management can then step in and take corrective action. On the other hand, they can be used to elicit higher performance. The performance standards are the carrots that management places before the unit manager to motivate him to achieve better results. Whenever he manages a nibble, the carrot is moved a little farther out and the manager runs faster. Systems such as management by objectives (MBO) have been developed to give unit managers a say in the establishment of these standards, so that they will be committed to them and therefore, the theory goes, strive harder to achieve them.

But this motivational aspect introduces a variety of problems. For one thing, given the right to participate in the setting of performance standards, the unit manager has a strong incentive to set the standards low enough to ensure that they can easily be met. And he also has an incentive to distort the feedback information sent up the MIS to make it look as though his unit has met a standard that it, in fact, missed. Second is the problem of choosing the planning period. There is, as noted, no direct link between the performance standards and specific decisions taken; it is only hoped that the manager will bear the standards in mind when he makes decisions. Long planning periods loosen the connection, and short ones defeat a prime purpose of the system—to give the manager freedom of action. The "flash reports" on the tenth of every month used by some corporations certainly keep the manager hopping after short-term results. But do they let him think beyond thirty days? The third problem of motivation arises with standards that cannot be realized for reasons beyond the manager's control—say, the bankruptcy of a major customer. Should the organization insist on honoring the agreement to the letter, and penalize the manager, or should it overrule the performance control system, in which case the system loses a good deal of its motivational punch?

Action planning

As we have seen, performance control is a key design parameter in market-based structures. But what happens in functional structures? Functional

---

[1]That is not to say, of course, that a performance control system can never be tight. It can specify so many detailed performance standards that the unit is left little room to maneuver. (We shall see examples of this later.) But, in general, performance controls are used in the market-based structure to maintain only the most general regulation of outputs.

work flows sequentially or reciprocally across them. This means that distinct organizational goals cannot easily be identified with any one unit. So aside from budgets and the like to control expenditures, performance control systems cannot really cope with the interdependencies of functional units. Other means must be found.

As we saw in Chapter 3, direct supervision effected through the superstructure and standardization of work processes effected through behavior formalization emerge as key mechanisms to coordinate the work in functional structures. These are preferred because they are the tightest available coordinating mechanisms. But sometimes they cannot contain all the interdependencies. And so the organization must turn to planning and control systems to standardize outputs, specifically, to action planning. Simon provides a dramatic example of what can happen when action planning fails to coordinate the remaining work-flow interdependences:

> In the first portion of the Waterloo campaign, Napoleon's army was divided in two parts. The right wing, commanded by the Emperor himself, faced Blucher at Ligny; the left wing, under Marshal Ney, faced Wellington at Quatre Bras. Both Ney and the Emperor prepared to attack, and both had prepared excellent plans for their respective operations. Unfortunately, both plans contemplated the use of Erlon's corps to deliver the final blow on the flank of the enemy. Because they failed to communicate these plans, and because orders were unclear on the day of the battle, Erlon's corps spent the day marching back and forth between the two fields without engaging in the action on either. Somewhat less brilliant tactical plans, coordinated, would have had greater success. (1957:193)

Two points should be noted about action planning. First, unlike performance control, action planning does not necessarily respect unit autonomy, nor does it necessarily map onto the system of grouping. Action plans specify decisions that call for specific actions—to market new products, build new factories, sell old machines. Some of the proposed actions may be taken within single units, but others can cut across unit boundaries.

Second, by its imposition of specific decisions, action planning turns out to be a less than pure form of standardizing outputs; more exactly, it falls between that and standardizing work processes. This point can be expressed in terms of a continuum of increasingly tight regulation, as follows:

- *Performance control* imposes general performance standards over a period of time, with no reference to specific actions.
- *Action planning* imposes specific decisions and actions to be carried out at specific points in time.

- *Behavior formalization* imposes the means by which decisions and actions are to be carried out.

So whereas performance control says, "Increase sales by 10 percent this year [in any way you care to]," action planning says, "Do it by introducing blue widgets." It, too, specifies outputs, but in a way that constitutes the specification of means. At the limit, action planning becomes behavior formalization—namely, the specification of the work flow: ". . . the plan may control, down to minute details, a whole complex pattern of behavior. The completed plan of the battleship will specify the design of the ship down to the last rivet. The task of the construction crew is minutely specified by this design" (Simon, 1957:231).

Action planning emerges as the means by which the nonroutine decisions and actions of an entire organization, typically structured on a functional basis, can be designed as an integrated system. All this is accomplished in advance, on the drawing board so to speak. Behavior formalization designs the organization as an integrated system too, but only for its routine activities. Action planning is its counterpart for the nonroutine activities, for the changes. It specifies who will do what, when, and where, so that the change will take place as desired.

The hierarchy of action planning and performance control systems

How do these two planning and control systems relate to the superstructure and to each other? Figure 4–2 shows performance control and action planning as two separate hierarchical systems, with certain "crossovers" between them. Performance control is shown as a system in which overall objectives at the top give rise to subobjectives, budgets, and other output standards, which in turn are elaborated into ever more detailed subobjectives, budgets, and standards until they emerge at the bottom of the structure as operating plans. The final outcome is, of course, organizational actions, but the connection between the plans and the actions is shown as a series of dotted lines to indicate that it is only indirect.

The arrows in the diagram are two-sided, to indicate that the performance control system may be not only top-down—where objectives decided at the strategic apex are elaborated into ever more detailed performance standards as they pass down the hierarchy—but also bottom-up, where the units at the bottom establish their own performance standards, and these are then aggregated up the hierarchy by unit, until they emerge at the strategic apex as composite standards—in effect, objectives for the whole organization. In actual practice, however, we would expect the performance control system to function most commonly, not in a purely top-down or bottom-up manner, but in a combination of the two. Some performance standards are elaborated down the hierarchy and others are aggregated up

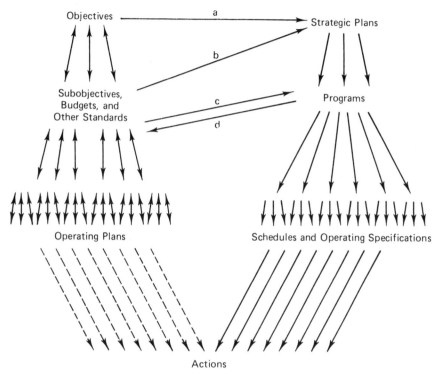

Performance Control System   Action Planning System

Objectives

Subobjectives, Budgets, and Other Standards

Operating Plans

Schedules and Operating Specifications

Programs

Strategic Plans

Actions

Figure 4-2. *Hierarchy of planning and control systems*

it; at each level, managers seek to impose standards on their employees, who propose less stringent ones instead. Through this kind of bargaining, there emerges a set of performance standards at all levels, composite and detailed.

The action planning system is essentially top-down. In theory, it begins with strategic planning, wherein the organization systematically assesses its strengths and weaknesses in terms of trends in the environment, and then formulates an explicit, integrated set of strategies it intends to follow in the future. These strategies are then developed into "programs," that is, specific projects—such as introducing a new product line, building a new factory, reorganizing the structure. These programs are, in turn, elaborated and scheduled, and eventually emerge as a set of specific operating specifications—to call on a customer, pour concrete, print an organigram—which evoke specific actions directly.

As shown in Figure 4–2, these two systems can be linked. At the top (line *a*), there is a crossover from performance objectives to strategic plans. According to the conceptual literature, the whole action planning process must begin with the specification of the overall objectives of the organization: it is believed that only with a knowledge of what the organization wants—operationalized in quantitative terms—can strategic plans be generated. The crossover from subobjectives or budgets to strategic plans (line *b*) is similar. Where there is unit autonomy, as in market-based structures, the strategic apex may develop overall objectives and then negotiate subobjectives and budgets with each of the units. These then become the objectives that initiate the action planning process in each unit.

A crossover also takes place from subobjectives and budgets to programs directly, shown by line *c*. This is more common in a functional structure, where a budget given to a department evokes specific programs rather than overall strategies. Thus, when the research department is told that its budget will be increased by $300,000 next year, it proceeds with plans to build the new laboratory it has been wanting.

The last crossover (line *d*) runs from programs to budgets and eventually to operating plans. This reflects the fact that the unit must assess the effect of all its proposed actions—the products to be marketed, machines to be bought, and so on—on its flow of funds (its budgets), the subobjectives it can reach, the manpower it must hire, and so on. In other words, the effect of specific actions on overall results must be assessed, hence the crossover from action planning to performance control.

Another crossover—perhaps the most important one, but not shown because of the nature of our diagram—is the overall feedback from performance control to action planning. As the organization assesses its performance, it initiates new action plans to correct the problems that appear.

Planning and control systems by part of the organization

Various forms of both action planning and performance control can be found at all levels of the hierarchy. In the case of the former, we have strategic planning and capital budgeting at the strategic apex and upper levels of the middle line, programming and PERT or CPM scheduling techniques at the middle levels, and production scheduling at the level of the operating core. In the case of performance control, we have already seen that objectives, budgets, and standards can be set for units and positions at any level, from the strategic apex to the operating core. At the top is the setting of overall organizational objectives; high up in the middle line are commonly found the financial reporting systems that treat major market units as profit or investment centers; elsewhere in the middle line are the standard costing systems to control aggregated performance and MBO systems to motivate line managers; and near the bottom, we find the operating plans and quality control systems.

However, our discussion also made clear that there are important differences by part of the organization. For example, although performance control can be used for individual positions—as when salespeople are given quotas, or machine operators quality control standards—we would expect it to be more commonly applied to units (and, of course, to the managers who supervise those units). Not so for action planning. We would expect action planning to apply to individual operators, as when a machinist is given specifications for the products he is to make.

Higher up in the hierarchy, we would expect the situation to be reversed. **The more global the responsibilities of a unit, the greater the propensity to control its overall performance rather than its specific actions.** For market-based units, as noted earlier, the performance control system is a critical device for control, whereas action planning is not. And since, as noted in the last chapter, the market basis for grouping is more common at higher than at lower levels in the structure, we find another reason why performance control would be favored over action planning in the upper reaches of the middle line. Of course, action planning systems may also be used at these levels where the basis for grouping is functional. As for the strategic apex, should it be subject to outside control (say, by a single owner), it may also have to respond to a performance control system. And if the basis for grouping the highest-level units is functional, then action planning may very well start right in the strategic apex.

Even though the technostructure is largely responsible for the design of all these planning and control systems, that does not mean that its own work is regulated by them. In fact, owing to the difficulty of standardizing the outputs of analytic work—activity that is usually carried out on a project or ad hoc basis—we would expect little use of performance controls in the technostructure. As for action planning, again the technocratic units do a good deal of it but seem to be only marginally affected by it themselves.

We would expect the use of planning and control systems to vary considerably in the support staff. Only those units that act as relatively autonomous entities and that have easily measured outputs—such as the cafeteria in the plant or the bookstore in the university—can be controlled primarily by performance standards. Some staff units with important interdependencies with other parts of the organization—such as the research department in the corporation—may be subject to action planning, at least to the extent that the line departments they serve are so subjected. And others, such as legal council, may experience little in the way of any planning and control system.

Liaison Devices

Often, neither direct supervision nor all three forms of standardization are sufficient to achieve the coordination an organization requires. In other words, important interdependencies remain after all the individual positions have been designed, the superstructure built, and the planning and control systems set in place. The organization must then turn to mutual adjustment for coordination. A customer complaint about poor service may, for example, require the sales and manufacturing managers to sit down together to work out new delivery arrangements.

Until recently, this kind of mutual adjustment was left largely to chance; at best, it took place informally, outside the formal organizational structure. But in recent years, **organizations have developed a whole set of devices to encourage liaison contacts between individuals, devices that can be incorporated into the formal structure.** In fact, these *liaison devices* represent the most significant contemporary development in organization design—indeed, the only serious one since the establishment of planning and control systems a decade or two earlier.

Since the 1960s, the popular literature of management has heralded each new liaison device as a major discovery. First it was "task forces," then "matrix structure," later the "integrators." But the reader was left in confusion: Were these just different names for the same phenomenon, or was each, in fact, a distinctly new contribution? And if so, did each bear any relation to the others? The writings of Jay Galbraith (1973) have re-solved many of these problems. Galbraith proposed a continuum of these liaison devices, from the simplest to the most elaborate: direct contact between managers, liaison roles, task forces, teams, integrating roles, managerial linking roles, and matrix organization. For purposes of our discussion, Galbraith's scheme has been reduced to four basic types of liaison devices—liaison positions, task forces and standing committees, integrating managers, and matrix structure.

Liaison positions

When a considerable amount of contact is necessary to coordinate the work of two units, a "liaison" position may be established formally to route the communication directly, bypassing the vertical channels. The position carries no formal authority, but because the incumbent serves at the crossroads of communication channels, he emerges as a nerve center of the organization with considerable power. Note that this power is informal, deriving from knowledge, not status. Some liaison positions serve between different line units—for example, the engineering liaison man who is a member of the engineering department but is physically located in the plant, the sales liaison person who mediates between the field sales force and the factory, or the purchase engineer who sits between purchasing and en-gineering. The latter are "instantly available to provide information to engineers whenever they need help in choosing components. They assist in writing specifications (thus making them more realistic and readable) and help expedite delivery of laboratory supplies and material for prototype models" (Strauss, 1962–63:180–81). Other liaison positions join line and staff groups; for example, the personnel specialists and accountants who counsel line departments while remaining responsive to their technocratic homes.

Task forces and standing committees

The meeting is the prime vehicle used in the organization to facilitate mutual adjustment. Some meetings are impromptu; people bump into each other in the hall and decide to have a "meeting." Others are scheduled on an ad hoc basis, as required. When the organization reaches the point of institutionalizing the meeting—that is, formally designating its participants, perhaps also scheduling it on a regular basis—the meeting may be considered to have become part of the formal structure. This happens when extensive and fairly regular contact—at least for a period of time—is required between the members of various units to discuss common concerns. Two prime liaison devices are used to institutionalize the meeting. **The task force is a committee formed to accomplish a particular task and then disband.** In contrast, **the standing committee is a more permanent interdepartmental grouping, one that meets regularly to discuss issues of common interest.** Many standing committees exist at middle levels of the organization, and others are formed at the strategic apex, a common one being the executive committee.

Integrating managers

When more coordination by mutual adjustment is required than liaison positions, task forces, and standing committees can provide, the organization may designate an integrating manager—in effect, a liaison position with formal authority. A new individual, sometimes with his own unit, is superimposed on the old departmental structure and given some of the power that formerly resided in the separate departments. Integrating managers can include brand managers in consumer-goods firms, responsible for the production and marketing of particular products; project managers in aerospace agencies, responsible for integrating certain functional activities; unit managers in hopsitals, responsible for integrating the activities of doctors, nurses, and support staff in particular wards, and so on.

The formal power of the integrating manager always includes some aspects of the decision processes that cut across the affected departments, but it never (by definition) extends to formal authority over the departmental personnel. (That would make the person department manager instead of integrating manager.) To control their behavior, therefore, the integrating manager must use his decisional authority and, more important, his powers of persuasion and negotiation. Galbraith lists three stages in the extension of the decisional power of the integrating manager. First, he can be given power to approve completed decisions—for example, to review the budgets of the departments. Second, he can enter the decision process at an earlier stage—for example, to draw up in the first place the budget that the departments must then approve. Third, he can be given control of the decision process, as when he determines the budget and pays the departments for the use of their resources.

Consider the brand manager in a consumer-goods firm. He is a kind of mini-general manager, responsible for the success of a single product. His performance is measured by how well it does in the marketplace. He must understand purchasing, manufacturing, packaging, pricing, distribution, sales, promotion, advertising, and marketing, and must develop plans for the brand, including sales forecasts, budgets, and production schedules. But the brand manager has no direct authority over the marketing or manufacturing departments. Rather, along with all the other brand managers of his firm, he negotiates with manufacturing to produce his brand and with marketing to sell it. If, however, he controls the budget for his brand, and has discretion in the use of it—for example, to contract its manufacture to different plants—he may have considerable power.

Whereas the brand manager is concerned with an existing or ongoing product, the project or program manager is concerned with bringing a new or embryonic undertaking to fruition—say, a new product or new facility. In both these cases, integrating managers with market orientations have been superimposed on functional structures to achieve work-flow coordination. But integrating managers with functional orientations can also be superimposed on market-based structures to encourage specialization, as when a manager concerned with the quality of programming is overlaid on a data-processing department formally organized on a project basis.

The job of integrating manager is not an easy one, the prime difficulty being to influence the behavior of people over whom he has no formal authority. The brand manager, for example, must persuade the manufacturing department to give priority to the production of his product and must encourage the sales department to promote his brand over the others, and the programming manager must encourage the programmers who report formally to project managers to increase the quality of their work. As Galbraith notes, what the integrating manager has at his command are contacts, information gained from serving at the crossroads of different channels, and the capacity to build up confidence and to encourage more effective decision making because of his broader perspective. The effective integrating manager appears to require a high need for affiliation and an ability to stand between conflicting groups and gain the acceptance of both without being absorbed into either.

Matrix structures

No single basis for grouping can contain all the interdependencies. Functional ones pose work-flow problems, market-based ones impede contacts among specialists, and so on. Standardization achieved through formalization of behavior, training and indoctrination, or planning and control systems can sometimes alleviate the problem, but important interdependencies often remain.

In our discussion to this point, we have seen at least three ways in which organizations handle this problem. These are shown in Figure 4–3. The first is to contain the residual interdependencies at the next higher level in the hierarchy; the second is to deal with the residual interdependencies in staff units (a dual structure is built—one line with the formal authority to decide, that contains the main interdependencies, the other staff, which advises on the residual interdependencies, as when market researchers or financial analysts advise the different product managers to help them coordinate their activities functionally); the third is, of course, to use one of the liaison devices already discussed, the organization in effect

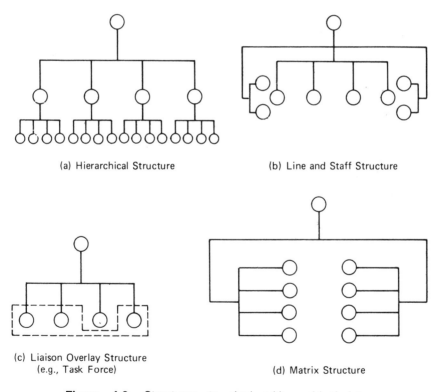

(a) Hierarchical Structure   (b) Line and Staff Structure

(c) Liaison Overlay Structure
    (e.g., Task Force)

(d) Matrix Structure

Figure 4-3. *Structures to deal with residual interdependencies*

85

preserving its traditional authority structure but superimposing, say, task forces to deal with the residual interdependencies.

Each one of these solutions favors one basis of grouping over another. Sometimes, however, the organization needs two (or even three) bases of grouping in equal balance. For example, an international firm may not wish to favor either a geographical or a product orientation in its structure, or a data-processing department or advertising agency may not wish to make a choice between a project orientation and an emphasis on specialization. Galbraith cites the case of the high-technology company whose products were undergoing continual change. Some managers argued for product divisions to deal with the complex problems of scheduling, replacing, and managing the new products, but others objected. The engineering manager felt that this would reduce the influence of his people just when he was experiencing morale and turnover problems. Management needed a product orientation as well as an improvement in the morale of the key specialists, both at the same hierarchical level. In these cases, organizations turn to the ultimate liaison device—*matrix structure.*

By using matrix structure, the organization avoids choosing one basis of grouping over another; instead, it chooses both. "In the simplest terms, matrix structure represents the effort, organizationally speaking, to 'have your cake and eat it, too'" (Sayles, 1976:5). But in so doing, the organization sets up a dual authority structure. As a result, **matrix structure sacrifices the principle of unity of command.** As shown in Figure 4–3(d), formal authority comes down the hierarchy and then splits, creating joint responsibilities and doing away with the notion of an unbroken chain of authority. To the classical writers, dual authority was anathema; it violated the principles and destroyed the neatness of the structure.[2] But as Galbraith notes, dual authority is hardly foreign to us: "Almost all of us were raised in the dual authority system of the family . . ." (1973:144). Similarly, in the matrix structure, different line managers are equally and jointly responsible for the same decisions and are therefore forced to reconcile between themselves the differences that arise. A delicate balance of power is created. To return to our example of the advertising agency, if the specialists need to be oriented to projects yet insist on being evaluated by their own kind, then matrix structure would have the evaluation decision made jointly by project and functional managers.

This balance of formal power is what distinguishes matrix structure from the other means of handling residual interdependencies, including the other liaison devices. It is one thing to have four product managers, each with a manufacturing, marketing, engineering, and personnel manager reporting to him, or four integrating managers, each seeking to coor-

---

[2]Frederick Taylor was a notable exception. His calls for functional authority of staff personnel were in this sense prophetic.

dinate the work of four functional managers with the line authority, or even to combine the latter into market-based task forces; it is quite another thing to force the product and functional managers to face each other, as in Figure 4–3(d), with equal formal power.

Nevertheless, Sayles (1976) notes in his review of matrix structure that in many contemporary organizations, the alternatives to it are simply too confusing:

> There are just too many connections and interdependencies among all line and staff executives—involving diagonal, dotted, and other "informal" lines of control, communication, and cooperation—to accommodate the comfortable simplicity of the traditional hierarchy, be it flat or tall. . . .
>
> Many companies, in fact, tie themselves in semantic knots trying to figure out which of their key groups are "line" and which "staff." (pp. 3, 15)

Sayles goes on to suggest that matrix structure is for organizations that are prepared to resolve their conflicts through informal negotiation among equals rather than recourse to formal authority, to the formal power of superiors over subordinates and line over staff. In effect, he seems to be telling us—picking up on Galbraith's point about the family—that matrix structure is for grown-up organizations. In fact, he believes that a great many organizations have already adopted some form of matrix structure, even if not in name.

Two kinds of matrix structures can be distinguished: a permanent form, where the interdependencies remain more-or-less stable and so, as a result, do the units and the people in them; and a shifting form, geared to project work, where the interdependencies, the market units, and the people in them shift around frequently. An example of *permanent matrix structure* can be found in the administration of some cities, where the functional citywide departments of parks, police, health, and so on, coordinate with the administrators of specific wards, and the two are jointly responsible for ensuring the quality of services to the city population. Some international companies have also moved toward this type of structure, typically putting the managers of geographical regions face to face with the managers of worldwide product lines. Reporting to both is a regional product manager, to whom in turn the functional managers report, as shown in Figure 4–4. A characteristic of the permanent matrix structure, evident in Figure 4–4, is that the chain of authority, once split, may reunite again, so that while one manager reports to two above him, his own subordinates report only to him.

The *shifting matrix structure* is used for project work, where the outputs change frequently, as in aerospace firms, research laboratories, and consulting think tanks. In these cases, the organization operates as a set of project teams (in effect, temporary market-based units) that draw their

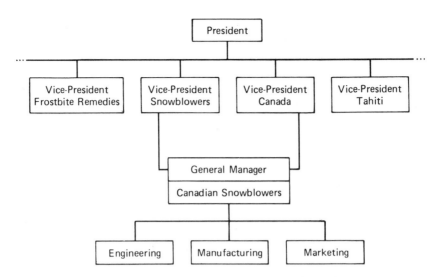

Figure 4-4. *A permanent matrix structure in an international firm*

members from the functional departments, which serve various "house-keeping" purposes. The National Aeronautics and Space Administration (NASA) has been a well-known user of such a structure. A fundamental characteristic of the teams used in the shifting matrix structure is that their leaders are full-fledged managers (of the market units), with formal authority (jointly shared with the managers of the functional units) over their members. That is what distinguishes them from the leaders of the task forces and the integrating managers described earlier. Those liaison devices were superimposed on a traditional line structure. This structure is matrix precisely because the task-force leaders take their place alongside the functional managers, sharing power equally with them.

Matrix structure has its share of problems. Although it seems to be a most effective device for developing new activities and for coordinating complex multiple interdependencies, it is no place for those in need of security and stability. Dispensing with the principle of unity of command creates considerable confusion, stress, and conflict, and requires from its participants highly developed interpersonal skills and considerable tolerance for ambiguity. There is also the problem of maintaining the delicate balance of power between the different sorts of managers. A tilt in one direction or the other amounts to a reversion to a traditional single-chain hierarchy, with the resulting loss of the benefits of matrix structure. However, a perfect balance without cooperation between the different managers can lead to so many disputes going up the hierarchy for arbitration that top management becomes overloaded. Then there is the problem of the cost of administration and communication in these structures. "The system demands that people have to spend far more time at meetings, discussing rather than doing work, than in a simpler authority structure. There simply is more communicating to be done, more information has to get to more people . . ." (Knight, 1976:126). Moreover, as we shall soon see, matrix structure requires many more managers than traditional structures do, thereby pushing up the administrative costs considerably.

A continuum of the liaison devices

Figure 4–5 summarizes our discussion of these four liaison devices—liaison positions, task forces and standing committees, integrating managers, and matrix structure. Again, the idea is borrowed from Galbraith and then modified. The figure forms a continuum, with pure functional structure at one end (that is, functional structure as the single chain of line authority) and pure market structure at the other. (Again, any other basis for grouping could be put at either end.) The first and most minor modification to either of the pure structures is the superimposition of liaison positions on it. Such positions generate a mild market orientation in the functional structure or a mild functional orientation in the market structure, thereby reducing slightly the informal power of the line managers (as shown by the diagonal line that cuts across the figure). A stronger modification is the superimposition of task forces or standing committees on either of the pure structures; the strongest modification, short of dispensing with the principle of unity of command, is the introduction of a set of integrating managers. As we have seen, such managers are given some formal decisional power—for example, control of important resources—and acquire considerable informal power. But the other managers, whether functional or market, retain their traditional line authority, including that over the personnel. Finally, standing midway between the two pure structures of Figure 4–5 is matrix structure, which represents an equal balance of power between the two. Dual authority replaces unity of command.

The liaison devices and the other design parameters

At a number of points, our discussion has hinted at the relationships between the liaison devices and the design parameters we have already discussed. Now let us focus on these relationships, looking first at the superstructure and then at the individual positions.

It is clear that the liaison devices can be used with any basis for grouping, since they are designed to override the limitations of using only a single one. Nevertheless, a review of the examples in the literature suggests that these devices are most often superimposed on functional groupings to introduce an orientation to markets.

As for unit size, as we saw earlier, liaison devices are the tools to

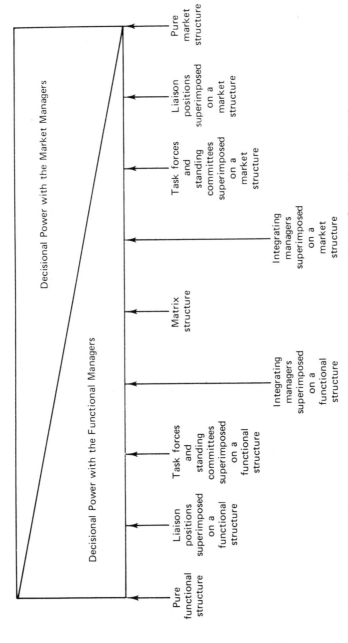

Figure 4-5. *A continuum of liaison devices (similar to Galbraith, 1973:114)*

encourage mutual adjustment by informal communication, and as we noted in Chapter 3, such communication requires face-to-face work groups of small size. Hence, we would expect that **the greater the use of the liaison devices, the smaller the average size of organizational units.** This should be especially pronounced for task forces and standing committees, as well as for temporary matrix structures, where the essential work is carried out in groups. Were we to consider the number of managers instead of unit size, the effect of the liaison devices should be even more pronounced. The addition of integrating managers ups the proportion of managers to nonmanagers significantly; the switch to matrix structure means the doubling of managers, more or less,[3] since many employees now have two bosses. So **certain of the liaison devices, especially matrix structure, result in a proliferation of the managers in the organization.**

Turning to the design of the individual positions, we would expect the liaison devices to be used where the organization cannot standardize its behaviors but must instead rely on mutual adjustment to coordinate its activities. In other words, there is less need for informal communication in bureaucratic structure, which means that **the liaison devices are tools primarily of organic structures.** They are flexible mechanisms to encourage loose, informal relationships. No doubt the milder liaison devices—liaison positions, task forces, and standing committees, those near the ends of the Figure 4–5 continuum—are sometimes superimposed on bureaucratic structures to reduce their inflexibility in places. But the use of the stronger liaison devices—integrating managers and matrix structure—so upset the traditional patterns of formalized behavior that the resulting structure can no longer be thought of as bureaucratic.

The liaison devices are generally used where work is, at the same time, (1) horizontally specialized, (2) complex, and (3) highly interdependent. If the work were not both horizontally specialized and interdependent, close coordination would not be necessary and the liaison devices would not be used. And if the work were not complex, the necessary coordination could be achieved largely by direct supervision or the standardization of work processes or outputs. Complex work can, of course, be coordinated by standardizing the skills used to do it—but only as long as the interdependencies are not great. Past some point of interdependence among specialized complex tasks, mutual adjustment is mandatory for coordination, and so the liaison devices are called upon to coordinate them.

---

[3]Assuming, that is, that nothing else changes. In the sense that those two managers must spend considerable time communicating with each other instead of supervising their employees, we might expect more rather than less. But in the sense that two people share the supervisory duties, we might expect less. To confound the issue, we shall see below and in Chapter 12 that matrix structure is associated with work that needs little direct supervision but intimate managerial involvement.

Of course, specialized complex tasks are professional ones, and so we should find a relation between professionalism (as well as training) and the use of the liaison devices. Indeed, many of our examples in this chapter have come from organizations that rely on professional expertise—aerospace agencies, research laboratories, and the like. Earlier it was suggested that there could be two kinds of professional organizations, one where the professionals function independently as individuals, and the other where they work together in groups. Now we see that the liaison devices are key design parameters in this second type of professional organization.

As for the relation between liaison devices and planning and control systems, to some extent at least, the use of these two lateral linkages is apt to be mutually exclusive. Unable to contain task interdependencies by the design of both individual positions and the superstructure, the organization would rely either on the standardization of outputs or the use of the devices of mutual adjustment. Consider, for example, how Sayles describes the organization that uses matrix structure. Its introduction of multiple sources of authority presupposed that its decisions "cannot be made by a well-programmed computer or small, expert planning groups" (1976:15); its "goals are, at once, multiple and conflicting and changing" (p. 16); the nature of its work interdependencies are such that "no accounting model" (p. 15) can balance the range of forces present in it. Rather, "the matrix forces decision making to be a constant process of interchange and trade-off, not only between the overall system and its specialized components and interest groups, but also between and among the specialists in the interest groups themselves" (p. 17). Clearly, planning and control systems cannot flourish in such an organization. In particular, performance control systems inappropriately require stable goals and units with only pooled interdependencies. And although some action planning may be feasible to deal with unit interdependencies, it must be general enough to allow for considerable adaptation through mutual adjustment. NASA used action planning to lay out the general schedule of the Apollo project, but so much additional coordination and adaptation were required that the space agency emerged from the project as a leader in the use of the liaison devices.

Liaison devices by part of the organization

The liaison devices appear to be best suited to the work carried out at the middle levels of the structure, involving many of the line managers as well as staff specialists. A standing committee may meet weekly to bring together the plant superintendent, sales manager, and head of purchasing; an engineer may be designated to a liaison position between a staff group in research and the line marketing department; a task force may be created, drawing middle-level members from the accounting, manufacturing, engineering, and purchasing departments, to investigate the feasibility of purchasing new equipment. And matrix structure, especially of the permanent kind, is commonly used where the power of middle-line managers representing two different bases for grouping must be balanced.

In general, given the nature of the work of middle managers—largely ad hoc but somewhat amenable to structure—we would often expect the set of liaison devices to be a most important design parameter of the middle line. At the very least, meetings abound in this part of the organization, many of them bringing together task forces and standing committees. Similarly, within staff units doing specialized, complex, and highly interdependent work—both in much of the technostructure and the upper levels of the support staff—we would expect the set of liaison devices to be a prime design parameter. Task forces and shifting matrix structure are especially well suited to the project work that often takes place in the technostructure. For example, a management science department may base its specialists in homogeneous groups (cost analysts, statisticians, economists, and so on) but deploy them in project teams to do their studies. And as we shall see later, organizations with many staff groups in close contact with middle-line units make such heavy use of the liaison devices that the staff/line distinction can break down and their three middle parts emerge as one amorphous mass of mutual-adjustment relationships.

As noted in earlier chapters, work in the operating core is coordinated primarily by standardization, with direct supervision as the backup coordinating mechanism. But in cases where the operating core is manned by professionals whose work interdependencies require them to function in teams—as in research centers and creative film companies—mutual adjustment is the key coordinating mechanism, and task forces and shifting matrix structures key design parameters.

Some use is also made of the liaison devices at the strategic apex. As we have seen, standing committees are common among senior managers; task forces are also used sometimes to bring them together with middle-line managers as well as senior staff personnel; likewise, liaison positions are sometimes designated to link the strategic apex to other parts of the organization, as when a presidential assistant is designated to maintain contact with a newly acquired subsidiary. But wider use of the liaison devices at the top of the organization is probably restricted by the very fluid and unprogrammed nature of the work there. Even the flexible liaison devices are simply too structured. As I have found in my own research, top managers often seem to prefer the informal telephone call or the impromptu meeting to the task force with its designated membership or the standing committee that meets on a regular basis.

UNTANGLING DECENTRALIZATION

The words *centralization* and *decentralization* have been bandied about for as long as anyone has cared to write about organizations. Yet they represent probably the most confused topic in management. The terms have been used in so many different ways that they have almost ceased to have any useful meaning.

Here we shall discuss the issue of centralization and decentralization exclusively in terms of power over the decisions made in the organization. **When all the power for decision making rests at a single point in the organization—ultimately in the hands of one person—we shall call the structure centralized; to the extent that the power is dispersed among many people, we shall call the structure decentralized.**

Logically, the subject of decentralization would seem to belong with the discussion of the design of the superstructure. Once the units have been designed, it seems appropriate to address the question of what decisions each should make. But it should be evident by now that all this logic—beginning with the mission, determining the positions, their specialization, formalization, and requirements for training and indoctrination, then grouping the positions to build the superstructure, after that determining the distribution of decisional power within it, and finally fleshing the whole thing out with the lateral linkages—has little to do with the practice of organizational design. The relationships among the design parameters are clearly reciprocal, not sequential. **The design parameters form an integrated system in which each is linked to all the others: change any one and all the others must be changed as well.** Decentralization is discussed last because it is the most complex of the design parameters, the one most in need of an understanding of all the others.

Why Decentralize a Structure?

What prompts an organization to centralize or decentralize its structure? As with most of the issues of structure, this one centers on the question of division of labor versus coordination. **Centralization is the tightest means**

of coordinating decision making in the organization. All decisions are made by one person, in one brain, and then implemented through direct supervision. Other reasons have been given for centralizing structures, but aside from the well-known one of lust for power, most of them amount to the need for coordination.

Why, then, should an organization decentralize? Simply because not all its decisions can be understood at one center, in one brain. Sometimes the necessary information just cannot be brought to that center. Perhaps too much of it is soft, difficult to transmit. How can the Baghdad salesperson explain the nature of his clients to the Birmingham manager? Sometimes the information can be transmitted to one center but cannot be comprehended there. How can the president of the conglomerate corporation possibly learn about, say, 100 different product lines? Even if a report were written on each, he would lack the time to study them all. Sometimes a sophisticated MIS gives the illusion of knowledge without the capacity to absorb it. Simon cites a newspaper report to tell a common story:

> The U.S. State Department, drowning in a river of words estimated at 15 million a month to and from 278 diplomatic outposts around the world, has turned to the computer for help. Final testing is under way on a $3.5 million combination of computers, high-speed printers and other electronic devices. Officials say these will eliminate bottlenecks in the system, especially during crises when torrents of cabled messages flow in from world troubled spots.
>
> When the new system goes into full operation this Fall, computers will be able to absorb cable messages electronically at a rate of 1,200 lines a minute. The old teletypes can receive messages at a rate of only 100 words a minute. (1968:622)

Simon concludes:

> A touching faith in more water as an antidote to drowning! Let us hope that Foreign Ministers will not feel themselves obliged to process those 1,200 lines of messages per minute just because they are there. (p. 622)

Perhaps the most common error committed in organizational design is the centralization of decision making in the face of such limitations. The top managers, empowered to design the structure, see errors committed below and believe that they can do better, either because they believe themselves smarter or because they think they can more easily coordinate decisions. Unfortunately, in complex conditions, this inevitably leads to a state known as "information overload": The more information the brain tries to receive, the less the total amount that actually gets through. People at the bottom of the hierarchy with the necessary knowledge end up having to defer to managers at the top who are out of touch with the reality of the situation.

Another, related reason for decentralization is that it allows the organization to respond quickly to local conditions. The transmission of information to the center and back takes time, which may be crucial. The Bank of America once advertised that, by having its "man-on-the-spot," presumably empowered to make decisions, it could provide better service to its clients.

And one last reason for decentralization is that it is a stimulus for motivation. Creative and intelligent people require plenty of room to maneuver. The organization can attract and retain such people, and utilize their initiative, only if it gives them considerable power to make decisions. Such motivation is crucial in professional jobs (and since these are the complex jobs, the professional organization has two good reasons to decentralize). Motivation is also a key factor in most managerial jobs, so some decentralization down the middle line is always warranted. Giving power to middle-line managers also trains them in decision making, so that some day one of them can take over the job of chief executive, where the most difficult decisions must be made.

Some Conceptual Cuts at Centralization/Decentralization

So far, all this seems clear enough. But that is only because we have not yet looked inside that black box called decentralization. The fact is that no one word can possibly describe a phenomenon as complex as the distribution of power in the organization. Consider the following questions:

- Which is more centralized: a library called "centralized" because it is in one place, although most of the decision-making power is dispersed to its department heads; or a "decentralized" library system, consisting of widely scattered satellite libraries, where the chief librarian of each guards all the power, sharing it with none of the other employees?

- How about the organization where decision-making power is dispersed to a large number of people but, because their decisions are closely monitored by a central individual who can fire them at a moment's notice, they make those decisions with careful assessment of his wishes? Or the case of the Jesuit priest or CIA agent who has complete autonomy in the field, except that he has been carefully indoctrinated to decide in a given way before he ever left the central headquarters? Are these organizations decentralized?

- In the United States, divisionalized corporations that rely on performance control systems for coordination are called "decentralized," whereas Americans are in the habit of calling the communist economies "centralized," even though they are organized like giant divisionalized corporations that rely on performance control systems for coordination. Which is it?

- Does standardization of the work process bring about centralization or decentralization? When a worker, because he is subject to a great many rules, is left free of direct supervision, can we say that he has power over his decisions? More generally, are bureaucracies centralized or decentralized? How about the one Crozier describes, where the workers force through rules that reduce the power of their managers over them, with the result that both end up in straitjackets?

- What about the case where a line manager has the authority to make a decision, but his advisors, by virtue of their superior technical knowledge, lead him into his choices? Or the case where the manager decides but, in executing the choices, his subordinates twist the outcome to their liking? Are these organizations centralized by virtue of the distribution of the formal power, or decentralized by virtue of the distribution of the informal?

- Finally, what about the organization where some decisions—say, those concerning finance and personnel—are made by the chief executive, and others—say, those in the areas of production and marketing—are dispersed to managers lower down? Is it centralized or decentralized?

The answer to these questions is that there is no simple answer, that unqualified use of the term *centralization* or *decentralization* should always be suspect. Yet a great deal of the research and discussion on organization structure has used them in just that way.

So the waters of decentralization are dirty. But before spilling them away, it may be worthwhile to see if we can find a baby in there.

Our list of questions seems to indicate two major points about the concept. First, **centralization and decentralization should not be treated as absolutes, but rather as two ends of a continuum.** The Soviet economy is not "centralized," just more centralized than a capitalist economy; the divisionalized firm is not "decentralized," just more decentralized than some firms with functional structures.[1] Second, much of the confusion seems to stem from the presence of a number of different concepts fighting for recognition under the same label. Perhaps it is the presence of two or even three babies in that bathwater that has obscured the perception of anyone.

---

[1]Although we shall see that the opposite is frequently the case, the rhetoric notwithstanding.

Below we discuss three uses of the term *decentralization* and retain two for our purposes. Each is discussed at length in the body of this chapter, and together they are used in a summary section to develop a framework of five basic kinds of decentralization commonly found in organizations.

Three uses of the term decentralization

The term *decentralization* seems to be used in three fundamentally different ways in the literature:

1. First is the dispersal of formal power down the chain of authority. In principle, such power is vested in the first instance in the chief executive at the strategic apex. Here it may remain, or the chief executive may choose to disperse it—*delegate* is a common synonym for this kind of decentralization—to levels lower down in the vertical hierarchy. **The dispersal of formal power down the chain of line authority will be called** *vertical decentralization.*

2. Decisional power—in this case, primarily informal—may remain with line managers in the system of formal authority, or it may flow to people outside the line structure—to analysts, support specialists, and operators. *Horizontal decentralization* **will refer to the extent to which nonmanagers control decision processes.**[2]

3. Finally, the term *decentralization* is used to refer to the physical dispersal of services. Libraries, copying machines, and police forces are "centralized" in single locations or "decentralized" to many, to be close to their users. But this "decentralization" has nothing per se to do with power over decision making (the satellite library, like the copying machine, may not make the decisions that most affect it). Thus, this third use of the term only serves to confuse the issue. In fact, we have already discussed this concept in Chapter 3, using the terms *concentrated* and *dispersed* instead of *centralized* and *decentralized.* In this book, the term *decentralization* will not be used to describe physical location.

This leaves us with two essential design parameters: vertical and horizontal decentralization. Conceptually, they can be seen to be distinct. Power can be delegated down the chain of authority and yet remain with line managers; the ultimate case of this vertical decentralization with hori-

---

[2]For purposes of our definition, managers of staff units are included among nonmanagers. Note that the term *horizontal* correctly describes this flow of power to analysts and support specialists as they are shown in our logo. The operators are, of course, shown below the vertical chain of authority but, for convenience, are also included in our definition of horizontal decentralization.

zontal centralization would give all the power to the first-line supervisors. Alternatively, senior staff people could hold all the power. Centralization of both types occurs when the strategic apex keeps all the power; decentralization of both sees power pass all the way down the chain of authority and then out to the operators.

But power over all decisions need not be dispersed to the same place. This gives rise to two other kinds of decentralization. **In selective decentralization, the power over different kinds of decisions rests in different places in the organization.** For example, finance decisions may be made at the strategic apex, marketing decisions in the support units, and production decisions at the bottom of the middle line, by the first-line supervisors. **Parallel decentralization refers to the dispersal of power for many kinds of decisions to the same place.** For example, finance, marketing, and production decisions would all be made by the division managers in the middle line.

But before we can begin our discussion of the kinds of decentralization found in organizations, we need to consider one more issue. Even within a single decision process, the power wielded by different people can vary. We need a framework to understand what control over the decision process really means.

What matters, of course, is not control over decisions per se but ultimately control over actions—what the organization actually does, such as marketing a new product, building a new factory, hiring a new mechanic. And actions can be controlled by more than just making choices. Power over any step in the decision process, from initiating the original stimulus to driving the last nail in the final execution of it, constitutes a certain power over the whole process.

Paterson provides us with a useful framework for understanding this issue. He depicts the decision process as a number of steps, as shown in modified form in Figure 5–1: (1) collecting *information* to pass on to the decision maker, without comment, about what can be done; (2) processing that information to present *advice* to the decision maker about what should be done; (3) making the *choice*—that is, determining what is intended to be done; (4) *authorizing* elsewhere what is intended to be done; and (5) doing it—that is, *executing* what is, in fact, done. The power of an individual is then determined by his control over these various steps. His power is

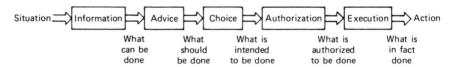

Figure 5-1. *A continuum of control over the decision process (similar to Paterson, 1969:150)*

maximized—and the decision process most centralized—when he controls all the steps: when he collects his own information, analyzes it himself, makes the choice, need seek no authorization of it, and then executes it himself. As others impinge on these steps, he loses power, and the process becomes decentralized.

Control over input information enables another person to select what factors will—and will not—be considered in the decision process. When information is filtered extensively, such control can be tantamount to control over the choice itself. More important still is the power to advise, since it directs the decision maker down a single path. Classical line/staff distinctions notwithstanding, there are times when the separation between giving advice and making the choice is fine indeed. History tells us of kings who were virtual figureheads, while their advisors—a Richelieu in France, a Rasputin in Russia—controlled the affairs of state. Control over what happens after the choice has been made can also constitute power. The right to authorize a choice is, of course, the right to block it or even change it. And the right to execute a choice once made often gives one the power to twist or even distort it. Newspapers carry accounts every day of how the "bureaucrats" misdirected the intentions of the politicians and ended up doing what they thought best in the first place. In effect, the decisions ended up being theirs.

And so, **a decision process is most decentralized when the decision maker controls only the making of the choice (the least he can do and still be called decision maker): In the organizational hierarchy, he loses some power to the information gatherers and advisors to his side, to the authorizers above, and to the executers below.** In other words, control over the making of choices—as opposed to control over the whole decision process—does not necessarily constitute tight centralization. With this in mind, let us now look at vertical and horizontal decentralization.

Vertical Decentralization

Vertical decentralization is concerned with the delegation of decision-making power down the chain of authority, from the strategic apex into the middle line. The focus here is on formal power—to make choices and authorize them—as opposed to the informal power that arises from advising and executing. Three design questions arise in vertical decentralization:

1. What decision powers should be delegated down the chain of authority?
2. How far down the chain should they be delegated?
3. How should their use be coordinated (or controlled)?

These three questions turn out to be tightly intertwined. Let us consider first some evidence on selective decentralization down the chain of authority. Dale (cited in Pfiffner and Sherwood, 1960:201) and Khandwalla (1973a) found that corporations tend to delegate power for manufacturing and marketing decisions farther down the chain of authority than they do power for finance and legal decisions. Lawrence and Lorsch (1967) found that power for a decision process tends to rest at that level where the necessary information can best be accumulated. For example, in the plastics industry, research and development decisions involved very sophisticated knowledge that was at the command of the scientist or group leader in the laboratory but was difficult to transfer up the hierarchy. Hence, these decisions tended to be made at relatively low levels in the hierarchy. In contrast, manufacturing decisions tended to be made at higher levels (plant manager), because the appropriate information could easily be accumulated there. Marketing decisions fell in between these two.

These findings, in effect, describe the organization as a system of work constellations, our fourth overlay of Chapter 1. Each constellation exists at that level in the hierarchy where the information concerning the decisions of a functional area can be accumulated most effectively. Combining these findings in Figure 5–2, we come up with four work constellations overlaid on our logo—a finance constellation at the top, a manufacturing constellation below that, then a marketing constellation, and finally the research and development one. Thus, **selective vertical decentralization is logically associated with work constellations grouped on a functional basis.** (Note that the decentralization in this case can be horizontal as well as vertical; staff groups at different hierarchical levels are shown involved in the top three constellations, and the fourth is exclusively staff.)

But such selective decentralization leaves important interdependencies to be reconciled, which raises the question of coordination and control. Direct supervision may be used to some extent, specifically by having the decisions of each work constellation authorized, and therefore coordinated, by the managers at the strategic apex. But too great a reliance on this form of coordination would be tantamount to recentralizing the decision processes and thereby canceling the advantages of selective decentralization. The same is true for the standardization of work processes or outputs, since that transfers power over the decision processes from all the constellations to the technostructure, which amounts to horizontal centralization instead of vertical decentralization. So although it may make some use of activity planning, in the final analysis, **the organization that is selectively decentralized in the vertical dimension will coordinate its decision making largely by mutual adjustment.** Specifically, it will place heavy emphasis on the use of the liaison devices.

The situation is quite different for parallel decentralization in the vertical dimension. This kind of decentralization does away with decision

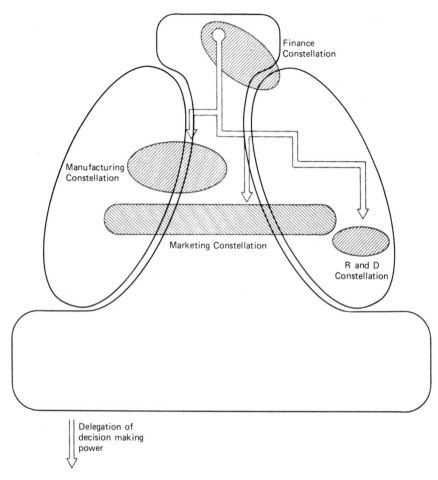

Figure 5-2. *Selective decentralization to functional work constellations*

interdependencies: power for the different functional decisions is focused at a single level in the hierarchy, specifically within units grouped on the basis of market. This is the structure known as "divisionalized" in the corporate sector. Each unit or division is decoupled from the others and given the power necessary to make all those decisions that affect its own products, services, or geographical areas. In other words, **parallel vertical decentralization is the only way to grant market-based units the power they need to function in a quasi-autonomous manner.** (Of course, such vertical decentralization must always be *somewhat* selective. That is, some decision-making power is always retained at the strategic apex. The divisionalized corporation typically delegates marketing and manufacturing

103

decisions to the divisions but keeps finance and acquisition decisions at the strategic apex.)

With the extensive autonomy of each market-based unit, there is no need to encourage mutual adjustment or action planning to coordinate work across them. What is important is to ensure that the autonomy is well used, that each market unit contributes to the goals considered important by the strategic apex. So the strategic apex faces the delicate task of controlling the behavior of its market units without restricting their autonomy unduly. Three coordinating mechanisms present themselves for such control—direct supervision and the standardization of skills and of outputs. (The standardization of work processes would obviously be too restrictive.)

There is some room for direct supervision, notably to authorize the major expenditures of the units and to intervene when their behavior moves way out of line. But too much direct supervision defeats the purpose of the decentralization: the strategic apex comes to manage the unit instead of its own manager. The standardization of skills, through training and indoctrination, can also be used to control the behavior of the manager of the market unit. He may, for example, be carefully indoctrinated and then sent out to run it with considerable autonomy. But there typically remains the need to monitor behavior—to find out when it is out of line. And that is typically left to the performance control system. **Parallel decentralization in the vertical dimension (to market-based units) is regulated primarily by performance control systems.** The units are given performance standards, and as long as they meet them, they preserve their autonomy.

But does parallel vertical decentralization to market-based units constitute "decentralization"? In the corporate world, the terms "divisionalization" and "decentralization" have been used synonomously ever since Alfred P. Sloan reorganized General Motors in the 1920s under the maxim "decentralized operations and responsibilities with coordinated control" (Chandler, 1962:160; see also Sloan, 1963). Faced with a structural mess left by William C. Durant, who had put the legal entity together through a series of acquisitions but had never consolidated it into a single organization, Sloan established product divisions with some operating autonomy but maintained tight financial controls at headquarters. A number of large corporations followed suit, and today the divisionalized structure is the most popular one among the largest American corporations. But does divisionalization constitute decentralization? Not at all; it constitutes the vesting of considerable decision-making power in the hands of a few people— the market unit managers in the middle line, usually near the top of it— nothing more. That is, **divisionalization constitutes a rather limited form of vertical decentralization.** These managers can, of course, delegate their power farther down the chain of authority, or out to staff specialists. But nothing requires them to do so. To paraphrase Mason Haire (1964:226), "decentralization" can give a manager the autonomy to run a "centralized" show![3] Thus, we should not be surprised when the same structure in a different context—the communist economy—is called centralized. A structure—capitalist or communist—in which a few division managers can control decisions that affect thousands or even millions of people can hardly be called decentralized, although it is certainly more so than one in which these decisions are made by even fewer managers at the strategic apex.

Horizontal Decentralization

Now we turn to the question of horizontal decentralization—namely, to the shift of power from managers to nonmanagers (or, more exactly, from line managers to staff managers, analysts, support specialists, and operators). An assumption in our discussion of vertical decentralization was that power—specifically formal power, or authority—rests in the line structure of the organization, in the first instance at the strategic apex. Vertical decentralization dealt with the delegation of that power down the chain of authority, at the will of the top managers.

When we talk of horizontal decentralization, we broaden the discussion in two regards. First, in discussing the transfer of power out of the line structure, we move into the realm of informal power, specifically of control over information gathering and advice giving to line managers and the execution of their choices, as opposed to the making and authorizing of these choices. And second, in discussing horizontal decentralization, we drop the assumption that formal power necessarily rests in the line structure, in the first instance at the strategic apex. Here formal power can rest elsewhere—for example, with operators who are empowered to elect the managers of the strategic apex.

Assuming the presence of managers, analysts, support staff, and operators, we can imagine a continuum of four stages of horizontal decentralization, listed below:

1. Power rests with a single *individual,* generally by virtue of the *office* he occupies (i.e., a manager).

2. Power shifts to the few *analysts* of the technostructure, by virtue of the influence their *systems* of standardization have on the decisions of others.

---

[3]But that raises a dilemma for the manager up above who prefers more decentralization. "Can he pull back the autonomy and order the subordinate to push decentralization down further? Or will this centralized intervention to further decentralization destroy the decentralization?" (Haire, p. 226)

3. Power goes to the *experts*—the analytic and support staff specialists, or the operators if they are professional—by virtue of their *knowledge*.

4. Power goes to *everyone* by virtue of *membership* in the organization.

Thus, in the most horizontally centralized organization, one person holds all the power, typically the top manager. Of course, even here, there can be variations according to how open that person is to advice. There is a difference between the "omnicompetent, aloof, imperial ruler," such as the Byzantine emperor, and the "omnicompetent but very accessible and responsive leader," such as a John F. Kennedy (Kochen and Deutsch, 1973:843). Hereafter, we find different degrees of horizontal decentralization, first to a few analysts whose systems control the behavior of others, then to all the experts with knowledge, and finally to everybody just because everybody is a member of the organization. The first case requires no further discussion; let us therefore consider the other three in turn.

Power to the analysts

When an organization relies on systems of standardization for coordination, some power must pass out from the line managers to the designers of those systems, typically the analysts of the technostructure. How much power, of course, depends on the extent and the kind of standardization. Obviously, the more the organization relies on systems of standardization for coordination, the greater the power of the analysts. Soviet government planners have more power than their American counterparts; the work-study analysts of an automobile company are more influential than those of a hospital. And the tighter the kind of standardization, the more powerful the analysts. By that token, job designers and work-study analysts—those who tell workers *how* to produce by standardizing their work processes—should typically have more power than production schedulers and planners—those who only tell them *what* and *when* to produce by standardizing their outputs. And trainers—those who teach people to produce by standardizing their skills—should have less power still. Thus, the factory worker would normally perceive the work-study analyst as the greatest threat to his autonomy, followed by the production scheduler and then the trainer.[4]

Who surrenders power to the analysts? Obviously, those whose work is standardized, such as the operator who loses the power to choose his work process, or the manager who loses the power to decide on his unit's

---

[4]However, to the extent that planners and trainers direct their efforts at people higher up in the structure, they can be more influential. Moreover, we should not forget that much of the training takes place outside the organization. We shall return to this point later in the chapter.

outputs. But so, too, do the managers of these people; as noted earlier, their jobs became institutionalized, technocratic standardization replacing their power of direct supervision.

This leads us to two important conclusions. First, **power to the analysts constitutes only a limited form of horizontal decentralization.** Only a few nonmanagers—these designers of the technocratic systems—gain some informal power, and that at the expense of the many operators and others whose behavior and outputs are standardized. And second, **this kind of limited horizontal decentralization in fact serves to centralize the organization in the vertical dimension, by reducing the power of the lower-line managers relative to those higher up.** In other words, **organizations that rely on technocratic standardization for coordination are rather centralized in nature, especially in the vertical dimension but also somewhat in the horizontal.**

Are bureaucracies centralized? This has been a controversial question in the research literature. As we have seen, the research has not been conclusive. Some researchers have argued that bureaucratic work standards, by limiting the power of the manager to exercise direct supervision, thereby give more power to the workers. The work of Crozier suggests quite a different conclusion: that both end up in a straitjacket, with decision-making power flowing up to a remote central headquarters.

We can sort out much of this confusion by discussing centralization in terms of our five coordination mechanisms. Those who see work rules as giving rise to decentralization seem to equate centralization with direct supervision: an organization is centralized if direct supervision is close; to the extent that work standards replace direct supervision, the organization becomes decentralized. But calling a bureaucracy decentralized because work rules instead of managers control the workers is like calling puppets purposeful because computers instead of people pull their strings.

Direct supervision may be the tightest coordinating mechanism, and therefore close control by managers may constitute the tightest form of horizontal centralization. Any move the individual makes can bring a rap on the knuckles from the boss: "That is not the way I expected you to do it." And standardization of work processes may provide the employee with more autonomy, since he knows what he can and cannot do. But that does not mean that it is a loose coordinating mechanism. Of course, if the rules are few, the employee has considerable discretion. But we are here discussing organizations where the rules are many—bureaucracies that rely on such rules for coordination, and so proliferate them. The important point is that reliance by the organization on any of the other coordinating mechanisms would yield its employees more freedom still in their work. That would happen if their outputs were standardized and they were allowed to choose their own work processes. Better still, if their work was coordinated by the standardization of skills, they would be trained and

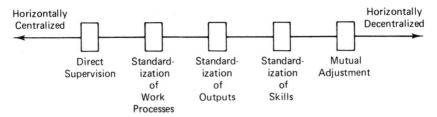

Figure 5-3. *The coordinating mechanisms on a continuum of horizontal decentralization*

indoctrinated before they started to work and thereafter would be left alone to choose their work processes and determine their outputs as they saw fit. And best of all would be the absence of standardization and direct supervision altogether; the employees would be completely free to work out their own coordination by mutual adjustment.

In other words, as shown in Figure 5–3, **the coordinating mechanisms form a continuum, with direct supervision the most horizontally centralizing and mutual adjustment the least, and with the three forms of standardization—first work processes, then outputs, finally skills—falling in between.** And because standardization of work processes falls next to direct supervision as the second most centralizing coordinating mechanism, we conclude that organizations that rely on this mechanism for coordination are relatively centralized. Specifically, such organizations give a certain amount of power to their analysts to design the standards, and as we have just concluded, such power to the analysts means vertical centralization coupled with only limited horizontal decentralization.

But to tie up a loose end, we cannot say that all bureaucracies are centralized. These particular bureaucracies are—the ones that rely on the standardization of *work processes* to coordinate the work of their unskilled operators. But earlier we came across a second kind of bureaucracy, one with professional operators who coordinate their work by the standardization of their skills. And because this coordinating mechanism falls near the decentralization end of our Figure 5–3 continuum, we can conclude that this second kind of bureaucracy is relatively *de*centralized in the horizontal dimension. We shall return to it below.

Power to the experts

In this stage of horizontal decentralization, the organization is dependent on specialized knowledge. So it must put its power where its knowledge is—namely, with the experts, whether they be in the technostructure, support staff, operating core, or, for that matter, middle line. "In the world of blind men, the one-eyed man is king." The surgeons dominate the operating rooms, the Wernher von Brauns rule the space agencies. In the previous discussion, there was only one recognized expert—the analyst—and his power was informal. But here the organization draws on the knowledge of a wider array of experts and begins to formalize more and more of the power it gives to them. The experts do not merely advise; they come to participate actively in making decisions.

How dependent the organization is on its experts and where they are found in its structure determine how much power they can accumulate. We can identify at least three types of expert power.

1   Informal expert power superimposed on a traditional authority structure. In the least horizontally decentralized type, the system of formal authority remains intact; that is, formal power remains in the hierarchy of line managers. But **to the extent that the organization has need of specialized knowledge, notably because certain decisions are highly technical ones, certain experts attain considerable informal power.** Thus, the maintenance men ruled the tobacco factories Crozier studied because only they could handle the one major source of uncertainty.

These experts made choices. Others gain informal power by virtue of the advice they give managers before choices are made, especially technical choices that the managers do not understand. The authorization step of decision making, often carried out as part of a capital budgeting process, lends itself to the manipulation of managers by experts. The sponsor of a decision or project, that person who first decided to proceed with it, has the expert knowledge of it but also has a strong commitment to see it authorized. The manager above, who must do the authorizing, can be more objective in his assessment of the project, but he lacks the detailed knowledge of it and the time to get it. So the situation is ripe for manipulation. In effect, systems of capital budgeting often fail because they cannot put the formal power for authorization where the required knowledge of the project is.

2   Expert power merged with formal authority. **As expertise becomes increasingly important in decision making, the distinction between line and staff—between the formal authority to choose on the one hand and the expertise to advise on the other—becomes increasingly artificial.** Eventually, it is done away with altogether, and line managers and staff experts join in task forces and standing committees to share decision-making power. A good example is the new-product group that brings together marketing, manufacturing, engineering, and research personnel from the technostructure, middle line, and support staff. Power within the group is based not on position but on expertise; each person participates according to the knowledge he can bring to the decision in question. This situation of expert power merged with formal authority amounts, therefore, to *selective* decentralization in the horizontal dimension, the experts having power for some decisions but not for others. In fact, reference back to Figure 5–2, where various functional work constellations were overlaid on our logo, suggests a link to selective decentralization in the vertical dimension. In other words, **selective decentralization seems to occur concurrently in both the horizontal and vertical dimensions.**

3   Expert power with the operators. In this third and most decentralized case of expert power, the operators themselves are the experts. And this expertise vests in them considerable power, which in turn decentralizes the organization in both dimensions: power rests in the operating core, at the bottom of the hierarchy with nonmanagers. Of course, expert operators are professional ones, which leads us to a rather important relationship, one that is well supported in the research: **the more professional an organization, the more decentralized its structure in both dimensions.** This brings the issue of bureaucracy and centralization into sharper focus. We can now see the two kinds of bureaucracy emerging clearly, one relatively centralized, the other decentralized. The first is bureaucratic by virute of the work standards imposed by its own technostructure. Its operating work is specialized but unskilled. It is relatively *centralized* both vertically and horizontally, because most of its decision-making power rests with its senior managers and the small number of analysts who formalize the behavior of everyone else. In the second, the operating core is staffed with professionals. It is bureaucratic by virtue of the standards imposed on it from the outside, by the professional associations that train its operators and later impose certain rules to govern their behavior. But because the professionals require considerable autonomy in their work, and because coordination is effected primarily by the standardization of skills—a coordinating mechanism shown near the decentralization end of the Figure 5–3 continuum—this second bureaucracy is rather decentralized in both dimensions. That is, power rests with the operators at the bottom of the hierarchy.

Power to everyone

The theme of our discussion so far has been that power in the hands of the managers constitutes horizontal centralization; that bureaucratization through the formalization of behavior puts some power into the technostructure and thereby constitutes a limited form of horizontal decentralization; and that the more that power is attributed to knowledge as opposed to position, the more the structure becomes horizontally decentralized, culminating in the professional organization whose operators control much of the decision making.

But, in theory at least, that is not the ultimate case of decentralization. Professional organizations may be meritocratic but they are not democratic. As long as knowledge is not uniformly dispersed, so too will power not be evenly distributed. One need only ask the orderlies (or even the nurses) of the hospital about their status vis-à-vis the doctors.

Decentralization is complete when power is based not on position or knowledge, but on membership. Everyone participates equally in decision making. The organization is democratic.

Does such an organization exist? The perfectly democratic organization would settle all issues by something corresponding to a vote or consensus. Managers might be elected to expedite the members' choices, but they would have no special influence in making them. Everyone would be equal. Certain volunteer organizations—such as Israeli kibbutzim or private clubs—approach this ideal, but can more conventional organizations?

"Industrial democracy" has received considerable attention in Europe recently. In Yugoslavia, workers own many of the enterprises and elect their own managers. In France, there has been much talk of "autogestion" (self-management). In Germany, half the seats on the boards of directors of the larger corporations are by law reserved for workers' representatives.

The evidence from these efforts suggests, however, that these steps do not lead to pure democratization, or anything close to it. Thus, in their excellent review of worker participation in eight countries of Europe, Asia, and the Middle East, Strauss and Rosenstein conclude:

1. Participation in many cases has been introduced from the top down as a symbolic solution to ideological contradictions;
2. Its appeal is due in large part to its apparent consistency with both socialist and human relations theory;
3. In practice it has only spotty success and chiefly in the personnel and welfare rather than in the production areas;
4. Its chief value may be that of providing another forum for the resolution of conflict as well as another means by which management can induce compliance with its directives. (1970:171)

These reviewers and others suggest that workers are not really interested in issues that do not pertain directly to their work. Most surprising, participation has been shown in some studies to strengthen the hand of top management at the expense of other groups, "to bypass middle management, to weaken the staff function, and to inhibit the development of professionalism" (p. 186). Paradoxically, industrial democracy seems to centralize the organization in both the vertical and horizontal dimensions. (A probable reason for this will be discussed in the next chapter.)

Crozier describes another kind of organizational democracy, which seems to have a similar effect. In this case, as noted earlier, the workers institute rules that delimit the power their superiors have over them. That renders the two equal—superior and subordinate are locked into the same straitjacket (except for the maintenance men of the tobacco factories, who exploited that last remaining bit of uncertainty). Power for decision making in turn reverts up to the organization's headquarters. The resulting structure is, in a sense, doubly bureaucratic—there being the usual rules to coordinate the work as well as special ones to protect the workers. And doubly bureaucratic in this case means, in the same sense, doubly centralized. So what results is a perverse kind of democracy indeed, the organization emerging as more bureaucratic and more centralized than ever, its extreme rigidity rendering it less able to serve its clients or to satisfy the higher-order needs of its workers.

These movements in organizational democracy have barely touched the United States. What has received considerable attention there instead is "participative management." In discussion of this concept, two of its propositions should be clearly distinguished. One, of a factual—that is, testable—nature, is that participation leads to increased productivity: "Involve your employees and they will produce more," management has been told by a generation of industrial psychologists. The other, a value proposition and so not subject to verification, is that participation is a value worthy in and of itself: "In a 'democratic' society, workers have the right to participate in the organizations that employ them." The American debate over participative management has focused almost exclusively on the first, factual proposition (although the proponents seem really to be committed to the second, value position). In the light of this focus, it is interesting that the factual proposition has not held up in much of the research. Studies by Fiedler (1966) and other have indicated that participation is not necessarily correlated with satisfaction or productivity. Those relationships depend on the work situation in question.

In any event, participative management can hardly be called democratization, since it is based on the premises that the line manager has the formal power and that he chooses to share it with his employees. He calls on them for advice and perhaps to share in the making of choices as well. But democracy does not depend on the generosity of those who hold formal power; instead, it distributes that power constitutionally throughout the organization.

So far, we have found little to encourage the proponents of organizational democracy. It may work in volunteer organizations, but attempts to achieve it in more conventional ones seem only to foster more centralization.

Before leaving the subject, we might mention another body of research that has shed light on the question. Social psychologists have conducted a number of "communication net" studies in which they have put a few subjects (often five) into networks of more or less restricted channels of communication, given them simple tasks to perform, and then watched what happened. In some networks, all the members had to pass their messages through one person (this was the hierarchical one); in others, they formed a circle and could communicate only with members to either side of them; in some, everyone could communicate freely with everyone else (the closest equivalent to democracy); and so on. Many of the results were expected—for example, that the hierarchical networks organized more quickly and made fewer errors, but that their members at the periphery enjoyed the task less than did the ones at the center. An unexpected finding, however, at least in one study (Guetzkow and Simon, 1954–55), was that the open-channel networks developed hierarchies by themselves (in 17 of 20 cases).

These findings suggest some interesting conclusions about horizontal decentralization. For one thing, the centralized organization may be more efficient under certain circumstances, particularly at early stages of the work. In contrast, the horizontally decentralized organization—the democratic one—seems better for morale. But the latter may sometimes be unstable, eventually reverting to a more hierarchical—and centralized—structure to complete its tasks. This, in fact, is exactly what the field studies indicate: that democratization leads, paradoxically, to centralization.

So the answer to our question about democracy seems to be negative. Attempts to make centralized organizations democratic—whether by having the workers elect the directors, encouraging them to participate in decision making, instituting rules to delimit the power of their managers, or establishing unrestricted communication channels—all seem to lead, one way or another, back to centralization. Note that all the experiments have taken place in organizations that do simple, repetitive, unskilled tasks. A laboratory group cannot be asked to design a thermonuclear reactor, let alone deliver a baby. Likewise, organizational democracy has not been a burning issue in research laboratories or hospitals; the attention has been focused on automobile plants, tobacco factories, and the like, organizations staffed largely with unskilled operators. Here is where the workers have had the least decision-making power and have been the most alienated. And here, unfortunately, is where attempts to tamper with the power system—to make it more democratic—seem to have failed the most dramatically.

Other organizations come closer to the democratic ideal—namely, those with professional operators, such as research laboratories and hospitals. They distribute their power widely. But not because anyone decided that participation was a good thing. And not so widely that every member shares power equally. Power follows knowledge in these organizations, which itself is distributed widely but unevenly. Thus, it seems that, at best, we shall have to settle for meritocracy, not democracy, in our nonvolunteer organizations, and then only when it is called for by tasks that are professional in nature.

Decentralization in Fives

Five distinct types of vertical and horizontal decentralization seem to emerge from our discussion. These can, in fact, be placed along a single continuum, from centralization in both dimensions at one end to decentralization in both at the other. There are shown in Figure 5–4, as distortions of our logo (where, it should be noted, the inflated size of a shaded part represents its special decision-making power, not its size in membership). Each of the five types of decentralization is discussed briefly below.

Type A: Vertical and Horizontal Centralization **Decisional power here is concentrated in the hands of a single individual, the manager at the top of the line hierarchy—namely, the chief executive officer.** Power bulges in Figure 5–4(a) at the strategic apex. **The chief executive retains both formal and informal power, making all the important decisions himself and coordinating their execution by direct supervision.** As such, he has little need to share his power with staffers, middle-line managers, or operators.

Type B: Limited Horizontal Decentralization (Selective) **In this type we find the bureaucratic organization with unskilled tasks that relies on standardization of work processes for coordination.** (Here is where the experiments in democratization have been concentrated.) The analysts play a leading role in this organization by formalizing the behavior of the other members, notably the operators, who consequently emerge as rather powerless. Standardization diminishes the importance of direct supervision as a coordinating mechanism, thereby reducing the power of the middle-line managers as well, particularly at the lower levels. As a result, **the structure is centralized in the vertical dimension; formal power is concentrated in the upper reaches of the line hierarchy, notably at the strategic apex.** (Should attempts be made to shift it to the operating core as part of a program of democratization, it immediately reverts to the strategic apex by virtue of election procedures.) **Because of their role in formalizing behavior, the analysts are, however, able to gain some informal power, which means limited horizontal decentralization.** Because the analysts are few relative to the other nonmanagers and their actions serve to reduce the power of the other nonmanagers, notably the operators, the horizontal decentralization turns out to be of the most limited kind. It is selective, in any event, since the analysts are involved only in the decisions concerning work formalization. Figure 5–4(b) shows power bulging at the strategic apex and slightly in the technostructure.

Type C: Limited Vertical Decentralization (Parallel) **Here we find the organization that is divided into market units, or divisions, to whose managers are**

delegated (in parallel) a good deal of formal power to make the decisions concerning their markets. But because that power need be delegated no farther down the chain of authority, the vertical decentralization is limited in nature. Likewise, because the division managers need not necessarily share their power with staff personnel or operators, the organization can be described as centralized in the horizontal dimension. Of course, the strategic apex retains ultimate formal power over the divisions. And because it coordinates their behavior by the standardization of outputs, effected by performance control systems designed in the technostructure, a few high-level planners retain some power as well. Thus, Figure 5–4(c) shows the major bulge

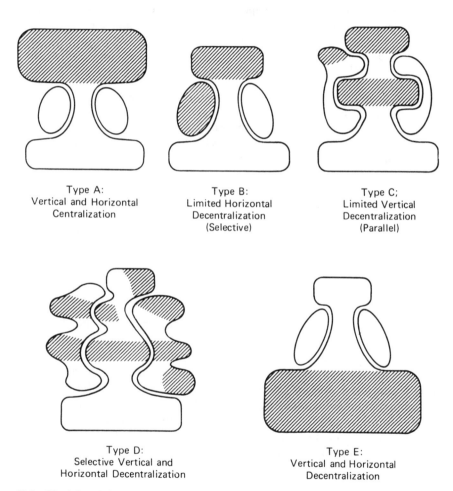

Type A:
Vertical and Horizontal
Centralization

Type B:
Limited Horizontal
Decentralization
(Selective)

Type C;
Limited Vertical
Decentralization
(Parallel)

Type D:
Selective Vertical and
Horizontal Decentralization

Type E:
Vertical and Horizontal
Decentralization

Note: The inflated size of the shaded parts indicates their special power in decision making, not their size in membership.

Figure 5-4. *Five types of decentralization*

well up in the middle line and minor ones in the strategic apex and at the top of the technostructure.

Type D: Selective Vertical and Horizontal Decentralization **Here we see our findings about selective decentralization in the two dimensions coming together. In the vertical dimension, power for different types of decisions is delegated to work constellations at various levels of the hierarchy. And in the horizontal dimension, these constellations make selective use of the staff experts, according to how technical the decisions are that they must make:** for some, the experts merely advise the line managers; for others, they join the managers on teams and task forces, sometimes even controlling the choices themselves. **Coordination within as well as between the constellations is effected primarily through mutual adjustment.** Power in Figure 5–4(d) bulges in various places (corresponding to Figure 5–2), notably in the support staff (especially as compared with the other four types), where a good deal of the organization's expertise lies.

Type E: Vertical and Horizontal Decentralization **Decision power here is concentrated largely in the operating core**—the only bulge in Figure 5–4(e)—**because its members are professionals, whose work is coordinated largely by the standardization of skills.** The organization is strongly decentralized in the vertical dimension because this power rests at the very bottom of the hierarchy. And it is strongly decentralized in the horizontal dimension, since this power rests with a large number of nonmanagers—namely, the operators. If another power center were to be identified, it would have to be shown apart, since the organization is forced to surrender a good deal of its control over decision processes to the professional schools that train its operators and the professional associations that control their standards.

Decentralization and the other design parameters

The relationship between our two forms of decentralization and the other seven design parameters has been discussed throughout this chapter; here we need merely review these findings briefly.

Decentralization is closely related to the design of positions. **The formalization of behavior takes formal power away from the operators and the managers who supervise them and concentrates it near the top of the line hierarchy and in the technostructure, thus centralizing the organization in both dimensions.** The result is Type A decentralization. **Training and indoctrination produce exactly the opposite effect: They develop expertise below the middle line, thereby decentralizing the structure in both dimensions** (Type E). Putting these two conclusions together, we can see that specialization of the unskilled type centralizes the structure in both dimensions, whereas specialization of the skilled or professional type decentralizes it in both dimensions.

We have also seen a number of relationships between decentralization and the design of the superstructure. **The use of market grouping leads to limited vertical decentralization of a parallel nature** (Type C): a good deal of power rests with the managers of the market units. No such definitive conclusion can be drawn for functional grouping. Types B and D are both typically functional structures, the first bureaucratic and rather centralized in both dimensions, the second organic—that is, reliant on mutual adjustment—and selectively decentralized in both dimensions. Similarly, Types A and E, at the two ends of our continuum, are often described as functional. Thus, we are led to the conclusion that **functional structure is possible with almost any degree of decentralization, in either dimension.**

The same conclusion can be drawn for unit size, or span of control. Too many other factors intervene. For example, large unit size may reflect extensive use of behavior formalization, in which case the structure is rather centralized in both dimensions (Type B). But it may also reflect extensive use of training and indoctrination, in which the structure is decentralized in both dimensions (Type E). It may also indicate the presence of market-based grouping, which results in limited vertical decentralization (Type C). Likewise, small unit size may indicate close supervision and centralization (of Type A), or the presence of small autonomous work teams and selective decentralization (of Type D).

As for the lateral linkages, we have seen that performance control systems are used primarily to control quasi-autonomous market units, and so are related to limited vertical decentralization (Type C). Action planning enables the strategic apex to control the important organizational decisions, although it must surrender some of its power to the staff planners, which results in Type B decentralization. In general, therefore, planning and control systems emerge as design parameters to effect modest or extensive centralization. And finally, the liaison devices are used primarily to coordinate the work within and between the selectively decentralized work constellations (Type D).

Decentralization by part of the organization

We have so far had little difficulty discussing each of the other design parameters by part of the organization. The same will not be true for the two kinds of decentralization, since the distribution of power is an organizationwide phenomenon. Nevertheless, some conclusions can be drawn.

By definition, vertical decentralization involves only the chain of authority—that is, the strategic apex and middle line. And here all kinds of patterns are possible. In some organizations, power remains at the strategic apex; in others, it is delegated to various levels in the middle line, sometimes selectively, sometimes in parallel; and in still other cases, power passes right to the bottom of the middle line, and perhaps beyond, to the operating core. If one generalization is in order, it is that classic authority patterns continue to dominate organizational power systems. That is, formal power resides in the first instance with the chief executive at the top of the hierarchy. From there it is delegated at his will. And formal power, vis-à-vis the informal, still matters a great deal in organizations. Thus, structures may tend to be more centralized in the vertical as well as the horizontal dimension than their situations call for. In other words, **there may be a tendency to retain somewhat more power than is necessary in the line structure, especially at the strategic apex.**

Horizontal decentralization, by definition, brings the other three parts of the organization—the technostructure, support staff, and operating core—into the power system. Again, we have seen all kinds of power distributions, from negligible staff groups to powerful ones, from weak operating cores to dominant ones. But one point is clear. All have informal power to the extent that they contain expertise. Staff groups do more than just advise when they have the knowledge needed to make technical decisions; operators accumulate power when they have the expertise needed to execute managerial decisions and when they are professionals—that is, when they perform jobs based on complex knowledge and skills. As a final point, we might note that *within* the technocratic units and the higher-level support units, where the work is essentially professional, we would expect to find a good deal of decentralization, from the staff managers to the staff specialists themselves.

We have now discussed our design parameters in some detail. We have seen the various forms each can take in the structure as well as the relation of each to the coordinating mechanisms. Direct supervision is effected through the design of the superstructure, notably the grouping into units, which creates the hierarchy of managerial positions. It is also strongly influenced by the design of the decision-making system—that is, by horizontal and vertical decentralization. Standardization of work processes is achieved through the formalization of behavior, standardization of skills through the establishment of training and indoctrination programs, and standardization of outputs through the use of planning and control systems. Finally, mutual adjustment is encouraged by the use of the liaison devices.

We have also begun to see some fundamental interrelationships among the design parameters. Some are mutually exclusive. For example, an organization may rely on prejob training or else it may formalize behavior through the use of on-the-job rules; it seldom does a great deal of both. Other design parameters are clearly used concurrently—for example, performance control systems and market-based grouping, or the liaison devices and organic structure. But more important, we have seen a good deal of indication that it is the clustering or configuring of many of these design parameters, not the interacting of any two, that seems to hold the key to understanding the structuring of organizations. But before we can discuss this clustering, we must put our design parameters into the context of the organization's situation.

FITTING DESIGN TO SITUATION

Given a set of design parameters at the command of the organization designer, how does he select them? How does he decide when to use a market and when a functional basis for grouping in the middle line, when to formalize behavior in the operating core and when to rely on training or the use of the liaison devices to encourage mutual adjustment, when to decentralize horizontally and when vertically?

Most of the contemporary research on organizational structuring has focused on these questions. This research has uncovered a set of what are called *situational* or *contingency factors,* organizational states or conditions that are associated with the use of certain design parameters. In this chapter we discuss these factors in four groups: the *age* and *size* of the organization; the *technical system* it uses in its operating core; various aspects of its *environment*, notably stability, complexity, diversity, and hostility; and certain of its *power* relationships. But before we discuss each, we must first comment on the notion of effectiveness in structural design.

Two Views of Organizational Effectiveness

A number of researchers have studied the relation between structure and performance, typically by comparing the structures of high- and low-performance firms. Their tendency has been to attribute effectiveness to the fit between certain design parameters and some situational factor—for example, the size of the organization, the technical system it uses, or the dynamic nature of its environment. One study, however, carried out by Khandwalla (1971, 1973b, 1974), found that effectiveness was dependent on the interrelationships among design parameters; in other words, on the use of different ones in a consistent or integrated manner.

121

These studies lead us to two important and distinct conclusions about structural effectiveness. The first we can label the *congruence* hypothesis: **effective structuring requires a close fit between the situational factors and the design parameters.** In other words, the successful organization designs its structure to match its situation. And the second we can call the *configuration* hypothesis: **effective structuring requires an internal consistency among the design parameters.** The successful organization develops a logical configuration of the design parameters.

Do these two hypotheses contradict each other? Not necessarily. Not as long as an organization's major situational factors—for example, its size on the one hand and its technical system on the other—do not call for design parameters that are mutually inconsistent. Where they do, the organization would have to trade off situational fit for consistency in its internal structure. But where they do not, the organization would simply select the structural configuration that best matches its situation. Of course, this situation is not something beyond the organization's control. That is, it can choose not only its design parameters, but certain aspects of its situation as well: it designs its own technical system, decides whether or not to grow large, gravitates to an environment that is stable or dynamic, and so on. Thus the situational factors can be clustered, too. This conclusion enables us to combine the two hypotheses into a single, *extended configuration* hypothesis: **effective structuring requires a consistency among the design parameters and contingency factors.**

Our preference, as has been evident, is for the extended configuration hypothesis. But before we can develop it, we need to consider the congruence hypothesis, because the research has shed a good deal of light on the relations between design and situation. These findings will in fact help us to develop the configurations and enable us to build the situational factors into them.[1]

In discussing these relationships in this chapter, we shall treat the situational factors as *independent* variables (that is, as given) and the design parameters as *dependent* ones (that is, to be determined). These assumptions will, of course, be dropped when we get to the configurations. As we argued earlier, because the configurations are systems, no one of their parts is independent or given; rather, each is integrated with, and hence dependent on, all the others.

In addition, we shall consider a set of *intermediate* variables in this chapter, through which the situational factors affect the design param-

[1]As discussed in the "Note to the Reader" at the outset of this book, we shall not discuss the evidence that supports these relationships here, only the findings themselves. The interested reader can turn for this evidence to the companion volume, H. Mintzberg, *The Structuring of Organizations; A Synthesis of the Research* (Englewood Cliffs, N.J.: Prentice-Hall, 1979), notably Chapters 13–16, where the four sets of situational factors are in turn discussed at length, in much the same format as below.

eters. These concern the work that is done in the organization and include the comprehensibility of the work (which most strongly affects specialization and decentralization); the predictability of the work (which most strongly affects standardization in its three forms, which means the design parameters of behavior formalization, planning and control systems, and training and indoctrination); the diversity of the work (which most strongly affects the choice of bases for grouping units, as well as behavior formalization and the use of liaison devices); and the speed with which the organization must respond to its environment (which most strongly affects decentralization, behavior formalization, and unit grouping).

We discuss age and size, technical system, and environment in two ways in this chapter—in terms of a set of hypotheses, each typically relating to a specific situational factor to one or more design parameters, and in terms of a framework or set of organizational types suggested by this set of hypotheses. (The power factors will be discussed only in terms of the hypotheses.) As we shall see, these types reinforce the findings of the earlier chapters that point the way to our configurations.

Age and Size

We have a considerable body of evidence on the effects of age and size on structure, most of which we can capture in five hypotheses, two concerning age and three size. After discussing each hypothesis, we shall see that we can clarify and synthesize them by looking at organizational aging and growth not as linear progressions, but as a sequence of distinct transitions between "stages of development."

Hypothesis 1: The older the organization, the more formalized its behavior.[2] Here we encounter the "we've-seen-it-all-before" syndrome, as in the case of the tenured college professor whose students follow his lecture word for word from the notebook of a previous student, or the government clerk who informs you that your seemingly unique problem is covered in Volume XXII, Page 691, Paragraph 14, a precedent set in 1915. As organizations age, all other things being equal, they repeat their work, with the result that it becomes more predictable, and so more easily and logically formalized.

Hypothesis 2: Structure reflects the age of founding of the industry. This curious hypothesis is suggested in the work of Arthur Stinchcombe

[2]We word these hypotheses factually, in terms of the findings of the research. Given that many also reflect analyses of organizational effectiveness, they might just as well have been worded prescriptively—for example, "The older the organization, the more its behavior *should* be formalized," or, "the more effective it will be *if* its behavior is formalized" (assuming in all cases, of course, no matter what the wording, that all other factors remain the same, an assumption that will prove important later, as we move into the discussion of configurations).

(1965), who studied contemporary organizations operating in industries founded in four different eras. He found a relation between age of industry and job specialization as well as the use of trained professionals in staff positions. For example, organizations of the prefactory era—farms, construction firms, retail stores, and the like—tend today to rely more heavily on family personnel, retaining a kind of craft structure, whereas those of the early nineteenth century—apparel, textiles, and so on—use virtually no unpaid family workers, but many clerks, a sign of bureaucracy. Those of the next era—railroads and coal mines—tend to rely heavily on professional managers in place of owner-managers, a second stage of "bureaucratization of industry," in Stinchcombe's opinion. And organizations whose industries date from the next era—motor vehicles, chemicals, electric utilities, and so on—are distinguished by the size of their staff departments and their use of professionals in their administrative structures. Stinchcombe stops here, but the obvious question concerns the industries of our era—aerospace, electronics, film making. Do they exhibit distinctive structural characteristics? Later we shall see clear evidence that they do indeed.

Hypothesis 3: The larger the organization, the more elaborate its structure—that is, the more specialized its tasks, the more differentiated its units, and the more developed its administrative component. This relationship would seem to spring from job specialization, from an organization's increasing ability to divide its labor as it adds employees and increases its volume of output. Thus, one study by a McGill MBA group found that while "grandpa" could do virtually everything in the family food store, when it became a full-fledged supermarket, there was a need to specialize: ". . . 'grandpa' handled the buying of produce. 'Grandma' supervised the store operations. 'Father' dealt with the procurement of the rest of the goods, whereas 'mother' handled the cash."[3] Likewise, with a greater division of labor, the units can be more extensively differentiated. In other words, increased size gives greater homogeneity of work within units but greater diversity of work between units. But the more differentiated the structure, the more emphasis that must be placed on coordination. Hence, the larger organization must use more, and more elaborate, coordination devices, such as a larger hierarchy to coordinate by direct supervision, more behavior formalization to coordinate by the standardization of work processes, more sophisticated planning and control systems to coordinate by output standardization, or more liaison devices to coordinate by mutual adjustment. All this means a more elaborate administrative component, with a sharper administrative division of labor. That means that we should expect sharper lines drawn between the operators who do the

---

[3]From a paper submitted to the author in Management Policy 701, McGill University, November 1969, by Selin Anter, Gilles Bonnier, Dominique Egre, and Bill Freeman.

work, the analysts who design and plan it, and the managers who coordinate it. Thus, although it is not uncommon for the president of a small company to roll up his sleeves and fix a machine, or to serve in the role of analyst in designing an inventory system, we would be surprised to see the president of a large company doing these things.

Typically, the industrial firm in mass production, as it grows, first develops its basic operating functions of production, marketing, and so forth. Then it elaborates its administrative hierarchy, particularly its technostructure. Later it tends to integrate vertically—that is, take over some of the activities of its suppliers and customers—and thereby further differentiate its structure along functional lines. Finally it diversifies—introduces new product lines—and expands its geographical markets, first domestically and then internationally. These last changes require the firm to further differentiate its structure, but this time along market lines; eventually, it superimposes a market grouping—product or geographical, or both—on its traditional functional structure.

In fact, this sequence of structural elaboration describes not only the individual business firm but also the whole of industrial society. At the turn of the century, the typical American firm was small, functionally structured, and with little administrative hierarchy; today, U.S. industry is dominated by giant divisionalized corporations with very elaborate administrative structures. In effect, whole societies of organizations grow and elaborate their structures over time. And this, of course, is the very point Stinchcombe was making. The forces of economic and technological development have brought new industries with new structures, as well as everlarger organizations, and all these changes have caused increasing structural elaboration.

Hypothesis 4: The larger the organization, the larger the average size of its units. Obviously, as an organization adds new employees, it must eventually form new units, each with a new manager, and it must also add more managers over these managers. In other words, it must elaborate its administrative hierarchy. Not so obvious is that this elaboration is moderated by an increase in average unit size. As organizations grow, they apparently call on their managers to supervise more and more employees. We can explain this in terms of the relation between size and specialization, discussed above. As positions in the organization become more specialized and the units more differentiated, each becomes easier to manage. It is one thing to supervise twenty operators all sewing red sweatshirts, or even twenty managers running identical supermarkets; it is quite another to supervise a like number of couturiers, each making a different dress, or a like number of department-store merchandise managers, with different and often overlapping product lines. Furthermore, not only is the work of like specialists more easily supervised, it is also more easily standardized. As a result, the manager's job can be partially institutionalized—replaced by technocratic systems of behavior formalizing or activity planning—thus reducing his workload and enabling him to supervise more people. Thus, to the extent that larger organization size means greater specialization, it also means larger unit size.

Hypothesis 5: The larger the organization, the more formalized its behavior. Just as the older organization formalizes what it has seen before, so the larger organization formalizes what it sees often. ("Listen, mister, I've heard that story at least five times today. Just fill in the form like it says.") More formally, the larger the organization, the more behaviors repeat themselves; as a result, the more predictable they become; and so the greater the propensity to formalize them. Furthermore, with increased size comes greater internal confusion, and perhaps lower morale owing to impersonalism. Management must find the means to make behavior more predictable, and so it turns to rules, procedures, job descriptions, and the like, all devices that formalize behavior. The findings of the last two hypotheses also suggest increasing formalization with increasing size. With their greater specialization, more unit differentiation, greater need for coordination (particularly by formal means), more elaborate administrative hierarchies, and sharper distinctions between operators, analysts, and managers, it follows that larger organizations will be more regulated by rules and procedures and make greater use of formal communication.

The relationships that we have been discussing in these last three hypotheses are summarized graphically in Figure 6–1.

Stages of structural development

Most of these relationships (including those of Figure 6–1, but excluding that of Stinchcombe), imply a kind of continuity—steady growth responded to by continuous changes in structure. But a good deal of other evidence, even though in some ways consistent with the conclusions above, suggests otherwise. Serious changes in structure tend to occur in spurts—in irregular transitions, equivalent to revolutions, following and followed by periods of relative stability in the design parameters.

William Starbuck argued this point eloquently back in 1965 with his "metamorphosis models," which viewed growth not as "a smooth continuous process" but as one "marked by abrupt and discrete changes" in condition and structure (p. 486). Changes more of kind than degree, these transitions bring fundamentally new ways to divide the organization's work and to coordinate it. Thus, just as the pupa sheds its cocoon to emerge as a butterfly, so too does the organic structure shed its informal relationships to emerge as a bureaucracy (hardly as delightful a metamorphosis). These models are generally referred to as ones of stages of growth or development.

A number have been proposed in the literature, but all seem to de-

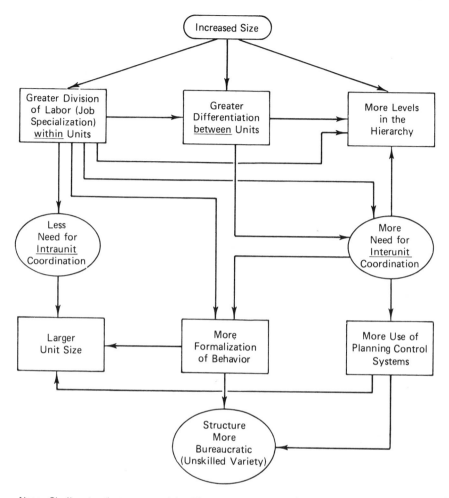

Note: Similar to that suggested in Blau and Schoenherr (1971); assumes conditions of technical system and environment held constant.

Figure 6-1. *Path diagram of the relationships between organizational size and structure*

scribe different aspects of the same sequence. Organizations generally begin their lives with nonelaborated, organic structures. Some begin in the *craft* stage and then shift to an *entrepreneurial* stage as they begin to grow, although more seem to begin in the entrepreneurial stage itself, led by powerful chief executives who coordinate largely by direct supervision.

As organizations in the entrepreneurial stage age and grow, they begin to formalize their structures and eventually make the transition to a new stage, that of *bureaucratic* structure. Jobs are specialized, hierarchies of authority built, and technostructures added to coordinate by standardization.

Further growth and aging often encourage these bureaucracies to diversify and then, like the overgrown amoeba, to split themselves into market-based units, or divisions, superimposed on their traditional functional structures, thus bringing them into a new stage, of *divisionalized* structure.

Finally, some recent evidence suggests that there may be another stage for some organizations, that of *matrix* structure, which transcends divisionalization and causes a partial reversion to organic structure.

Of course, not all organizations need pass through all these stages. But many do seem to go through a number of them in the sequence presented, sometimes stopping at some intermediate stage. The reader will recall the story of Ms. Raku and Ceramico, a typical if apocryphal one, introduced on the first pages of this book.

Technical System

It has been difficult up to this point to keep from discussing technology as a factor in organization design. Clearly, structure is tightly intertwined with it. But before considering how, we must make quite clear what we mean by the terms we shall use.

Technology is a broad term that has been used—and abused—in many contexts. We prefer to avoid it. For its broader meaning—essentially, the knowledge base of the organization—we shall use the term *complexity* and discuss it under environment. Here we shall focus on a narrower interpretation of technology—namely, the instruments used in the operating core to transform the inputs into outputs, which we shall call the *technical system* of the organization. Note that the two concepts are distinct. Accountants, for example, apply a relatively complex technology (that is, base of knowledge), with a simple technical system—often no more than a sharp pencil. Alternatively, most people drive automobiles without ever knowing what goes on under the hood; in other words, they use a fairly complex technical system with hardly any technological knowledge at all.

In discussing the effect of the technical system on the structural parameters, we find it convenient to introduce our framework or organizational types first, and then turn to hypotheses.

Woodward's study of unit, mass, and process production

We have already referred to Joan Woodward's pathbreaking analysis of the effects on structure of different forms of technical systems used in industry. Woodward focused on three basic systems of production—unit (essentially custom), mass (of many standard items), and process (the intermittent or continuous flow of fluids). These systems also relate to stages and eras, unit production in good part predating the Industrial Revolution, mass production being largely associated with it, and process production being largely a phenomenon of the twentieth century. Woodward found some marked relationships between these three systems of production and various of the design parameters. Specifically, in moving from unit to mass to process production:

- The span of control of the chief executives increased.
- The span of control of middle managers decreased.
- The ratio of managers to nonmanagers increased (from an average of 1 to 23, to 1 to 16, to 1 to 8); also, their qualifications rose (process organizations had more graduates, more managerial training, and more promotion from within).
- The ratio of clerical and administrative personnel to production personnel (indirect salaried to hourly paid) increased (from 1 to 1, to 4 to 1, to 9 to 1).
- The number of levels of management in the production department increased.

Moreover:

- The span of control of the first-line supervisors was highest in mass-production firms (about 48, compared with about 13 in process firms and 23 in unit-production firms).
- The mass-production firms had the smallest proportion of skilled workers.
- The mass-production firms were bureaucratic in structure, whereas the process- and unit-production firms tended to be organically structured.

But what distinguishes this study from the others is not these random observations but the way Woodward used them to paint an integrated picture of three distinctly different organizational structures associated with the three technical systems.

Unit production

The firms that manufactured individual units, prototypes, and large equipment in stages exhibited a number of characteristics in common. Most important, because their outputs were ad hoc or nonstandard, the unit producers' operating work could likewise not be standardized or for-

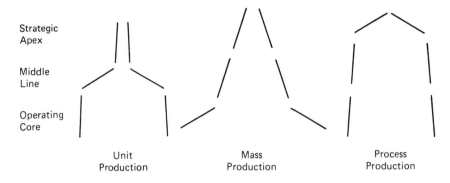

Strategic Apex

Middle Line

Operating Core

Unit Production

Mass Production

Process Production

Note: Shapes denote narrow, intermediate, and wide spans of control as Woodward described them.

Figure 6-2. *Spans of control at three levels in three technical systems (based on the findings of Woodward, 1965)*

malized, and so their structures were organic. Any coordination that could not be handled by mutual adjustment among the operators themselves was resolved by direct supervision by the first-line managers. Being directly responsible for production, the first-line managers worked closely with the operators, typically in small work groups. This resulted in a narrow span of control at the first level of supervision. (The spans of control for the three different structures at three levels in the hierarchy are shown symbolically in Figure 6–2.) Woodward characterizes unit production as craft in nature, with the structure built around the skills of the workers in the operating core.

These characteristics, in turn, meant little elaboration of the administrative structure. With most of the coordination in the unit-production firms being ad hoc in nature, handled by mutual adjustment among the operators or direct supervision by the first-line managers, there was little need for an elaborate managerial hierarchy above them or a technostructure beside them. Thus, of the three forms of production, the unit type had the smallest proportion of managers and, as can be seen in Figure 6–2, the widest span of control at the middle levels. At the strategic apex, however, the span of control tended to be narrow, a reflection perhaps of the ad hoc nature of the business. Not assured of a steady stream of orders, as in more routine production, the top managers had to spend more time with customers and so could not supervise as many people.

Mass production

If the structures of the unit-production firms were shaped by the nonstandard nature of their technical systems, those of the mass producers were shaped by the standard nature of theirs. Here mass standardized production led to formalized behavior, which led to all the characteristics of the classic bureaucracy. Operating work was routine, unskilled, and highly formalized. Such work required little direct supervision, resulting in wide spans of control for the first-line supervisors. The administration contained a fully developed technostructure to formalize the work. Woodward notes that the mass producers, unlike the other two, conformed to all the patterns of the traditional literature—clearly defined work duties, emphasis on written communication, unity of command, span of control at top levels often in the 5–7 range, a rigid separation of line and staff, and considerable action planning, long-range at the strategic apex (owing to the long product development cycles), short-range at lower levels (primarily to deal with sales fluctuations).

Moreover, Woodward found the structures of the mass-production firms to be the most segmented of the three and the most riddled with hostility and suspicion. She identifies three major points of conflict: (1) between the technical and social systems of the operating core, which gives rise to conflict that Woodward considers fundamentally irreconcilable, even in the well-run mass-production organization; (2) between the short-range focus of the lower-level managers and the long-range focus of the senior managers; (3) and between the line and staff groups in the administrative structure, one with authority, the other with expertise.

Hunt (1970:171–72) refers to this second Woodward group as "performance" organizations, in contrast to the other two, which he calls "problem-solving" organizations. In Hunt's view, whereas the unit producers handled only exceptions and the process firms were concerned only with exceptions, the mass producers experienced fewer exceptions, these were of a less critical nature, and many of them could be handled by formal routines. These mass-production performance organizations spent their time fine-tuning their bureaucratic machines.

Process production

In firms built for the continuous production of fluid substances, Woodward found another structure again. What would cause these firms to be different from the mass producers? And why should Hunt describe them as problem solvers, concerned only with exceptions?

The answer seems to lie in a metamorphosis of structure when a technical system becomes so regulating that it approaches the state of automation. Mass production is often highly mechanized, but, if Woodward's findings are a fair guide, seldom to the point of automation. The result is work that is highly regulated—simple, routine, and dull—requiring a large contingent of unskilled operators. And this, in turn, breeds an obsession with control in the administrative structure: supervisory, especially technocratic, personnel are required to watch over and standardize the work of uninterested operators. With automation—which Woodward's findings suggest to be more common in process production—comes a dramatic reduction in the number of unskilled operators tied directly to the pace of production. Some giant oil refineries, for example, can be operated by six people, and even they only serve as monitors; the technical system runs itself.

With this change in the operating work force comes a dramatic change in structure: the operating core transcends a state of bureaucracy—in a sense, it becomes totally bureaucratic, totally standardized, but without the people—and the administration shifts its orientation completely. The rules, regulations, and standards are now built into machines, not workers. And machines never become alienated, no matter how demeaning their work. So out goes the need for direct supervision and technocratic standardization and with it the obsession with control. And in comes a corps of technical specialists, to design the technical system and then maintain it. In other words, automation brings a replacement in the operating core of unskilled workers directly tied to the technical system by skilled workers to maintain it, and in the middle levels of the structure a replacement of managers and technocratic staff who control the work of others by a support staff of professional designers who control their own work. And these changes dissolve many of the conflicts of the mass-production firms. Alienated operators no longer resist a control-obsessed management. Even at the strategic apex, "the company executives are increasingly concerned not with running today's factory, but with designing tomorrow's" (Simon, 1977:22–23). And staff need no longer battle line. This classical distinction—between those who advise and those who choose—becomes irrelevant when it is the control of machines that is at stake. Who gives orders to a machine, its staff designer or its line supervisor? Logically, decisions are taken by whoever has the specialized knowledge needed to make them, whether they be called line or staff.

With these points made, the Woodward findings about the process-production firms fall neatly into place, at least assuming that they are highly automated.[4] She found that the process producers' structures were generally organic in nature. Their operating cores consisted mostly of skilled, indirect workers, such as the service people who maintained the equipment. As in the unit-production firms, the first-level supervisory spans of control were narrow, again a reflection of the need for skilled operators to work in "small primary working groups." This led to a "more intimate and informal" relationship between operator and supervisor than

---

[4]This assumption does not always appear to hold. For example, steel companies in process production require large operating work forces. In these cases, as we shall see later, the structures take on the form of the mass producers. So the Woodward findings really seem to hold for automated production, not for process production per se, although that is where automation is most common.

in the mass-production firms, "probably a contributing factor to better industrial relations" (p. 60).

Of Woodward's three types, the process producers relied most on training and indoctrination, and had the highest ratios of administrators to operators, a reflection of the extensive use of support staff who designed the technical systems and also carried out functions such as research and development. They, too, tended to work in small groups—teams and task forces—hence the finding of narrow spans of control at middle levels as well. Woodward also found that the line/staff distinction was blurred in the process firms, it being "extremely difficult to distinguish between executive and advisory responsibility" (p. 65). In some firms, the staff specialists were incorporated into the line structure; in others, "the line of command seemed to be disintegrating, executive responsibility being conferred on specialist staff" (p. 65). But it made little real difference; in any event, the line managers had training and knowledge similar to that of the staff specialists, and the two in fact interchanged jobs regularly.

These firms also exhibited a sharp separation between product development and operations, resulting in a structure with two independent parts: an inner ring of operations with fixed facilities, short-range orientation, and rigid control built into the machinery; and an outer ring of development—both product and process—with a very long-range orientation, loose control, and an emphasis on social relations. This two-part structure served to reduce conflict, first because it detached the technical and social systems from one another, unlike mass production, which put them into direct confrontation (here people could be free while machines were tightly controlled), and second, because it served to decouple the long- and short-range orientation. Another major source of conflict in the mass-production firms was reduced with the blurring of the line/staff distinction.

At the strategic apex of the process-production firms, Woodward found a tendency to use "management by committee" instead of by single decision makers. This was far less true of unit and mass producers. Yet she also found wide spans of control at the strategic apex, a finding that might be explained by the ability of the specialists lower down to make many key decisions, thereby freeing the top managers to supervise a large number of people. Perhaps the high-level committees served primarily to ensure coordination, by authorizing the choices made lower down.

To conclude, the dominant factor in the process-production firms Woodward studied seems to have been the automation of their technical systems. Automation appears to place an organization in a "postbureaucratic" state: the technical system is fully regulating, but of machines, not people, and the social system—largely outside the operating core—need not be controlled by rules and so can emerge as an organic structure, using mutual adjustment among the experts, encouraged by the liaison devices, to achieve coordination. Thus, the real difference between

Woodward's mass and process producers seems to be that although both sought to regulate their operating work, only the latter could automate it. In having to regulate people, the mass producers developed a control mentality that led to all kinds of conflict; in regulating machines, the process producers experienced less conflict.

With these findings in mind, we can now present three basic hypotheses about the relationships between structure and technical system.

Hypothesis 6: The more regulating the technical system, the more formalized the operating work and the more bureaucratic the structure of the operating core. As the technical system becomes more regulating—that is, broken down into simple, specialized tasks that remove discretion from those who have to use it—the operating work becomes more routine and predictable; as a result, it can more easily be specialized and formalized. Control becomes more impersonal, eventually mechanical, as staff analysts who design the work flow increasingly take power over it away from the unskilled workers who operate it and the managers who supervise them. We saw all these relationships clearly in Woodward's mass-production firms. But what about those in process production? As Woodward described it, this technical system was almost completely regulating—that is, automated. Yet she characterized the structures of these firms as organic. But she meant the administrative structures, where the people were found. Their operating cores were, in a sense, almost perfectly bureaucratic; that is, in production (if not maintenance), their operating work was perfectly standardized; it just did not involve people.

Hypothesis 7: The more sophisticated (difficult to understand) the technical system, the more elaborate the nonoperating structure—specifically, the larger and more professional the support staff, the greater the selective decentralization (to that staff), and the greater the use of liaison devices (to coordinate the work of that staff). If an organization is to use complex machinery, it must hire staff specialists who can understand that machinery, who can design, purchase, and modify it; it must give them considerable power to make decisions concerning that machinery; and they, in turn, must work in teams and task forces to make those decisions. Hence, we would expect organizations with sophisticated technical systems to have a high proportion of support staff, to rely heavily on the liaison devices at middle levels, to favor small units there, and to decentralize selectively—that is, give the support staff power over the technical decisions. All these conclusions are suggested in the Woodward study; specifically, in the absence of an elaborate staff structure in the unit-production firms, generally with the least sophisticated technical systems, and in the presence of all these features in the process firms, generally with the most sophisticated technical systems.

Hypothesis 8: The automation of the operating core transforms a bureaucratic administrative structure into an organic one. We have already discussed this hypothesis at some length in terms of Woodward's process producers. Organizations dominated numerically by unskilled operators doing routine work are riddled with interpersonal conflicts. As Woodward notes, these stem largely from the inherent incompatibility of the social and technical systems: often, what is good for production is simply not good for the producer. As a result, mass-production firms develop an obsession with control—a belief that the workers must be constantly watched and pushed if they are to get their work done. Moreover, the control mentality spills over the operating core and affects all levels of the hierarchy, from the first level of supervision to the strategic apex. Control becomes the watchword of the organization. Top managers watch over middle managers, middle managers watch over operators and staff specialists, and staff specialists design systems to watch over everyone. Automation does not simply bring about more regulation of the activities of the operating core; as we saw, it eliminates the source of many of the social conflicts throughout the organization.[5] Moreover, drawing on our last hypothesis, automated technical systems, typically being the most sophisticated, require the largest proportion of staff specialists. These people tend to communicate among each other informally and to rely for coordination on the liaison devices. And these, of course, are the most flexible of the design parameters. Thus, automation of the operating core breeds all kinds of changes in the administrative structure that drive it to the organic state.

This leads us to an interesting social implication: that one apparent solution to the problems of impersonal bureaucracy is not less regulation of operating tasks but more, to the point of automating them. Automation seems to humanize the traditional bureaucratic structure, something that democratization proves unable to do.[6]

Environment

We have so far discussed the influence on structure of factors intrinsic to the organization itself—its age, its size, and the technical system it uses in its operating core. But every organization also exists in a milieu to which it must respond when designing its structure. Now we consider situational factors associated with this milieu; first the characteristics of the general environment, then specific aspects of the system of power faced by the organization.

[5]New conflicts, however, arise in the organization with an automated operating core, as we shall see later, notably among the different specialists. But these do not regenerate the control mentality; rather, they arise in the absence of it.

[6]But we might ask whether automation has the opposite effect for the clients, further standardizing and impersonalizing the products and services they receive.

What does the word *environment* really mean? The dictionary is as vague as the literature of management: "the aggregate of surrounding things, conditions, or influences . . ." (*Random House Dictionary*). So environment comprises virtually everything outside the organization—its "technology" (the knowledge base it must draw upon); the nature of its products, customers, and competitors; its geographical setting; the economic, political, and even meteorological climate in which it must operate; and so on. What the literature does do, however, is focus on certain dimensions of organizational environments, four in particular:

1   Stability. An organization's environment can range from *stable* to *dynamic*, from that of the wood carver whose customers demand the same pine sculptures decade after decade, to that of the detective squad that never knows what to expect next. A variety of factors can make an environment dynamic, including unstable government, unpredictable shifts in the economy, unexpected changes in customer demand or competitor supply, client demands for creativity or frequent novelty as in an advertising agencies, rapidly changing technologies as in electronics manufacturing, even weather that cannot be forecasted, as in the case of open-air theater companies. Notice that *dynamic* here means unpredictable, not variable; variability may be predictable, as in steady growth of demand.

2   Complexity. An organization's environment (here, its "technology") can range from *simple* to *complex*, from that of the manufacturer of folding boxes who produces his simple products with simple knowledge, to that of the space agency that must utilize knowledge from a host of the most advanced scientific fields to produce extremely complex outputs. Clearly, the complexity dimension affects structure through the intermediate variable of the comprehensibility of the work to be done. Note that rationalized knowledge, no matter how complex in principle, is here considered simple because it has been broken down into easily comprehended parts. Thus, automobile companies face relatively simple product environments by virtue of their accumulated knowledge about the machines they produce.

3   Market Diversity. The markets of an organization can range from *integrated* to *diversified*, from that of an iron mine that sells its one commodity to a single steel mill, to those of a trade commission that seeks to promote all a nation's industrial products all over the world. Market diversity may result from a broad range of clients, of products and services, or of geographical areas in which the outputs are marketed. Clearly, market diversity affects the structure through the intermediate variable of the diversity of the work to be done.

4   Hostility. Finally, an organization's environment can range from *munificent* to *hostile*, from that of a prestige surgeon who picks and chooses his patients, through that of a construction firm that must bid on all its contracts, to that of an army fighting a war. Hostility is influenced by competition, by the organization's relations with unions, government, and other outside groups, and by the availability of resources to it. Of course, hostile environments are typically dynamic ones. But extreme hostility has a special effect on structure that we wish to distinguish. Hostility affects structure especially through the intermediate variables of the speed of necessary response.

What matters about environment in the design of structure is its specific effect on the organization. In other words, it is not the environment per se that counts but the organization's ability to cope with it—to predict it, comprehend it, deal with its diversity, and respond quickly to it. That is why, for example, when discussing the complexity dimension, we noted that if the organization is able to rationalize what seems to be a complex product into a system of simple components, its product environment can be called simple. Also, although it is convenient to discuss an organization's environment as uniform—a single entity—the fact is that every organization faces multiple environments. The products may be complex but the marketing channels simple, the economic conditions dynamic but the political ones stable. Often, however, it is a reasonable approximation to treat the environment as uniform along each of its dimensions, either because some of its more placid aspects do not really matter to the organization or, alternatively, because one active part of the environment is so dominant that it affects the entire organization. We shall proceed under this assumption in the first four hypotheses presented below, each considering one of the dimensions, taking up the case of contradictory demands from the environment in the fifth hypothesis.

Hypothesis 9: The more dynamic the environment, the more organic the structure. In peacetime, or well back from the battlefield in wartime, armies tend to be highly bureaucratic institutions, with heavy emphasis on planning, formal drills, and ceremony, close attention being paid to discipline. On the battlefield, at least the modern one, there is the need for greater flexibility, and so the structure becomes less rigid. This is especially so in the dynamic conditions of guerrilla warfare. It stands to reason that in a stable environment, an organization can predict its future conditions and so, all other things being equal, can easily insulate its operating core and standardize its activities there—establish rules, formalize work, plan actions—or perhaps standardize its skills instead. But this relationship also extends beyond the operating core. In a highly stable environment, the whole organization takes on the form of a protected, or undisturbed system, which can standardize its procedures from top to bottom. Alternatively, faced with uncertain sources of supply, unpredictable customer demand, frequent product change, high labor turnover, unstable political conditions, or rapidly changing technology (knowledge), the organization cannot easily predict its future, and so it cannot rely on standardization for coordination. It must use a more flexible, less formal coordinating mechanism instead—direct supervision or mutual adjustment. In other words, it must have an organic structure.

Note the wording of Hypothesis 9: Dynamic environments lead to organic structures, instead of stable environments leading to bureaucratic ones. This wording was chosen to highlight the asymmetrical nature of the relationship—that dynamic conditions have more influence on structure than do static ones. Specifically, there is evidence to suggest that a dynamic environment will drive the structure to an organic state despite forces of large size and regulating technical system that act in the opposite direction, whereas a stable environment will not override the other situational factors—the structure will be bureaucratic to the extent called for by these other factors.

Hypothesis 10: The more complex the environment, the more decentralized the structure. Before proceeding with discussions of this hypothesis, it will be useful to clarify the distinction between environmental stability and complexity.

Conceptually, it is not difficult to distinguish between these two dimensions of environment. The dice roller easily comprehends his game, yet he cannot predict its outcome. His environment is simple but dynamic. So, too, is that of the dress manufacturer, who easily comprehends his markets and technologies yet has no way to predict style or color from one season to the next. In contrast, the clinical surgeon spends years trying to learn his or her complicated work, yet undertakes it only when rather certain of its consequences. This environment is complex but stable. Despite this, perhaps because many organizations face environments that are simple and stable or complex and dynamic, these two dimensions have often been confused. Yet we shall soon see that important types of organizations face, in one case, simple and dynamic, and in another, complex and stable environments. Again we can turn to our coordinating mechanisms to help resolve the confusion.

Our tenth hypothesis suggests that the complexity dimension has a very different effect on structure from the stability one. Whereas the latter affects bureaucratization, the former affects decentralization. One of the problems in disentangling Hypotheses 9 and 10, aside from the fact that the two environmental variables often move in tandem, is that the most bureaucratizing of the coordinating mechanisms—the standardization of work processes—also tends to be rather centralizing, whereas one of the most organic—mutual adjustment—tends to be the most decentralizing. The relationship between the five coordinating mechanisms and bureaucratization was discussed in Chapter 2, that between the mechanisms and decentralization in Chapter 5. Figure 6–3 summarizes these two discus-

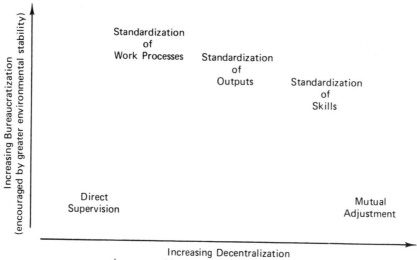

Figure 6-3. *Coordinating mechanisms on scales of decentralization and bureaucratization*

sions, with the coordinating mechanisms of increasing bureaucratization shown along the ordinate and those of increasing decentralization along the abscissa (the latter is, in fact, a replication of Figure 5–3).

We can draw on an argument of Galbraith to use the coordinating mechanisms as shown in Figure 6–3 to disentangle the two hypotheses, and thereby to develop more support for each. Galbraith argues that coordination is most easily achieved in one brain. Faced, therefore, with a simple environment, the organization will tend to rely on one brain to make its key decisions; in other words, it will centralize. Should that environment also be stable, according to Hypothesis 9 it will be in the organization's best interests to standardize for coordination—in other words, to bureaucratize. As can be seen in Figure 6–3, the organization will select the standardization of work processes for coordination, the mechanism that enables it to maintain the tightest centralization within a bureaucratic structure. But should its simple environment be dynamic instead of stable, the organization can no longer bureaucratize but must, rather, remain flexible—organic. So, as Figure 6–3 shows, it will rely on direct supervision for coordination, the one mechanism of the five that enables it to have a structure that is both centralized and organic.

What about the organization faced with a complex environment? This introduces problems of comprehensibility. In Galbraith's terms, one brain can no longer cope with the information needed to make all the decisions. It becomes overloaded. So the organization must decentralize: The top manager must give up a good deal of his power to others—other managers, staff specialists, sometimes operators as well. Now, should that complex environment be stable, Hypothesis 9 would lead us to expect a bureaucratic structure—in other words, one that relies on standardization for coordination. In that case, the problem becomes to find a coordinating mechanism that allows for standardization with decentralization. And the solution emerges with a quick glance at Figure 6–3: the organization chooses the standardization of skills. Should the complex environment instead be dynamic, the organization seeks a coordinating mechanism that is both decentralizing and organic. Mutual adjustment is the obvious choice.

What emerges from this discussion are two kinds of bureaucratic and two kinds of organic structures, in each case a centralized one for simple environments and a decentralized one for complex environments. That, in fact, corresponds exactly to the conclusion that emerged repeatedly in our discussion of the design parameters. There, for example, we encountered two fundamentally different bureaucracies, a centralized one for unskilled work, a decentralized one for professional work. Now we see that the former operates in a simple environment, the latter in a complex one, in both cases stable. We shall return to these four types shortly.

Hypothesis 11: The more diversified the organization's markets, the greater the propensity for it to split into market-based units (given favorable economies of scale). Here we propose a relationship between a third environmental variable—market diversity—and a third design parameter—the basis for grouping units. Hypothesis 11 indicates that the organization that can identify distinctly different markets—products or services, geographical regions, or clients—will be predisposed to split itself into high-level units on this basis, and to give each control of a wide range of the decisions affecting its own markets. This amounts to what we called in Chapter 5 limited vertical decentralization, a good deal of the decision-making power being delegated to the managers of the market units. In simple terms, diversification breeds divisionalization.

There is, however, one key impediment to divisionalization, even when markets are diverse, and that is the presence of a common technical system or critical function that cannot be segmented. In divisionalization, each market unit requires its own distinct operating core. This it cannot have when economies of scale dictate a single, unified technical system. Some technical systems can be split up even though of very small scale, and others must remain intact despite massive size. A bakery operating in two states with total sales of, say, $2 million may find it worthwhile to set up a division with its own plant in each, whereas an aluminum producer with sales 100 times as great may, despite a diversity of customers in all fifty states and a variety of end products (foil, sheets, construction components, and so on), be forced to retain a functional structure because it can afford only one smelter.

Likewise, the presence of a function critical to all the markets in common impedes true divisionalization, as in the case of purchasing in the retail chain or investment in the insurance business. The organization still splits itself into market-based units, but it concentrates the critical function at headquarters. This reduces the autonomy of the market units, leading to an incomplete form of divisionalization. In fact, as we shall see in Chapter 11, this is most common when the diversity is based on client or region rather than on product or service, common outputs giving rise to important interdependencies among the different clients or regions.

We can explain Hypothesis 11 in terms similar to those used to explain Hypothesis 10. The organization that must comprehend information about many different aspects of its market environment eventually finds it convenient to segment that environment into distinct markets if it can and to give individual units control over each. In this way it minimizes the coordination of decision making that must take place across units. We must, however, make a clear distinction between environmental diversity and complexity, even though both increase the informational load on the decision makers and thereby encourage some kind of decentralization. A simple environment can be very diverse, as in the case of a conglomerate firm that operates a number of simple businesses, whereas a complex environment may focus on an integrated market, as in the case of the NASA of the 1960s that had one overriding mission—to put a man on the moon before 1970.[7] In fact, for reasons that we shall discuss in Chapter 11, divisionalization appears to be better suited to simple diversified markets than to complex ones.

Hypothesis 12: Extreme hostility in its environment drives any organization to centralize its structure temporarily.[8] Again, we can explain this in terms of our coordinating mechanisms. Direct supervision is the fastest and tightest means of coordination—only one brain is involved. All members of the organization know exactly where to send information; no time is wasted in debate; authority for action is clearly defined; one leader makes and coordinates all the decisions. As we saw in Chapter 5, the more centralized communication networks organized themselves more quickly and required less communication to make decisions. When an organization faces extreme hostility—the sudden loss of its key client or source of supply, severe attack by the government, or whatever—its very survival is threatened. Since it must respond quickly and in an integrated fashion, it turns to its leader for direction.

---

[7]NASA, of course, had other missions—for example, to launch weather satellites. But the Apollo project was dominant in the 1960s.

[8]It seems reasonable to hypothesize further that extreme hostility drives the organization to organic structure as well, in that hostile environments are unpredictable ones, requiring flexible responses. However, no evidence was found regarding this relationship.

But what of the organization in a complex environment that faces extreme hostility? The complexity requires it to decentralize in order to comprehend the environment, yet the hostility demands the speed and coordination of a centralized response. Forced to choose, the organization presumably centralizes power temporarily, in order to survive. This enables it to respond to the crisis, even if without due regard for its complexity. With some luck, it may be able to ride it out. But should the crisis persist, the organization may simply be incapable of reconciling the two opposing forces. It may simply expire.

Hypothesis 13: Disparities in the environment encourage the organization to decentralize selectively to differentiated work constellations. No organization has ever existed in an environment uniformly dynamic, complex, diverse, or hostile across its entire range. But the organization need not respond to every contingency in its environment either. Some are exigent, demanding responses; others are placid, requiring none. Dynamic economic conditions may require organic structure even though the political environment is stable; hostility from the union in an otherwise munificent environment may require temporary centralization followed by a return to decentralization. But what happens when one contingency does not dominate, when disparities in the environment call for different responses in the design of the structure? Take the case of mixed competition in the large oil company:

> Mobil Oil and Exxon may compete furiously at the intersection of two streets in any American town, but neither of them is really threatened by this marginal competition. They work very closely together in the important matter of oil depletion allowances, our foreign policy about the Mideast, federal tax policies, the pollution issues, and private transit versus mass transit. . . . Where, then, is the furious rate of competition? At the lower levels in the organization—the levels of the regional manager who moves prices up and down a fraction and the station manager who washes the windshields and cleans the rest rooms. (Perrow, 1974:41)

What this example suggests is that disparities in the environment encourage the organization to differentiate its structure, to create pockets—what we earlier referred to as work constellations—to deal with different aspects of the environment (different "subenvironments").[9] Each constellation is located according to the effect of its subenvironment on the organization—near the top if the effect is universal, farther down if it is local. The managers at the top of the oil company can attend to cooperation

---

[9]This is, of course, akin to the tendency to divisionalize when markets are diverse, except that here the disparities cut across different environmental dimensions, and the response is to differentiate the structure along functional lines (and often vertically), instead of market lines (and horizontally).

while those in the regions deal with the competition. Each work constellation is given power over the decisions required in its subenvironment, and each is allowed to develop the structure its decision processes require. For example, one constellation of an organization may be organically structured to handle dynamic conditions, and others, operating in stable subenvironments, may be structured bureaucratically. We saw this earlier in the case of the new venture teams isolated from the rest of their structures. Thus, disparities in the environment encourage the organization to differentiate its structure and to use selective decentralization in both the vertical and horizontal dimensions. In other words, it can centralize and decentralize at the same time.

This is clearly illustrated by the McGill MBA group study of the Canadian subsidiary of a European recording company. There were two sharply differentiated constellations here. One, at the strategic apex, comprised the top managers sent from the European headquarters. They handled liaison with it, the financial affairs of the company, and some of the production problems, all relatively stable and simple issues. But the marketing decisions—in particular, what Canadian stars and songs to record—required intimate knowledge of the local scene, of the tastes of the Canadian consumers, both English and French, and of Canadian entertainment personalities. It also required a very different orientation to decision making. With a product life cycle of three months ("there is nothing quite so dead as yesterday's number one hit on the hit parade") and with the most dynamic of supply markets (recording artists being "notoriously hard to get along with"), marketing required a free-wheeling style of decision making, in sharp contrast to that of the rather straightlaced European executives. Thus, a second work constellation was created below the first and given complete and undisputed power over marketing decisions. It worked in a structure for which the word "organic" seemed an understatement.[10]

An organizational type for each of four environments

Our discussion of the environment again supports our contention that we learn more by focusing on distinct types of structures found under specific conditions than by tracing continuous relationships between structural and situational variables. Hypotheses 9 and 10, although initially stated in terms of continuous relationships, seem more powerful when used to generate specific types of structures found in specific kinds of environments. In particular, four basic types emerge from that discussion, shown in matrix form as follows:

[10]From a paper submitted to the author by Alain Berranger and Philip Feldman in Management Policy 276–661, McGill University, November 1972.

	Stable	Dynamic
Complex	Decentralized Bureaucratic (standardization of skills)	Decentralized Organic (mutual adjustment)
Simple	Centralized Bureaucratic (standardization of work processes)	Centralized Organic (direct supervision)

Simple, stable environments give rise to centralized, bureaucratic structures, the classic organizational type that relies on standardization of work processes (and the design parameter of formalization of behavior) for coordination. Examples are Woodward's mass-production manufacturing firms and Crozier's tobacco company. Lawrence and Lorsch so describe certain container firms, operating in simple, stable environments, that standardized their products and processes, introduced changes slowly, and coordinated at the top of the hierarchy where information could easily be consolidated and understood. In fact, one container firm that tried to do the opposite—to use the liaison devices to coordinate by mutual adjustment lower down—exhibited lower performance than the others. Apparently, it just confused a simple situation, like four people in a car all trying to decide which way to drive downtown.

Complex, stable environments lead to structures that are bureaucratic but decentralized, reliant for coordination on the standardization of skills. Because their work is rather predictable, the organization can standardize; and because that work is difficult to comprehend, it must decentralize. Power must flow to the highly trained professionals of the operating core who understand the complex but routine work. Typical examples of this are general hospitals and universities.[11]

When its environment is dynamic but nevertheless simple, the organization requires the flexibility of organic structure, but its power can remain centralized. Direct supervision becomes its prime coordinating mechanism. This is characteristic of the entrepreneurial firm, which seeks a niche in the marketplace that is simple to understand yet dynamic enough

[11]We must, therefore, take issue with the conclusion of Beyer and Lodahl that, "If the knowledge taught at the university were a fixed commodity that changed little from year to year, centralization of authority and bureaucratic decision making would be as efficient and effective for universities as for other organizations with stable environments and technologies." (1976:109) Bureaucratic yes, centralized no. Even a university that taught only Latin, Ancient Greek, and Sanskrit would not centralize. These three bodies of knowledge are stable, but together they are too much for central administrators to comprehend. Thus, to the extent that universities teach stable bodies of knowledge—and most of the time, even scientific knowledge remains relatively stable—they bureaucratize and *decentralize*.

144

to keep out the bureaucracies. In such a place, the entrepreneur can maintain a tight personal control, not even having to share his power with a technostructure.

When the dynamic environment is complex, the organization must decentralize to managers and specialists who can comprehend the issues, yet allow them to interact flexibly in an organic structure so that they can respond to unpredictable changes. Mutual adjustment emerges as the prime coordinating mechanism, its use encouraged by the liaison devices. Research studies have described NASA during the Apollo project, the Boeing Company, and plastics firms in general in this way. (Note, in Stinchcombe's terms, that these are all organizations of our age.)

Market diversity, as discussed in Hypothesis 11, can be viewed as a third dimension—in effect, as a separate condition superimposed on the two-dimensional matrix. These four types of structures will tend to be functional if their markets are integrated, market-based (at least at the highest level of grouping) if they are diversified (assuming favorable economies of scale and an absence of critical functions). Since, as we saw in Chapter 4, coordination in the market-based structure is achieved by the standardization of outputs, effected through performance control systems, we are able to account for our fifth and last coordinating mechanism in this third dimension.

Similarly, Hypothesis 12 can be viewed as imposing another special condition on the two-dimensional matrix. Extreme hostility drives each of the four types to centralize its structure temporarily, no matter what its initial state of decentralization. (Two, of course, are already rather centralized.)

All these conditions assume uniform environments, or at least ones that can be treated as uniform, owing to the dominance of a single characteristic. They are either complex or simple, stable or dynamic, integrated or diversified, extremely hostile or not. Uniformity, in turn, produces consistent use of the design parameters in the structure. Hypothesis 13 drops the assumption of uniformity, indicating that disparities in the environment encourage the organization to respond with a differentiated structure. It sets up work constellations, decentralizes power selectively to them, locates each according to the effect of its decisions on the organization, and allows it to design its internal structure according to the demands of its particular subenvironment.

Power

Organizations do not always adopt the structures called for by their impersonal conditions—their ages and sizes, the technical systems they use, the stability, complexity, diversity, and hostility of their environments. A number of *power* factors also enter into the design of structure, notably the presence of external control of the organization, the personal needs of its various members, and the fashion of the day, embedded in the culture in which the organization finds itself (in effect, the power of social norms). Three hypotheses describe a number of the findings about these power factors:

Hypothesis 14: The greater the external control of the organization, the more centralized and formalized its structure. A number of studies of both public and private organizations have provided evidence that outside control of them—whether directly by specific owners or indirectly, say, by a major supplier on whom they are dependent—tends to concentrate their decision-making powers at the top of their hierarchies and to encourage greater than usual reliance on rules and regulations for internal control. All this, in fact, seems logical enough. The two most effective means to control an organization from the outside are (1) to hold its most powerful decision maker—its chief executive officer—responsible for its actions, and (2) to impose clearly defined standards on it, transformed into rules and regulations. The first centralizes the structure; the second formalizes it.

Moreover, external control forces the organization to be especially careful about its actions. Because it must justify its behaviors to outsiders, it tends to formalize them. Formal, written communication generates records that can be produced when decisions are questioned. Rules ensure fair treatment to clients and employees alike. External control can also act to bureaucratize the structure by imposing on it more sweeping demands than usual for rationalization. For example, whereas the autonomous firm can deal with its suppliers and clients in the open market, the subsidiary may be informed by headquarters that it must purchase its supplies from a sister subsidiary, and moreover that managers of the two subsidiaries must sit down together to plan the transfers in advance so that no surplus or shortages will result. Or a parent organization or government might insist on standards being applied across the whole range of organizations it controls. It may demand anything from the use of a common logo, or corporate symbol, to a common management information system or set of purchasing regulations. Entrepreneurial firms with organic structures that are purchased by larger corporations are often forced to develop organigrams, specify job descriptions and reporting relationships more clearly, and adopt action planning and a host of other systems that bureaucratize their structures.

To conclude, Hypothesis 14 indicates that when two organizations are the same age and size, use the same technical system, and operate in the same environment, the structure of the one with the greater amount of external control—by government, a parent organization, the unions, or whatever—will be more centralized and more formalized. This, of course, raises all kinds of interesting issues in societies that find more and more of their autonomous organizations being gobbled up by giant conglomerations—big business, big government, big labor. The loss of autonomy means not only the surrender of power to the external controller but also significant changes within the structure of the organization itself, no matter what its intrinsic needs—more power concentrated at its strategic apex, tighter personnel procedures, more standardization of work processes, more formal communication, more regulated reporting, more planning and less adapting. In other words, centralization of power at the societal level leads to centralization of power at the organizational level, and to bureaucratization in the use of that power.

Hypothesis 15: The power needs of the members tend to generate structures that are excessively centralized. All members of the organization typically seek power—if not to control others, at least to control the decisions that affect their own work. The managers of the strategic apex promote centralization in both the vertical and horizontal dimensions; the managers of the middle line promote vertical decentralization, at least down to their own levels, and horizontal centralization to keep power within the line structure; the analysts and the support staff favor horizontal decentralization, to draw power away from the line managers; and the operators seek vertical and horizontal decentralization, all the way down to the operating core.

But the dice of this power game are loaded. To function effectively, organizations typically require hierarchical structures and some degree of formal control. And these naturally put power in the hands of the line managers, as opposed to the staff specialists or the operators, and aggregate that power at the top of the hierarchy, in the hands of the managers of the strategic apex. We have seen that various situational factors—such as a sophisticated technical system and environmental complexity—call for a sharing of central power. But to the extent that the line managers, notably the senior ones, relish power, the structure can easily become excessively centralized. That is, more power can be concentrated at its top than the factors of age, size, technical system, and environment would normally call for (at least until the resulting inefficiencies catch up with the organization).

Hypothesis 16: Fashion favors the structure of the day (and of the culture), sometimes even when inappropriate. Stinchcombe's research, discussed in Hypothesis 2, suggests that there is such a thing as "the structure of the day"—that is, the one favored by industries founded in a given period. But his research also shows that structures transcend periods; in other words, that some organizations retain structures favored in previous periods. The implication of this is that when a new structure comes along, it is appropriate for some organizations but not for others.

This point has, apparently, been lost on a good many organizations, because fashion—the power of the norms of the culture in which the organization finds itself—seems to play an important role in structural design. We might like to believe that organizations are influenced only by factors such as age, size, technical system, and environment, not by what Jones, Inc., is doing next door. But there is too much evidence to the contrary.

Part of the problem probably lies with the business periodicals and consulting firms eager to promote the latest fad. As Whistler (1975) has noted, "There is still money to be made, and notoriety to be gained, in peddling universal prescriptions. In economic terms, the demand is still there, in the form of executives who seek the gospel, the simple truth, *the one best way*" (1975:4). Paris has its salons of haute couture; likewise, New York has its offices of "haute structure," the consulting firms that bring the latest in high structural fashion to their clients—long-range planning (LRP), management information systems (MIS), management by objectives (MBO), organization development (OD).

In the 1960s, the management media heralded "the coming death of bureaucracy," to use the title of an article by Warren Bennis (1966). And many organizations took this seriously, some to their regret. Thus, when Lawrence and Lorsch describe the low-performance container firm that tried to use integrators—one of the very fashionable tools of organic structure—in a simple, stable environment, we find fashion extracting its toll in inappropriate structural design. Since Bennis's article, it has become evident that bureaucracies will not die. Not as long, at least, as organizations grow old and large, mass-produce their outputs, and find simple, stable environments to nurture their standards. The fact is that articles would not be published and speakers would not attend conferences to tell of "the one best way" if the printers and airlines were not structured as bureaucracies. Today, few would deny that bureaucracies are alive, if not well.

Throughout this century, the swings between centralization and decentralization at the top of large American corporations have resembled the movements of women's hemlines. But the trend toward the use of divisionalization has been consistent, ever since du Pont and General Motors first made it fashionable in the 1920s. Thus, Rumelt found in a study of the Fortune 500 strong support not only for Chandler's (1962) well-known proposition that "structure follows strategy" but for another, that "structure also follows fashion" (1974:149). The use of the divisionalized form increased from 20 percent in 1949 to 76 percent in 1969; but not all of it was explained by market diversification, as Hypothesis 11 would have us believe: "Until the early 1960s the adoption of product-division structures was strongly contingent upon the administrative pressures created by diversification but . . . in more recent years divisionalization has become accepted as the norm and managements have sought reorganization along product-division lines in response to normative theory rather than actual administrative pressure" (p. 77).

Of course, fashionable structure need not be inappropriate structure.

Fashion reflects new advances in organizational design, advances that suit some organizations with older structures. Once the divisionalized form became established, it was appropriately adopted by most diversified companies that had been structured along functional lines.[12] Indeed, those that failed to do so were saddled with structures that suddenly became out of date—less effective than the new alternative. Much like the dowager who always dresses as she did in her heyday, so too the organization may cling to a structure appropriate to days gone by. Thus, one study found that in the absence of competitive pressures, some European companies did not divisionalize even though they were diversified. Placid environments enabled them to retain outdated, ineffective structures (Franko, 1974).

This finding also suggests that structural fashion is in some sense culture-bound. What is all the rage among the Fortune 500 (the largest U.S. corporations) may simply look odd to the Fortune 200 (the largest non–U.S. corporations). West Virginians and Westphalians may simply have different preferences for structure. This is another way of saying that culture, working through fashion, is another factor that influences structural design.

The literature provides evidence for this too, for example, that certain European societies—such as the German—take better to bureaucracy than does the American, or that the Japanese place much heavier emphasis on indoctrination than do most other people.

In contemporary American culture, we see quite different trends in structural fashion. Coming quickly into vogue, close behind the divisionalized form, is project structure, what Bennis and Slater (1964) and then Toffler (1970) have called "ad-hocracy"—in essence, selectively decentralized organic structure that makes heavy use of the liaison devices. One can hardly pick up a management journal without reading about task forces, integrating managers, matrix structure. Clearly, this structure corresponds well to the calls for the destruction of bureaucracy, to the democratic norms prevalent in American society, and to its increasingly better-educated work force. But although this may be the structure of our age—well-suited to new, "future-shocked" industries such as aerospace and think-tank consulting—it may be wholly inappropriate for most older industries. It, too, is no panacea. Like all the structures before it, themselves once fashionable, it suits some organizations and not others. It is to be hoped that those others will not opt for project structure, as did one of Lawrence and Lorsch's container firms, just because it is fashionable.

To conclude our discussion of the situational factors, we note that different ones tend to affect the structure at different levels, although a

---

[12]In fact, there is reason to argue that the real fashion was the strategy of diversification; divisionalization then became the appropriate structural response.

number can affect the same design parameter (as in the case of formalization of behavior, which is affected by age, size, technical system, environmental stability, and culture). The factors of age and size, although significant at all levels, seem most pronounced in the middle of the structure; that is where, by creating changes in the favored mechanism of coordination, they produce extensive structural elaboration. The technical system, being housed in the operating core, clearly has its greatest effect there. But it has important selective effects elsewhere as well—for example, at middle levels requiring an extensive support staff when it is sophisticated. The environmental factors seem to have exactly the opposite effect from the technical-system ones. It is the managers and staff specialists at and near the strategic apex, those who must function continuously at the organization's boundaries, who are most affected by the environmental dimensions. These dimensions also importantly affect the structure in the middle, but have only a selective effect on the operating core, which the rest of the structure in fact tries to seal off from direct environmental influence. Finally, the power factors seem to cut across all levels of the structure, but only on a selective basis. External control, member needs for power, fashion, and culture sometimes modify the structures that would otherwise result from consideration of only the factors of age, size, technical system, and environment.

7

DESIGN AS CONFIGURATION

Throughout this book, ever since the introduction of the five coordinating mechanisms in its first pages, we have seen growing convergences in its findings. For example, the standardization of work processes was seen in Chapter 1 to relate most closely to the view of the organization as a system of regulated flows. Then in Chapter 2, we saw these two linked up to the design parameter of behavior formalization in particular and the traditional kind of bureaucratic structure in general, where the operating work is highly specialized but unskilled. In the next chapter, we found that the operating units of such structures are large, and that they tend to be grouped by function, as do the units above them in the middle line. In Chapter 5, there emerged the conclusion that decentralization in these structures tends to be of the limited horizontal type, where power resides primarily at the strategic apex and secondarily in the technostructure that formalizes everyone else's work. Then in the last chapter, we found that this combination of the design parameters is most likely to appear in larger and mature organizations, specifically in their second stage of development; in organizations that use mass production technical systems, regulating but not automated; in organizations operating in simple, stable environments; and in those subject to external control. Other such convergences appeared in our findings. In effect, **the elements of our study— the coordinating mechanisms, design parameters, and situational factors—all seem to fall into natural clusters, or configurations.**

It will be recalled that in our discussion of the effective structuring of organizations in the last chapter, two hypotheses were put forward. The congruence hypothesis, which postulates that effective organizations select their design parameters to fit their situation, was the subject of that chapter. Now we take up the configuration hypothesis, which postulates that effective organizations achieve an internal consistency among their design parameters as well as compatibility with their situational factors—in effect, configuration. It is these configurations that are reflected in the convergences of this book.

How many configurations do we need to describe all organizations? The mathematician tells us that p elements, each of which can take on n forms, lead to p^n possible combinations. With our various design parameters, that number would grow rather large. Nevertheless, we could start building a large matrix, trying to fill in each of the boxes. But the world does not work that way. There is order in the world, but it is a far more profound one than that—a sense of union or harmony that grows out of the natural clustering of elements, whether they be stars, ants, or the characteristics of organizations.

The number "five" has appeared repeatedly in our discussion. First there were five basic coordinating mechanisms, then five basic parts of the organization, later five basic types of decentralization. Five is, of course, no ordinary digit. "It is the sign of union, the nuptial number according to the Pythagoreans; also the number of the center, of harmony and of equilibrium." The *Dictionnaire des Symboles* goes on to tell us that five is the "symbol of man . . . likewise of the universe . . . the symbol of divine will that seeks only order and perfection." To the ancient writers, five was the essence of the universal laws, there being "five colors, five flavors, five tones, five metals, five viscera, five planets, five orients, five regions of space, of course five senses," not to mention "the five colors of the rainbow." Our modest contribution to this impressive list is five configurations of structure and situation. These have appeared repeatedly in our discussion; they are the ones described most frequently in the literature.[1]

In fact, the recurrence of the number "five" in our discussion seems not to be coincidental, for it turns out that there is a one-to-one correspondence among all our fives. In each configuration, a different one of the coordinating mechanisms is dominant, a different part of the organization plays the most important role, and a different type of decentralization is used.[2] This correspondence is summarized in the following table:

---

[1]Quotes from *Dictionnaire des Symboles,* sous la direction de Jean Chevalier avec la collaboration de Alain Gheerbrant (Editions Robert Laffont, 1969), p. 208; my translation from the French. The obsolescence of most of their fives is not of central concern to us here and now; it simply suggests that we often begin with quintets before we proceed to more elaborate typologies.

[2]At the risk of stretching my credibility, I would like to point out that this neat correspondence was not fabricated. Only after deciding on the five configurations was I struck by the correspondence with the five coordinating mechanisms and the five organizational parts. Slight modification in the typology of decentralization (which rendered it more logical) was, however, suggested by the five configurations.

Structural Configuration	Prime Coordinating Mechanism	Key Part of Organization	Type of Decentralization
Simple Structure	Direct supervision	Strategic apex	Vertical and horizontal centralization
Machine Bureaucracy	Standardization of work processes	Technostructure	Limited horizontal decentralization
Professional Bureaucracy	Standardization of skills	Operating core	Vertical and horizontal decentralization
Divisionalized Form	Standardization of outputs	Middle line	Limited vertical decentralization
Adhocracy	Mutual adjustment	Support staff*	Selective decentralization

*We shall see in Chapter 12 that there are two basic types of Adhocracies. In the second type—more like the Professional Bureaucracy—the operating core is also a key part.

We can explain this correspondence by considering the organization as being pulled in five different directions, each by one of its parts. (These five pulls are shown in Figure 7–1.) Most organizations experience all five of these pulls; however, to the extent that conditions favor one over the others, the organization is drawn to structure itself as one of the configurations.

■ Thus, the strategic apex exerts a pull for centralization, by which it can retain control over decision making. This it achieves when direct supervision is relied upon for coordination. To the extent that conditions favor this pull, the configuration called *Simple Structure* emerges.

■ The technostructure exerts its pull for standardization—notably for that of work processes, the tightest form—because the design of the standards is its raison d'être. This amounts to a pull for limited horizontal decentralization. To the extent that conditions favor this pull, the organization structures itself as a *Machine Bureaucracy*.

■ In contrast, the members of the operating core seek to minimize the influence of the administrators—managers as well as analysts—over their work. That is, they promote horizontal and vertical decentralization. When they succeed, they work relatively autonomously, achieving whatever coordination is necessary through the standardization of skills. Thus, the operators exert a pull for professionalism—that is, for a reliance on outside training that enhances their skills. To the extent that condi-

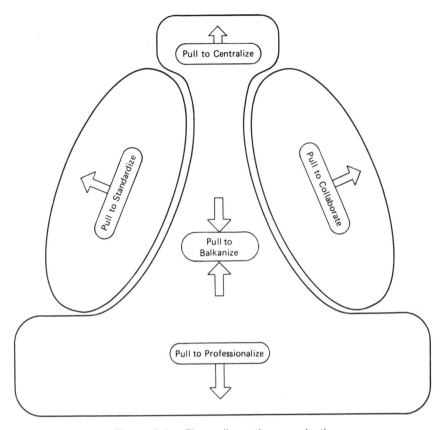

Figure 7-1. *Five pulls on the organization*

tions favor this pull, the organization structures itself as a *Professional Bureaucracy.*

■ The managers of the middle line also seek autonomy but must achieve it in a very different way—by drawing power down from the strategic apex and, if necessary, up from the operating core, to concentrate it in their own units. In effect, they favor limited vertical decentralization. As a result, they exert a pull to Balkanize the structure, to split it into market-based units that can control their own decisions, coordination being restricted to the standardization of their outputs. To the extent that conditions favor this pull, the *Divisionalized Form* results.

■ Finally, the support staff gains the most influence in the organization not when its members are autonomous but when their collaboration is called for in decision making, owing to their expertise. This happens when the organization is structured into work constellations to which power is decentralized selectively and that are free to coordinate within and between themselves by mutual adjustment. To the extent that conditions favor this pull to collaborate, the organization adopts the *Adhocracy* configuration. (See Chapter 12.)

Consider, for example, the case of a film company. The presence of a strong director will favor the pull to centralize and encourage the use of the Simple Structure. Should there be a number of strong directors, each pulling for his or her own autonomy, the structure will probably be Balkanized into the Divisionalized Form. Should the company instead employ highly skilled actors and cameramen, producing complex but standard industrial films, it will have a strong incentive to decentralize further and use the Professional Bureaucracy structure. In contrast, should the company employ relatively unskilled personnel, perhaps to mass-produce spaghetti westerns, it will experience a strong pull to standardize and to structure itself as a Machine Bureaucracy. But if, instead, it wishes to innovate, resulting in the strongest pull to collaborate the efforts of director, designer, actor, and cameraman, it would have a strong incentive to use the Adhocracy configuration.

These five configurations are the subject of the remaining chapters of the book. The description of each in the next five chapters serves two purposes. First, it enables us to propose a fundamental way to categorize organizations—and the correspondences that we have seen give us some confidence in asserting that fundamentality. And second, by allowing us to draw together the material of the first six chapters, the descriptions serve as an excellent way to summarize and, more important, to *synthesize* the findings of this book.

In describing these configurations, we drop the assumption that the situational factors are the independent variables, those that dictate the choice of the design parameters. Instead, we shall take a "systems" approach now, treating our configurations of the contingency and structural parameters as "gestalts," clusters of tightly interdependent relationships. There is no dependent or independent variable in a system; everything depends on everything else. Large size may bureaucratize a structure, but bureaucracies also seek to grow large; dynamic environments may require organic structures, but organizations with organic structures also seek out dynamic environments, where they feel more comfortable. Organizations—at least effective ones—appear to change whatever parameters they can—situational as well as structural—to maintain the coherence of their gestalts.

Each of the five chapters that follows describes one of the configurations, drawing its material from every chapter of this book. Each chapter begins with a description of the basic structure of the configuration: how it uses the coordinating mechanisms and the design parameters, as well how it functions—how authority, material, information, and decision processes flow through its five parts. This is followed by a discussion of the conditions of the configuration—the factors of age, size, technical system, environment, and power typically associated with it. (All these conclusions are summarized in Table 12–1.) Here, also, we seek to identify well-known examples of each configuration, and to note some common hybrids it forms with other configurations. Finally, each chapter closes with a discussion of some of the more important social issues associated with the configuration. It is here that I take the liberty usually accorded an author of explicitly injecting my own opinions into the concluding section of his work.

One last point before we begin. Parts of this section have an air of conclusiveness about them, as if the five configurations are perfectly distinct and encompass all of organizational reality. That is not true, as we shall see in a sixth and concluding chapter. Until then, the reader would do well to proceed under the assumption that every sentence in this section is an overstatement (including this one!). There are times when we need to caricature, or stereotype, reality in order to sharpen differences and so to better understand it. Thus, the case for each configuration is overstated to make it clearer, not to suggest that every organization—indeed any organization—exactly fits a single configuration. Each configuration is a *pure* type (what Weber called an "ideal" type), a theoretically consistent combination of the situational and design parameters. Together the five may be thought of as bounding a pentagon within which real organizations may be found. In fact, our brief concluding chapter presents such a pentagon, showing within its boundaries the hybrids of the configurations and the transitions between them. But we can comprehend the inside of a space only by identifying its boundaries. So let us proceed with our discussion of the configurations.

8

THE SIMPLE STRUCTURE

Prime Coordinating Mechanism:	Direct supervision
Key Part of Organization:	Strategic apex
Main Design Parameters:	Centralization, organic structure
Situational Factors:	Young, small; nonsophisticated technical system; simple, dynamic environment; possible extreme hostility or strong power needs of top manager; not fashionable

Consider an automobile dealership with a flamboyant owner, a brand-new government department, a middle-sized retail store, a corporation run by an aggressive entrepreneur, a government headed by an autocratic politician, a school system in a state of crisis. In most ways, these are vastly different organizations. But the evidence suggests that they share a number of basic structural characteristics. We call the configuration of these characteristics the *Simple Structure.*

Description of the Basic Structure

The Simple Structure is characterized, above all, by what is not—elaborated. Typically, it has little or no technostructure, few support staffers, a loose division of labor, minimal differentiation among its units, and a small managerial hierarchy. Little of its behavior is formalized, and it

157

makes minimal use of planning, training, and the liaison devices. It is, above all, organic. In a sense, Simple Structure is nonstructure: it avoids using all the formal devices of structure, and it minimizes its dependence on staff specialists. The latter are typically hired on contract when needed, rather than encompassed permanently within the organization.

Coordination in the Simple Structure is effected largely by direct supervision. Specifically, power over all important decisions tends to be centralized in the hands of the chief executive officer. Thus, the strategic apex emerges as the key part of the structure; indeed, the structure often consists of little more than a one-person strategic apex and an organic operating core. The chief executive tends to have a wide span of control; in fact, it is not uncommon for everyone else to report to him. Grouping into units—if it exists at all—more often than not is on a loose functional basis, with the coordination between units left to the chief executive. Likewise, communication flows informally in this structure, most of it between the chief executive and everyone else. Thus, a group of McGill MBA students commented in their study of a small manufacturer of pumps, "It is not unusual to see the president of the company engaged in casual conversation with a machine shop mechanic. These types of specialties enable the president to be informed of a machine breakdown even before the shop superintendent is advised."[1] The work flow too tends to be flexible, with the jobs of the operating core being relatively unspecialized and interchangeable.

Decision making is likewise flexible, with the centralization of power allowing for rapid response. Strategy formulation is, of course, the sole responsibility of the chief executive. The process tends to be highly intuitive and nonanalytical, often thriving on uncertainty and oriented to the aggressive search for opportunities. It is not surprising, therefore, that the resulting strategy—seldom made explicit—reflects the chief executive's implicit vision of the place of the organization in its environment. In fact, that strategy is often a direct extrapolation of his personal beliefs, an extension of his own personality.

Handling disturbances and innovating in an entrepreneurial way are perhaps the most important aspects of the chief executive's work. But considerable attention is also given to leadership—a reflection of the importance of direct supervision—and to monitoring for information to keep himself well informed. In contrast, the more formal aspects of managerial work—figurehead duties, for example—are of less significance, as are the need to disseminate information and allocate resources internally, since power and information remain in the strategic apex of the Simple Structure.

[1]From a paper submitted to the author in Management Policy 701, McGill University, 1970, by S. Genest and S. Darkanzanli.

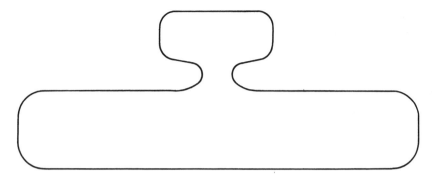

Figure 8-1. *The Simple Structure*

Figure 8–1 shows the Simple Structure symbolically, in terms of our logo, with a wide span of control at the strategic apex, no staff units, and an insignificant middle line.

Conditions of the Simple Structure

Above all, **the environment of the Simple Structure tends to be at one and the same time simple and dynamic.** A simple environment can be comprehended by a single individual, and so enables decision making to be controlled by that individual. A dynamic environment means organic structure: Because its future state cannot be predicted, the organization cannot effect coordination by standardization. Another condition common to Simple Structures is a technical system that is both nonsophisticated and nonregulating. Sophisticated ones require elaborate staff support structures, to which power over technical decisions must be delegated, and regulating ones call for bureaucratization of the operating core.

Among the conditions giving rise to variants of the Simple Structure, perhaps the most important is stage of development. The *new organization* tends to adopt the Simple Structure, no matter what its environment or technical system, because it has not had the time to elaborate it administrative structure. It is forced to rely on leadership to get things going. Thus, we can conclude that **most organizations pass through the Simple Structure in their formative years.**

Many *small organizations,* **however, remain with the Simple Structure beyond this period.** For them, informal communication is convenient and effective. Moreover, their small size may mean less repetition of work in the operating core, which means less standardization. Of course, some organizations are so small that they can rely on mutual adjustment for coordination, almost in the absence of direct supervision by leaders. They constitute a hybrid we can call the *simplest structure*, a Simple Structure with the open lateral communication channels of the Adhocracy.

Another variant—the crisis organization—appears when extreme hostility forces an organization to centralize, no matter what its usual structure. The need for fast, coordinated response puts power in the hands of the chief executive and serves to reduce the degree of bureaucratization as well. (Of course, highly elaborated organizations do not eliminate their technostructures and middle lines when faced with a crisis. But they may temporarily set aside their power over decision making.) James D. Thompson (1967) describes a special case of crisis organization, what he calls the *synthetic organization*. This is temporary, set up to deal with a natural disaster. The situation is new, and the environment is extremely hostile, hence the emphasis on leadership. (Of course, permanent organizations that specialize in disaster work, such as the Red Cross, would be expected to develop standardized procedures and so to use a more bureaucratic form of structure.)

Personal needs for power produce another variant, which we call the *autocratic organization*. When a chief executive hoards power and avoids the formalization of behavior as an infringement on his right to rule by fiat, he will, in effect, design a Simple Structure for his organization. The same result is produced in the *charismatic organization*, when the leader gains power not because he hoards it but because his followers lavish it upon him. Culture seems to figure prominently in both these examples of Simple Structure. The less industrialized societies, perhaps because they lack the educated work forces needed to man the administrative staff jobs of bureaucratic structures, seem more prone to build their organizations around strong leaders who coordinate by direct supervision. The forces of autocracy or charisma can sometimes drive even very large organizations of developed societies toward the Simple Structure, as in the Ford Motor Company in the late years of its founder.

Another factor that encourages use of the Simple Structure is owner-management, since this precludes outside control, which encourages bureaucratization. The classic case of the owner-managed organization is, of course, the *entrepreneurial firm*. In fact, **the entrepreneurial firm seems to be the best overall illustration of the Simple Structure, combining almost all of its characteristics—both structural and situational—into a tight gestalt.** The classic entrepreneurial firm is aggressive and innovative, continually searching for the risky environments where the bureaucracies fear to tread. But it is also careful to remain in market niches that the entrepreneur can fully comprehend. In other words, it seeks out environments that are both dynamic and simple. Similarly, the entrepreneurial firm is careful to remain with a simple, nonregulating technical system, one that allows its structure to remain organic and centralized. The firm is usually small, so that it can remain organic and the entrepreneur can retain tight control. Often, it is also young, in part because the attrition rate among entrepreneurial firms is high, in part because those that survive tend to switch to a more bureaucratic configuration as they age. The entrepreneur tends to be autocratic and sometimes charismatic as well; typically, he has founded his own firm because he could not tolerate the controls imposed upon him by the bureaucracies in which he has worked. Inside the organization, all revolves around the entrepreneur. Its goals are his goals, its strategy his vision of its place in the world. Most entrepreneurs loath bureaucratic procedures—and the technostructures that come with them—as impositions on their flexibility. So their unpredictable maneuvering keeps their structures lean, flexible, and organic.

Some Issues Associated with Simple Structure

In the Simple Structure, decisions concerning strategy and operations are together centralized in the office of the chief executive. **Centralization has the important advantage of ensuring that strategic response reflects full knowledge of the operating core. It also favors flexibility and adaptability in strategic response: only one person need act.** But **centralization can also cause confusion between strategic and operating issues.** The chief executive can get so enmeshed in operating problems that he loses sight of strategic considerations. Alternatively, he may become so enthusiastic about strategic opportunities that the more routine operations wither for lack of attention and eventually pull down the whole organization. Both problems occur frequently in entrepreneurial firms.

The Simple Structure is also the riskiest of the configurations, hinging on the health and whims of one individual. One heart attack can literally wipe out the organization's prime coordinating mechanism.

Like all the configurations, restricted to its appropriate situation, the Simple Structure usually functions effectively. Its flexibility is well suited to simple, dynamic environments, to extremely hostile ones (at least for a time), and to young and small organizations. But lacking a developed administration, the Simple Structure becomes a liability outside its narrow range of conditions. Its organic state impedes it from producing the standardized outputs required of an environment that has stabilized or an organization grown large, and its centralized nature renders it ineffective in dealing with an environment that has become complex. Unfortunately, however, when structural changes must come, the only person with the power to make them—the chief executive himself—often resists. The great strength of the Simple Structure—its flexibility—becomes its chief liability.

One great advantage of Simple Structure is its sense of mission. Many people enjoy working in a small, intimate organization, where its leader—often charismatic—knows where he is taking it. As a result, the organization tends to grow rapidly, the world being, so to speak, at its feet. Employees can develop a solid identification with such an organization. **But other people perceive the Simple Structure as highly restrictive.** Because one person calls all the shots, they feel not like the participants on an exciting journey, but like cattle being led to market for someone else's benefit.

As a matter of fact, the broadening of democratic norms beyond the political sphere into that of organizations has rendered the Simple Structure unfashionable in contemporary society. Increasingly, it is being described as paternalistic, sometimes autocratic, and is accused of distributing organizational power inappropriately. Certainly, our description identifies Simple Structure as the property of one individual, whether in fact or in effect. There are no countervailing powers in this configuration, which means that the chief executive can easily abuse his authority.

There have been Simple Structures as long as there have been organizations. Indeed, this was probably the only structure known to those who first discovered the benefits of coordinating their activities in some formal way. But in some sense, Simple Structure had its heyday in the era of the great American trusts of the late nineteenth century, when powerful entrepreneurs personally controlled huge empires. Since then, at least in Western society, the Simple Structure has been on the decline. Between 1895 and 1950, according to one study (cited in Pugh et al., 1963–64:296), the proportion of entrepreneurs in American industry has declined sharply, whereas that of "bureaucrats" in particular and administrators in general has increased continuously.

Today, many view the Simple Structure as an anachronism in societies that call themselves democratic. Yet it remains a prevalent and important configuration, and will, in fact, continue to be so as long as new organizations are created, some organizations prefer to remain small and informal while others require strong leadership despite larger size, society prizes entrepreneurship, and many organizations face temporary environments that are extremely hostile or more permanent ones that are both simple and dynamic.

9

THE MACHINE BUREAUCRACY

Prime Coordinating Mechanism:	Standardization of work processes
Key Part of Organization:	Technostructure
Main Design Parameters:	Behavior formalization, vertical and horizontal job specialization, usually functional grouping, large operating-unit size, vertical centralization and limited horizontal decentralization, action planning
Situational Factors:	Old, large; regulating, nonautomated technical system; simple, stable environment; external control; not fashionable

A national post office, a security agency, a steel company, a custodial prison, an airline, a giant automobile company: all these organizations appear to have a number of structural characteristics in common. Above all, their operating work is routine, the greatest part of it rather simple and repetitive; as a result, their work processes are highly standardized. These characteristics give rise to the *Machine Bureaucracies* of our society, the structures fine-tuned to run as integrated, regulated machines.

This is the structure closest to the one Max Weber first described, with standardized responsibilities, qualifications, communication channels, and work rules, as well as a clearly defined hierarchy of authority. It is the structure that Stinchcombe showed to arise from the Industrial Revolution, the one that Woodward found in the mass-production firms, Crozier in the tobacco monopoly, Lawrence and Lorsch in the container firm.

Description of the Basic Structure

A clear configuration of the design parameters has held up consistently in the research: highly specialized, routine operating tasks; very formalized procedures in the operating core; a proliferation of rules, regulations, and formalized communication throughout the organization; large-sized units at the operating level; reliance on the functional basis for grouping tasks; relatively centralized power for decision making; and an elaborate administrative structure with a sharp distinction between line and staff.

The operating core

The obvious starting point is the operating core, with its highly rationalized work flow. As a result of this, the operating tasks are simple and repetitive, generally requiring a minimum of skill and little training—often taking only hours, seldom more than a few weeks, and usually in-house. This leads to a sharp division of labor in the operating core—to narrowly defined jobs, specialized both vertically and horizontally—and to an emphasis on the standardization of work processes for coordination. Thus, formalization of behavior emerges as the key design parameter. Because the workers are left with little discretion in their work, there is little possibility for mutual adjustment in the operating core. The use of direct supervision by first-line managers is limited by the fact that standardization handles most of the coordination. Thus, very large units can be designed in the operating core. (There is, however, as we shall see below, need for another kind of direct supervision.)

The administrative component

The tight regulation of the operating work—in effect, the sealing off of the operating core from disruptive environmental influence—requires that the administrative structure be highly elaborated. First is the middle line, which is fully developed, especially well above the operating core, and is sharply differentiated into functional units. The managers of this middle line have three prime tasks. One is to handle the disturbances that arise among the highly specialized workers of the operating core. Although standardization takes care of most of the operating interdependences, ambiguities inevitably remain, and these give rise to conflicts. These cannot easily be handled by mutual adjustment among the operators, since informal communication is inhibited by the extensive standardization. So they tend to be handled by direct supervision, the orders of first-line managers. And because many of these conflicts arise between operators adjacent to each other in the work flow, the natural tendency is to bring adjacent operators under common supervision—in other words, to group the operators into units that deal with distinct parts of the work flow, which results in the functional basis for grouping operating units. For the same reason, this functional grouping gets mirrored all the way up the hierarchy, from the production and maintenance departments, which look to the plant manager to resolve many of their conflicts, to the manufacturing and marketing vice-presidents, who often expect the same of the company president.

A second task of the middle-line managers, which also explains why they are grouped on functional bases, is to work in a liaison role with the analysts of the technostructure to incorporate their standards down into the operating units. Their third task is to support the vertical flows in the structure—the aggregation of the feedback information up the hierarchy and the elaboration of the action plans that come back down. All these tasks of the middle-line managers require personal contacts—with their subordinates, the analysts, and their own superiors—which limit the number of people they can supervise. Hence, units above the operating core tend to be rather small in size and the overall administrative hierarchy rather tall in shape.

The technostructure must also be highly elaborated. In fact, Stinchcombe identified the birth of this structure in early nineteenth-century industries such as textiles and banking with the growth of technocratic personnel. **Because the Machine Bureaucracy depends primarily on the standardization of its operating work processes for coordination, the technostructure—which houses the analysts who do the standardizing—emerges as the key part of the structure.** This is so despite the fact that the Machine Bureaucracy sharply distinguishes between line and staff. To the line managers is delegated the formal authority for the operating units; the technocratic staff—officially, at least—merely advises. But without the standardizers—the cadre of work-study analysts, job-description designers, schedulers, quality control engineers, planners, budgeters, MIS people, accountants, operations researchers, and many, many more—the structure simply could not function. Hence, despite their lack of formal authority, considerable informal power rests with the analysts of the technostructure—those who standardize *everyone else's* work.

The informal power of the technostructure is gained largely at the expense of the operators, whose work the analysts formalize to a high degree, and of the first-line managers, who would otherwise supervise the operators directly. Such formalization institutionalizes the work of these managers, removing much of their power to coordinate and putting it into the systems designed by the analysts. The first-line manager's job can, in fact, become so circumscribed that he can hardly be said to function as a manager at all (that is, as someone who is *in charge* of an organizational unit). The classic case is the foreman on the assembly line, although earlier we had the example of the branch managers of the large Canadian banks, and Jay (1970:66) describes the same phenomenon in his job as head of a program production department in the BBC television service.

The emphasis on standardization extends well beyond the operating core of the Machine Bureaucracy, and with it follows the analysts' influence. In other words, **rules and regulations permeate the entire Machine Bureaucracy structure; formal communication is favored at all levels; decision making tends to follow the formal chain of authority.** In no other configuration does the flow of information and decision making more closely resemble the system of regulated flows presented in our second overlay of Chapter 1, with commands amplified down the vertical chain and feedback information aggregated up it. (This is not to suggest that the work of the senior managers is rigid and formalized, but rather that at every hierarchical level, behavior in the Machine Bureaucracy is *relatively* more formalized than that in the other configurations.)

A further reflection of this formalization is the sharp divisions of labor all over the Machine Bureaucracy. We have already discussed job specialization in the operating core and the sharp division between line and staff. In addition, the administrative structure is sharply differentiated from the operating core. Unlike the case with the Simple Structure, here managers seldom work alongside operators. And the division of labor between the analysts who design the work and the operators who do it is equally sharp. In general, **of the five configurations, it is the Machine Bureaucracy that most strongly emphasizes division of labor and unit differentiation, in all their forms—vertical, horizontal, line/staff, functional, hierarchical, and status.**

In general, then, the Machine Bureaucracy functions most clearly in accord with the classical principles of management: formal authority filters down a clearly defined hierarchy, throughout which the principle of unity of command is carefully maintained, as is the rigid distinction between line and staff. Thus, the real error of the classical theorists was not in their principles per se, but in their claim that these were universal; in fact, they apply only to this and one other of the five configurations.[1]

---

[1]That other one is, as we shall see, the Divisionalized Form. But to be fair to the classicists, at the time of Fayol's first major statement of his views (1916), one and possibly two of the other three structural configurations hardly existed. The Adhocracy is really a post–World War II structural innovation, and the Professional Bureaucracy developed during this century. We can fault Fayol only for ignoring the Simple Structure, although his followers (some right up

The obsession with control

All this suggests that **the Machine Bureaucracy is a structure with an obsession—namely, control.** A control mentality pervades it from top to bottom. Three quotations illustrate this, each from a different hierarchical level. First, near the bottom, consider how a Ford Assembly Division general foreman describes his work:

> I refer to my watch all the time. I check different items. About every hour I tour my line. About six thirty, I'll tour labor relations to find out who is absent. At seven, I hit the end of the line. I'll check paint, check my scratches and damage. Around ten I'll start talking to all the foremen. I make sure they're all awake, they're in the area of their responsibility. So we can shut down the end of the line at two o'clock and everything's clean. Friday night everybody'll get paid and they'll want to get out of here as quickly as they can. I gotta keep 'em on the line. I can't afford lettin' 'em get out early.
> We can't have no holes, no nothing. (quoted in Terkel, 1972:186)

At the middle level, the issues may be different, but the control mentality remains the same: ". . . a development engineer is not doing the job he is paid for unless he is at his drawing board, drawing, and so on. Higher management . . . cannot trust subordinates when they are not demonstrably and physically 'on the job'" (Burns, 1971:52–53). And at the strategic apex:

> When I was president of this big corporation, we lived in a small Ohio town, where the main plant was located. The corporation specified who you could socialize with, and on what level. (His wife interjects: "Who were the wives you could play bridge with.") The president's wife could do what she wants, as long as it's with dignity and grace. In a small town they didn't have to keep check on you. Everybody knew. There are certain sets of rules. (quoted in Terkel, 1972:406)

The obsession with control reflects two central facts about these structures: First, **attempts are made to eliminate all possible uncertainty, so that the bureaucratic machine can run smoothly, without interruption.** The operating core must be sealed off from external influence so that the standard outputs can be pumped off the assembly lines without disruption—hence the need for rules from top to bottom. Second, **by virtue of their design, Machine Bureaucracies are structures ridden with conflict; the control systems are required to contain it.** The magnified divisions of labor, horizontal and vertical, the strong departmental differentiation, the

---

to the time of this writing) can be criticized more strongly because they ignored the important structural innovations that were developing all around them.

rigid distinction between line and staff, the motivational problems arising from the routine work of the operating core, all these permeate the structure with conflict. As Woodward noted, in these types of organizations, the ideal social and technical systems simply do not correspond:

> Technical ends may best be served by conflict and pressure. Many of the conflicts that occurred in the firms studied seemed to be constructive by making a contribution to end results, and it was certainly not true to say that the most successful firms were those with the best relationships and closest identification between the staff and the company. (p. 45)

Hence, the development of the ubiquitous control mentality. The problem in the Machine Bureaucracy is not to develop an open atmosphere where people can talk the conflicts out, but to enforce a closed, tightly controlled one where the work can get done despite them.

The obsession with control also helps to explain the frequent proliferation of support staff in these structures. Many of the staff services could be purchased from outside suppliers. But that would expose the Machine Bureaucracy to the uncertainties of the open market, leading to disruptions in the systems of flows it so intently tries to regulate. So it "makes" rather than "buys." That is, it envelops as many of these support services as it can within its own boundaries in order to control them, everything from the cafeteria in the factory to the law office at headquarters.

The strategic apex

The managers at the strategic apex of these organizations are concerned in large part with the fine-tuning of their bureaucratic machines. Hunt notes, as we saw earlier, that these are "performance organizations," not "problem-solving" ones. Theirs is a perpetual search for more efficient ways to produce given outputs. Thus, the entrepreneur function takes on a very restricted form at the strategic apex.

But all is not strictly improvement of performance. **Just keeping the structure together in the face of its conflicts also consumes a good deal of the energy of top management.** As noted earlier, conflict is not *resolved* in the Machine Bureaucracy; rather, it is *bottled up* so that the work can get done. And as in the case of the bottle, the seal is applied at the top; ultimately, it is the top managers who must keep the lid on the conflicts through their role of handling disturbances.

Direct supervision is another major concern of top management. Formalization can do only so much at the middle levels, where the work is more complex and unpredictable than in the operating core. The coordination between the highly differentiated middle-level units—for example, between engineering, marketing, and manufacturing in the mass-production firm—often requires a flexible mechanism. The obvious choice would seem to be mutual adjustment. But its use is limited by the various blocks to informal communication—status differences between line and staff and between managers at different levels of the hierarchy, sharp differentiation between units at the same level of the hierarchy, and the general emphasis on formal communication and vertical reporting relationships. (In terms of our continuum of Figure 4–5, only the mildest liaison devices tend to be used in these structures—liaison positions and perhaps standing committees, but not matrix structure and the like. The latter would destroy the chain of authority and the principle of unity of command, elements of central importance to the basic configuration.) So there remains the need for a good deal of direct supervision at the top. Specifically, the managers of the strategic apex must intervene frequently in the activities of the middle line to effect coordination there. The top managers are the only generalists in the structure, the only managers with a perspective broad enough to see all the functions—the means—in terms of the overall ends. Everyone else in the structure is a specialist, concerned with a single link in the chain of activities that produces the outputs.

All this leads us to the conclusion that **considerable power in the Machine Bureaucracy rests with the managers of the strategic apex.** That is, these are rather centralized structures; in fact, they are second in this characteristic only to the Simple Structure. The *formal* power clearly rests at the top; hierarchy and chain of authority are paramount concepts. But so also does much of the *informal* power, since that resides in knowledge, and only at the top of the hierarchy does the segmented knowledge come together. The managers of the middle line are relatively weak, and the workers of the operating core have hardly any power at all (except, as we shall see later, to disrupt the operations). **The only ones to share any real informal power with the top managers are the analysts of the technostructure, by virtue of their role in standardizing everyone else's work.** Hence, we can conclude that the Machine Bureaucracy is centralized in the vertical dimension and decentralized only to a limited extent in the horizontal one.

Strategy making

Strategy in these structures clearly emanates from the strategic apex, where the perspective is broad and the power is focused. **The process of strategy making is clearly a top-down affair, with heavy emphasis on action planning.** In top-down strategy making, all the relevant information is ostensibly sent up to the strategic apex, where it is formulated into an integrated strategy. This is then sent down the chain of authority for implementation, elaborated first into programs and then into action plans.

Two main characteristics of this strategy-making system should be noted. First, it is intended to be a fully rationalized one, as described in our second overlay of Chapter 1. All the decisions of the organization are meant to be tied into one tightly integrated system. Exceptions flow up the chain of authority, to be handled at the level at which their effect is contained in a single unit, ultimately at the strategic apex if they cut across major functions. In turn, the resulting decisions flow down the chain for implementation in specific contexts. The structure that emerges is not so much one of work constellations, where groups at different levels make different kinds of decisions, as one of a hierarchy of ends and means, where managers at successively lower levels make the same kinds of decisions but with different degrees of specificity. For example, production decisions made at the vice-presidential level may concern what sum of money should be spent on new machinery; at the plant level, which machines to buy; and at the foreman level, how these machines are to be installed. Second, unique to this structure is a sharp dichotomy between formulation and implementation in strategy making. The strategic apex formulates and the middle line and operating core implement. At least, in theory. We shall come to practice momentarily.

Figure 9–1 shows the Machine Bureaucracy symbolically, in terms of our logo, with a fully elaborated administrative and support structure—both staff parts of the organization being focused on the operating core—and large operating units but narrower ones in the middle line to reflect the tall hierarchy of authority.

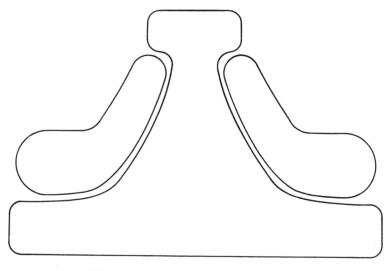

Figure 9-1. *The Machine Bureaucracy*

Conditions of the Machine Bureaucracy

We began our discussion of the basic structure with the point that the work flow of the Machine Bureaucracy is highly rationalized, its tasks simple and repetitive. Now we can see that such **machine bureaucratic work is found, above all, in environments that are simple and stable.** The work of complex environments cannot be rationalized into simple tasks, and that of dynamic environments cannot be predicted, made repetitive, and so standardized.

In addition, **the Machine Bureaucracy is typically found in the mature organization, large enough to have the volume of operating work needed for repetition and standardization, and old enough to have been able to settle on the standards it wishes to use.** This is the organization that has seen it all before and has established a standard procedure to deal with it. Machine Bureaucracies are clearly the second stage of structural development, as we described in Chapter 6, the consequences of Simple Structures that grow and age.

Machine Bureaucracies tend also to be identified with regulating technical systems, since these routinize work and so enable it to be formalized. These technical systems range from the very simple to the moderately sophisticated, but not beyond. Highly sophisticated technical systems require that considerable power be delegated to staff specialists, resulting in a form of decentralization incompatible with the machine bureaucratic structure. Nor can the technical system be automated, for that would do away with routine operating work and so lead to another configuration. Thus, although the organization may make heavy use of mechanization and computers because its work is standardized, it remains a Machine Bureaucracy only as long as these do not displace a work force dominated by unskilled operators.

Mass-production firms are perhaps the best known Machine Bureaucracies. Their operating work flows form integrated chains, open at one end to accept raw material inputs, and after that functioning as closed systems that process the inputs through sequences of standardized operations until marketable outputs emerge at the other end. These horizontal operating chains are typically segmented into links, each of which forms a functional department that reports up the vertical chain of authority. Even in some enormously large mass-production firms, the economies of scale are such that functional structures are maintained right up to the top of the hierarchy. Likewise, in process production, when the firm is unable to automate its operations but must rely on a large work force to produce its outputs, it tends to adopt a functional Machine Bureaucratic structure.[2]

[2]The contradiction here with Woodward, who describes the structure of process production firms as organic, appears to stem from an assumption in her work that process technical systems are always largely automated.

Figure 9–2 shows the organigram of a large steel company, functional right to its top level of grouping.

In the case of the giant Machine Bureaucracies, an interesting shift occurs in the relationship between environmental stability and structural formalization: the former becomes the dependent variable. These organizations have great vested interests in environmental stability; without it, they cannot maintain their enormous technical systems. So whereas once upon a time they may have bureaucratized because their environments were stable, as they grew large they found themselves having to stabilize their environments because they were bureaucratic. As Worthy notes, ". . . there were external pressures on the enterprise itself that had to be organized and controlled before scientific management could come into its own" (1959:76). Thus, giant firms in industries such as transportation, tobacco, and metals are well known for their attempts to control the forces of supply and demand—through the use of advertising, the development of long item-supply contacts, sometimes the establishment of cartels, and, as noted earlier, the envelopment of support services. They also adopt strategies of "vertical integration"; that is, they extend their production chains at both ends, becoming their own suppliers and customers. In this way, they are able to bring some of the forces of supply and demand within their own planning processes, and thereby regulate them. In effect, when it gets large enough, the Machine Bureaucracy can extend its control into its environment, seeking to regulate whatever out there can disturb its routine operations.

Of course, the Machine Bureaucracy configuration is not restricted to large, or manufacturing, or even private-enterprise organizations. Some small manufacturers—for example, certain producers of discount furniture and paper products—prefer this structure because their operating work is simple and repetitive. Many service firms—what we can call *white-collar bureaucracies*—use it for the same reason, even though their operations are not integrated into single chains. Strings of assembly-line workers are replaced in the insurance company by grids of office clerks, in the telephone company by rooms of switchboard operators, in the bank by rows of tellers. The outputs of these service firms may differ from those of the factories—as does the color of their workers' collars—but their operating work, being equally routine and nonprofessional, is no less amenable to formalization. The large hotel, for example, lends itself to the machine bureaucratic form because its structure is tied right into its permanent physical facilities. Once the hotel is built, its location and size, as well as the nature of its rooms (in effect, its product-market strategy), are largely fixed. Thereafter, its success depends primarily on how effectively it can regulate its operations to the satisfaction of its customers. Those customers have definite expectations—not for surprise but for stability. Thus, a few years ago, one of the giant hotel chains ran a series of print advertisements under the

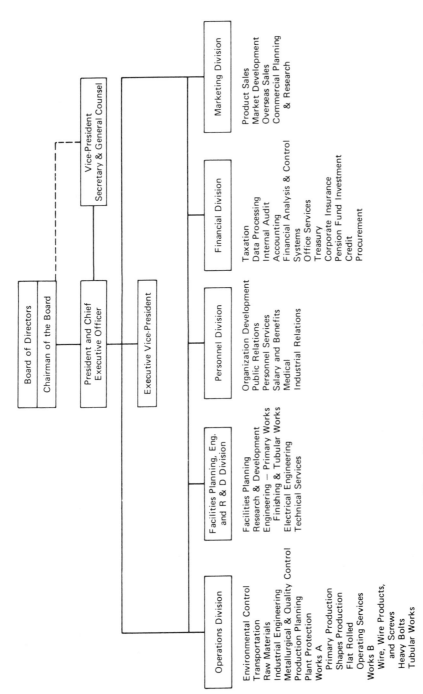

Figure 9-2. *Organigram of a large steel company*

theme, "At every Holiday Inn, the best surprise is no surprise." In one, George J. Fryzyan III, business insurance consultant, exclaimed, "The room was clean. The TV worked. Everything worked. Amazing." After more praise, he added, "It's got something to do with those 152 standards at every Holiday Inn. . . ." Machine Bureaucracies are well suited to ensuring that nothing can possibly go wrong.

One McGill MBA group studied a security agency with 1,200 part-time guards and nine full-time managers. The guards, paid at or near the minimum wage, were primarily older, retired men. Their work was extremely routine and simple—for example, guarding school crossings and patrolling buildings after hours. Correspondingly, everything was absolutely routinized and the structure was remarkably bureaucratic. Uniforms were worn, ranks were used, a tight code of discipline was in force, a manual specified general regulations in minute detail, and each job also had its own equally specific regulations. And this formalization of behavior was not restricted to the guards. When the firm embarked on an acquisition campaign, it drew up a procedure to evaluate candidates that seemed like a page out of its operations manual.

This organization was not a Machine Bureaucracy in the pure sense, since it lacked an elaborate administrative hierarchy. There were few middle managers and almost no analysts. In effect, the tasks of the organization were so simple and stable that management itself could work the procedures out and then let them be, almost in perpetuity. Hence, there was no need for a technostructure. The structure was really a hybrid between Simple Structure and Machine Bureaucracy, which we might call the *simple bureaucracy*: centralized, highly bureaucratic, but with no elaboration of the administrative structure. Thus, **given extremely simple and almost perfectly stable work, the Machine Bureaucracy can shed most of its administrative component.**

Another condition often found with many Machine Bureaucracies is external control. Hypothesis 14 indicated that the more an organization is controlled externally, the more its structure is centralized and formalized, the two prime design parameters of the Machine Bureaucracy. External control is often most pronounced in government agencies, giving rise to a common example of this configuration, which we can call the *public machine bureaucracy.* Many government agencies—such as post offices and tax collection departments—are bureaucratic not only because their operating work is routine but also because they are accountable to the public for their actions. Everything they do must seem to be fair, notably their treatment of clients and their hiring and promotion of employees. So they proliferate regulations.

Since control is the forte of the Machine Bureaucracy, it stands to reason that organizations in the business of control—regulatory agencies, custodial prisons, police forces—are drawn to this configuration, sometimes in spite of contradictory conditions.[3] These constitute a variant we call the *control bureaucracy*. Another condition that drives the organization to the machine bureaucratic structure is the special need for safety. Organizations that fly airplanes or put out fires must minimize the risks they take. Hence, these *safety bureaucracies* formalize their procedures extensively to ensure that these are carried out to the letter. Few people would fly with an airline that had an organic structure, where the maintenance men did whatever struck them as interesting instead of following precise checklists and the pilots worked out their procedures for landing in foggy weather when the need arose. Likewise, a fire crew cannot arrive at a burning house and then turn to the chief for orders or decide among its members who will connect the hose and who will go up the ladder. The environments of these organizations may seem dynamic, but in fact most of their contingencies are predictable—they have been seen many times before—and so procedures for handling them have been formalized. (Of course, an unexpected contingency forces the crew to revert to organic structure.) We can also call organizations such as fire departments *contingency bureaucracies*. They exist not to provide routine services, but to stand ready in the event of the need for nonroutine ones. But because these services are critical, the organizations must plan elaborate procedures to respond quickly and efficiently to every contingent event that can be anticipated. Their operators then spend their time practicing these procedures and waiting around for an event to occur, hopefully one of the contingencies anticipated.

Finally, we note that fashion is no longer a condition that favors the Machine Bureaucracy configuration. This structure was the child of the Industrial Revolution. Over the course of the last two centuries—particularly at the turn of this one—it seems to have emerged as the dominant configuration. But the Machine Bureaucracy is no longer fashionable. As we shall soon see, it is currently under attack from all sides.

Some Issues Associated with Machine Bureaucracy

No structure has evoked more heated debate than the Machine Bureaucracy. As one of its most eminent students has noted:

> On the one hand, most authors consider the bureaucratic organization to be the embodiment of rationality in the modern world, and, as such, to be

---

[3]In Chapter 10 we shall see that many police forces, which for other reasons seem as though they should be structured as Professional Bureaucracies, are in fact drawn toward Machine Bureaucracy because of the control orientation and the need for public accountability.

intrinsically superior to all other possible forms of organization. On the other hand, many authors—often the same ones—consider it a sort of Leviathan, preparing the enslavement of the human race. (Crozier, 1964:176)

Weber, of course, emphasized the rationality of this structure; in fact, the word *machine* comes directly from his writings:

> The decisive reason for the advance of bureaucratic organization has always been its purely technical superiority over any other form of organization. The fully developed bureaucratic mechanism compares with other organizations exactly as does the machine with the non-mechanical modes of production.
>
> Precision, speed, unambiguity, knowledge of the files, continuity, discretion, unity, strict subordination, reduction of friction and of material and personal costs—these are raised to the optimum point in the strictly bureaucratic administration. . . (Gerth and Mills translation, 1958:214)

A machine is certainly precise; it is also reliable and easy to control; and it is efficient—at least when restricted to the job it has been designed to do. These are the reasons many organizations are structured as Machine Bureaucracies. In fact, these structures are the prime manifestations of our society's high degree of specialization; moreover, they are the major contributors to our high material standard of living. Without Machine Bureaucracies, automobiles would be reserved for the rich and travelers would fly at their own peril. No structure is better suited to mass production and consistent output, none can more efficiently regulate work. Our society—such as it is—simply could not function without these structures. **When an integrated set of simple, repetitive tasks must be performed precisely and consistently by human beings, the Machine Bureaucracy is the most efficient structure—indeed, the only conceivable one.**

But in these same advantages of machinelike efficiency lie all the disadvantages of these structures. Machines consist of mechanical parts; organizational structures also include human beings—and that is where the analogy breaks down. First, we shall discuss the human problems that arise in the operating core when people see themselves as more than just mechanical factors of production. Second, we shall discuss the coordination problems that arise in the administrative center when conflicts cannot be resolved by standardization. But in another sense, the machine analogy holds up and helps us to define a third set of problems—those of adaptability at the strategic apex. Machines are designed for specific purposes; they are difficult to modify when conditions change.

Human problems in the operating core

James Worthy, when an executive of Sears, Roebuck, wrote a penetrating and scathing criticism of Machine Bureaucracy in his book, *Big Business and Free Men*. Worthy traces the root of the human problems in these structures to the "scientific management" movement that swept America, and later the Soviet Union,[4] in the first third of this century. He sees its founder, Frederick W. Taylor, as the epitome of the personality drawn to the Machine Bureaucracy.

> His virtual obsession to control the environment around him was expressed in everything he did: in his home life, his gardening, his golfing; even his afternoon stroll was not a casual affair but something to be carefully planned and rigidly followed. Nothing was left to chance if in any way chance could be avoided. . . .
>
> From his writings and his biography one gets the impression of a rigid, insecure personality, desperately afraid of the unknown and the unforseen, able to face the world with reasonable equanimity only if everything possible has been done to keep the world in its place and to guard against anything that might upset his careful, painstaking plans. (1959:74–75)

Worthy acknowledges Taylor's contribution to efficiency, narrowly defined. Worker initiative did not, however, enter into his efficiency equation. Taylor "visualized the role of people within the organization in precisely the same manner as he visualized the component parts of a mechanism. 'A complicated and delicately adjusted machine' was a favorite figure of speech" (pp. 65–66). So efficient organizations came to be described as "smoothly running machines," the organigrams as "blueprints," and the time-and-motion-study analyst's role as "human engineering" (pp. 66–67). The problem was that "the methods of engineering have proved inappropriate to human organization" (p. 67). The assumption, as Emery (1971) has put it, that "we'll get the engineering system straight and simply tie the social system to it" (p. 186), created its own set of difficulties. Taylor's pleas to remove "all possible brain work" (Worthy, p. 67) from the shop floor also removed all possible initiative from the people who worked there: ". . . the machine has no will of its own. Its parts have no urge to independent action. Thinking, direction—even purpose—must be provided from outside or above" (p. 79). **Treating people as "means," as "categories of status and function rather than as indi-**

---

[4]There it had its "fullest flowering," encouraged by Lenin "as a means for accelerating industrial production" (p. 77). Worthy notes further the "interesting parallels between communism and scientific management. In both cases workers are seen as means rather than ends, doers rather than planners or initiators; to be manipulated—by persuasion if possible, by coercion if necessary—in other interests and for other needs than their own" (p. 78). Worthy also makes the link in the other direction, from regulated structure to centralized government. Writing of the American distrust for national planning, he comments, "But let there be a serious downturn in business, let the present smooth functioning of markets collapse under the blows of economic adversity, and the habit of mind that thinks in terms of mechanistic organization of the enterprise will make it easy to think in terms of mechanistic organization of the economy" (p. 79).

viduals," had the "consequence of destroying the meaning of work it-self." And that has been "fantastically wasteful for industry and society" (p. 70). Organizations have paid dearly for these attitudes in the various forms of worker resistance—absenteeism, high turnover rates, sloppy workmanship, strikes, even outright sabotage.

Studs Terkel's (1972) fascinating book, *Working*, in which "people talk about what they do all day and how they feel about what they do" provides chapters of evidence on workers' responses to Machine Bureaucracies. Here is how a steelworker discusses his job:

> I don't know who the guy is who said there is nothing sweeter than an unfinished symphony. Like an unfinished painting and an unfinished poem. If he creates this thing one day—let's say, Michelangelo's Sistine Chapel. It took him a long time to do this, this beautiful work of art. But what if he had to create this Sistine Chapel a thousand times a year? Don't you think that would even dull Michelangelo's mind? Or if da Vinci had to draw his anatomical charts thirty, forty, fifty, sixty, eighty, ninety, a hundred times a day? Don't you think that would even bore da Vinci? (p. xxxvii)

Undoubtedly. Unless he had the temperament of Babe Secoli, a checker in a Chicago supermarket with a very different perspective on machine bureaucratic work:

> We sell everything here, millions of items. From potato chips and pop—we even have a genuine pearl in a can of oysters. It sells for two somethin'. Snails with the shells that you put on the table, fanciness. There are items I never heard of we have here. I know the price of every one. Sometimes the boss asks me and I get a kick out of it. . . .
>
> You sort of memorize the prices. It just comes to you. I know half a gallon of milk is sixty-four cents; a gallon, $1.10. You look at the labels. A small can of peas, Raggedy Ann. Green Giant, that's a few pennies more. I know Green Giant's eighteen and I know Raggedy Ann is fourteen. . . . You just memorize. On the register is a list of some prices, that's for the part-time girls. I never look at it.
>
> I don't have to look at the keys on my register. I'm like the secretary that knows her typewriter. The touch. My hand fits. The number nine is my big middle finger. The thumb is number one, two and three and up. The side of my hand uses the bar for the total and all that.
>
> I use my three fingers—my thumb, my index finger, and my middle finger. The right hand. And my left hand is on the groceries. They put down their groceries. I got my hips pushin' on the bottom and it rolls around on the counter. When I feel I have enough groceries in front of me, I let go of my hip. I'm just movin'—the hips, the hand, and the register, the hips, the hand, and the register. . . (As she demonstrates, her hands and hips move in the manner of an Oriental dancer.) You just keep goin', one, two, one, two. If you've got that rhythm, you're a fast checker. Your feet are flat on the floor and you're turning your head back and forth. . . .

I'm a couple of days away, I'm very lonesome for this place. When I'm on a vacation, I can't wait to go, but two or three days away, I start to get fidgety. I can't stand around and do nothin'. I have to be busy at all times. I look forward to comin' to work. It's a great feelin'. I enjoy it somethin' terrible. (pp. 282, 286)

The difference between the da Vincis in the steel mills and the Secolis in the supermarkets is that some people take to routine work and others abhor it. Some simply appreciate regularity in their work—perhaps, like Secoli, because it gives them a chance to get to know it well, or perhaps because it satisfies a need for order and security. But others, either because their need is to do creative, self-actualizing work or because they dislike being told what to do, cannot tolerate the work offered them in Machine Bureaucracies.

As long as everybody can find the work that best suits him or her, there is no problem. But apparently, not everyone can. There appear to be more jobs in the Machine Bureaucracies of our society than people happy to fill them, and too few in the more popular structures. Thus, one study in an automobile assembly plant found that 69 percent of the workers complained of monotony, 87 percent wanted to find a job with higher skills and more responsibility, variety, and freedom; most claimed they stayed because of what they could earn, only 6 percent because they liked the work (cited in Melcher, 1976:85).

And time is not on the side of the Machine Bureaucracy. Rising educational levels raise work asperations—that is, bring out the need for self-actualization at the expense of the need for security. Moreover, the welfare system has taken care of certain security needs, giving the worker the option of doing nothing without starving. The result is that today's Machine Bureaucracies are experiencing more and more resistance from people who simply do not want to be there, at least in societies like America. Whether the same phenomenon is occuring in countries like, say, Switzerland, where the people seem to relish order and regularity, is not clear. (And the problem is not restricted to the operating core. Successful American middle-aged executives—no longer tolerant of the control mentality—seem also to be quitting in increasing numbers, after years of struggling to get to where they are.) Clearly, in the view of a growing portion of the work force, Machine Bureaucracies are becoming unacceptable places to spend their working lives.

Taylor was fond of saying, "In the past the man has been first; in the future the system must be first" (quoted in Worthy, 1959:73). Prophetic words, indeed. Modern man seems to exist for his systems; many of the organizations he created to serve him have come to rule him. The consumer seems to find cheap goods in the marketplace on Saturday only if he is willing to squander his talents as a producer from Monday to Friday. Mass consumption in return for dreary production.

But even the consumption is affected, by what one writer (Thompson, 1961) has referred to as the "bureaupathologies"—the dysfunctional behaviors of these structures, which lead to higher prices, shoddy workmanship, and indifferent or rude treatment of customers. Sometimes the consequences are bizarre. A story in the December 17, 1971, issue of *Time* magazine told what happens when specialization drives workers to displace ends in favor of means. Firemen in Genoa, Texas, set fire to abandoned buildings because they were bored. Explained one, "We'd hang around the station on the night shift without a thing to do. We just wanted to get the red light flashing and the bells clanging."

The various bureaupathologies reinforce each other to form vicious circles. The displacement of ends in favor of means, the mistreatment of clients, the various manifestations of worker alienation—all lead to a tightening of the controls on behavior. The implicit motto of the Machine Bureaucracy seems to be, "When in doubt, control." All problems are to be solved by the turning of the technocratic screws. But since this is what caused the bureaupathologies in the first place, more of it serves only to magnify the problems, leading to the imposition of further controls, and so on. How far this can go is perhaps best illustrated by a firm that intervened to reverse the process. When Marks and Spencer, the U.K. retail chain, dispensed with inventory replacement cards, sales receipts, time clocks, and other control procedures, the owners estimated that the firm was able to eliminate 8,000 of its 28,000 jobs and to save 26 million pieces of paper annually (Becker and Gordon, 1966–67:331–32).

But not every organization can wipe out most of its control system in one fell swoop. So other means have been tried—by the organization or its workers—to reverse the vicious circles, everything from job enlargement to outright democratization. As discussed in Chapter 2, job enlargement (or "enrichment"), where the workers are given a wider variety of tasks to perform and perhaps control over the design of those tasks as well, does not seem to hold a great deal of promise for major improvement of the work. No doubt the engineering orientation has led to excessive specialization in many cases. When the human factor is finally plugged into the performance equation—that is, when the worker's initiative is taken into account—it clearly becomes worthwhile to enlarge many jobs. But the question is, How far? And the answer seems to be, Not very. As we have emphasized in this chapter, the nature of the Machine Bureaucracy's work reflects above all the regulating characteristic of the organization's technical system and the stability and simplicity of its environment. The obsession with control is a response to these conditions, albeit often an excessive one. As long as these conditions remain—in essence, **as long as society demands cheap, mass-produced goods and services—a great many jobs will remain pretty much as they are now—that is, minimally affected by job enlargement.** Braverman (1974) puts it rather brutally: "Taylorism dominates the world of production; the practitioners of 'human relations' and 'industrial psychology' are the maintenance crew for the human machinery" (p. 87).

If the human problems in the operating core of Machine Bureaucracy cannot be solved by job enlargement, what are the prospects for democratization instead? Here, too, the evidence (discussed in Chapter 5) is discouraging, and for the same reason: **democratization does not eliminate the fundamental conflict in the Machine Bureaucracy between engineering efficiency on the one hand and individual satisfaction on the other.** Giving the workers the right to vote for directors periodically does not change the realities of their everyday work. (It might, however, somewhat change their attitudes to that work, infusing a dose of ideology into an otherwise utilitarian situation. A sense of ownership might reduce the feelings of alienation.) As we saw in Chapter 5, such democratization seems to centralize the structure further. Indeed, these effects can be predicted from our Hypothesis 14, since, in electing the directors, the workers constitute a force for external control. That hypothesis indicated that external control not only centralizes a structure but also bureaucratizes it.

Nowhere is this result clearer than in Crozier's (1964) description of another kind of democracy—a judicial type—where the workers impose rules in order to dilute their bosses' control over them. As we noted earlier, this turns out to be a perverse kind of democracy indeed. With the bosses constrained by the rules, power passes up the hierarchy, and the structure becomes significantly more centralized. And with workers' rules countering managers' rules, the structure also becomes more bureaucratic, at everybody's expense. The workers end up being locked into an even tighter straitjacket, albeit of their own design. The clients lose, too. Those of the ordinary Machine Bureaucracy can at least take solace in the fact that the rules are for their benefit—to encourage more efficient production. The additional rules of the bureaucracies Crozier describes have nothing to do with efficiency; they serve to protect the worker. As we shall soon see, like all rules, they act to inhibit innovation and adaptation. Where the workers are organized to fight the intrusions of management, change becomes well-nigh impossible. Judicial democratization catches the client in a tug of war between worker and manager. The organization burns up more of its energy in its own conflicts, with less left over to produce outputs for the clients.

The discouraging conclusion is that the Machine Bureaucracy creates major human problems in the operating core, ones for which no solutions are apparent. Joan Woodward had it right when she argued that in these structures, there is an irreconcilable conflict between the technical and social systems. What is good for production simply is not good for people. Fundamental change will apparently have to come, not through the front door of direct confrontation or legislation, but through the back door of changed conditions to which the organization must respond. Specifically, nothing short of automation of the technical system (or of an environment becoming more complex or dynamic) seems able to alleviate the social problems of the Machine Bureaucracy.

We do, of course, have one other choice as a society: to reduce our demand for cheap, mass-produced goods and services. As we shall see in Chapter 10, craft organizations, structured as Professional Bureaucracies, can sometimes produce the same outputs as Machine Bureaucracies but with less social turmoil and much higher quality. The question is whether we are prepared to pay the price: stoneware dishes replaced every generation instead of plastic ones replaced every year, an occasional dress hand-woven in a studio instead of frequent ones mass-produced in a factory, a Ferrari every twenty years instead of a Ford every two. Of course, should the vicious circles intensify to the point where life in the Machine Bureaucracy becomes so intolerable that nobody will work there, we shall have no other choice. Perhaps the system will end up serving man after all, despite himself.

Coordination problems in the administrative center

Since the operating core of the Machine Bureaucracy is not designed to handle conflict, many of the human problems that arise there spill over into the administrative structure. Again, Worthy (1959) says it best:

> The organization was set up like a machine and it had to be operated like a machine. But because its components were human rather than mechanical, the task of controlling and directing it taxed the ingenuity of the scientific managers. The elaborate contrivances of the modern industrial organization, the masses of paper work and red tape, the layers on layers of supervision, the luxuriant growth of staff—all these are evidence of the difficulty of controlling human organizations in terms of mechanistic principles. (p. 72)

It is one of the ironies of the Machine Bureaucracy that to achieve the control it requires, it must mirror the narrow specialization of its operating core in its administrative structure. "By his sweeping redivision of labor as between workers and management, Taylor so increased the burden on management that a considerable further division of labor within management became essential" (pp. 67–68). And this administrative division of labor, in turn, leads to a sharp differentiation of the administrative structure and narrow functional orientations. This in turn means problems of communication and coordination. Thus, one Harvard Business School case describes the three years of convoluted effort General Motors went through, with no sign of success, just to coordinate the purchase of work gloves across its units (Bennett, 1977).

The fact, as noted earlier, is that the administrative structure of the Machine Bureaucracy is ill-suited to the use of mutual adjustment. All the communication barriers in these structures—horizontal, vertical, status, line/staff—impede informal communication. "Each unit becomes jealous of its own perogatives and finds ways to protect itself against the pressure or encroachments of others" (Worthy, 1950:176).

Narrow functionalism not only impedes coordination; it also encourages the building of private empires. In such structures, it is difficult to associate any particular function with overall output or performance. Hence, when a manager calls for more personnel—more cost analysts, more clerks, more sales managers—no one can be quite sure whether the claim is legitimate. So there emerges a competition among the managers to build bigger and more powerful units, a competition stimulated by the bureaucratic rule that associates salary with number of subordinates. This encourages the building of top-heavy organizations, often more concerned with the political games to be won than the clients to be served. A Machine Bureaucracy free of market forces—for example, a government regulatory agency with an ensured budget and vague performance goals—can become virtually a closed system, responsible to no one and producing nothing, forever spinning its administrative wheels in great busyness.

But if mutual adjustment does not work—generating more political heat than cooperative light—how does the Machine Bureaucracy resolve its coordination problems in the administration? Instinctively, it tries standardization—for example, by tightening job descriptions or proliferating rules. But standardization is not suited to handling the nonroutine problems of the administrative center. Indeed, it only makes them worse, undermining the influence of the line managers and increasing the conflict. So **to reconcile the coordination problems that arise in its administrative center, the Machine Bureaucracy is left with only one coordinating mechanism, direct supervision.** Specifically, nonroutine coordination problems between units are "bumped" up the line hierarchy for reconciliation, until they reach a common level of supervision. This, of course, results in the centralization of power for decision making at the upper levels of the hierarchy, ultimately at the strategic apex. And this in turn results in a host of new problems. In effect, **just as the human problems in the operating core become coordination problems in the administrative center, so too do the coordination problems in the administrative center become adaptation problems at the strategic apex.**

Adaptation problems at the strategic apex

As long as its environment remains perfectly stable, the Machine Bureaucracy faces no great difficulty of adaptation. Its standard procedures handle the routine problems of coordination, and nonroutine ones do not arise.

But no organization can expect that much stability. Environments inevitably change, generating new nonroutine problems. When these become frequent in the Machine Bureaucracy, the managers at the strategic apex quickly become overloaded. Every organigram—and our logo as well—shows a narrowing of the middle line as it approaches the strategic apex. The propensity to pass nonroutine problems up the line hierarchy causes a bottleneck at the top during times of change, which forces the senior managers to make their decisions quickly. But how can they do so when these are decisions that arose elsewhere in the organization, in places where the top managers lack intimate contact?

In theory, the Machine Bureaucracy is designed to account for this problem. It has a management information system (MIS) that aggregates information up the hierarchy, presenting the people at the top with concise summaries of what goes on down below—the perfect solution for the overloaded top manager. Except that much of the information is the wrong kind.

A number of problems arise in the MIS. For one thing, in the tall administrative structure of the Machine Bureaucracy, information must pass through many levels before it reaches the top. Losses take place at each one. Not only natural losses. The fact that the transfers are vertical— between people on different status levels of the hierarchy—means that intentional distortions of information also occur. Good news gets highlighted and bad news blocked on its way up. Probably a greater problem is the MIS's emphasis on "hard" (quantitative), aggregated information. A good deal of evidence suggests that it is not this kind of information top managers need to make their strategic decisions as much as it is soft, specific information.

Often the MIS data are too late as well. It takes time for events to get reported as official "facts," more time for these to get accumulated into reports, and more time still for these to pass up the hierarchy until they finally reach the top manager's desk. In the perfectly stable environment, he can perhaps wait; in a changing one, he cannot. A military commander wants to know about the enemy's movements as they are taking place, not later, when they are reflected in some official measure like casualties in a battle. Likewise, the corporate president wants to be told that his most important customer was seen playing golf yesterday with his major competitor; he does not want to find out about it six months later in the form of a negative variance on a sales report. Gossip, hearsay, speculation—the softest kinds of information—warn the manager of impending problems; the MIS all too often records for posterity that these problems have long since arrived. Moreover, a good deal of important information never even gets into the MIS. The mood in the factory, the conflict between two managers, the reasons for a lost sale—this kind of rich information never becomes the kind of fact that the traditional MIS can handle. So **the information of the MIS, by the time it reaches the strategic apex—after being** filtered and aggregated through the levels of the administrative hierarchy—is often so bland that the top manager cannot rely on it. In a changing environment, that manager finds himself out of touch.

The obvious solution for the top managers is to bypass the MIS and set up their own informal information systems, ones that can bring them the rich, tangible information they need, quickly and reliably. They are inclined to establish their own networks of contacts and informers, both inside and outside the organization, and expose themselves to as much first-hand information as possible. But getting such information takes time. And that, of course, was the problem in the first place—the bottleneck at the strategic apex of the Machine Bureaucracy in a changed environment. So a fundamental dilemma faces the top managers of the Machine Bureaucracy as a result of the centralization of the structure and the emphasis on reporting through the chain of authority. In times of change, when they most need to spend time getting the "tangible detail," they are overburdened with decisions coming up the hierarchy for resolution. They are therefore reduced to acting superficially, with inadequate, abstract information.

The essential problem lies in one of the major tenets of the Machine Bureaucracy, that strategy formulation must be sharply differentiated from strategy implementation. The first is the responsibility of top management; the second is to be carried out by everyone else, in hierarchical order. Nowhere in practice is this dichotomy sharper than in the military, with "strategy" focusing on the general direction of armies and "tactics" on the particular deployment of men and materiel. And nowhere are its dangers better illustrated than in the infamous battle of Passchendaele of World War I, where 300,000 British troups went over the trenches to become casualties: "No senior officer from the Operations Branch of the General Headquarters, it was claimed, ever set foot (or eyes) on the Passchendaele battlefield during the four months that battle was in progress. Daily reports on the condition of the battlefield were first ignored, then ordered discontinued. Only after the battle did the Army chief of staff learn that he had been directing men to advance through a sea of mud" (Feld, 1959:21).

The formulation-implementation dichotomy presupposes two fundamental conditions in order to work effectively: that (1) the formulator has full information, or at least information as good as that available to the implementor, and (2) the situation is sufficiently stable or predictable to ensure that there will be no need for *re*formulation during implementation. The absence of either condition should lead to a collapse of the dichotomy, to proceeding with formulation and implementation concurrently, in an adaptive rather than a planning mode.

The top manager who cannot get the necessary information simply cannot formulate a sensible strategy. The Machine Bureaucracy is designed on the questionable assumption that even in times of change, the MIS will bring the necessary information up to the top of the hierarchy. The conditions of the mud are only the most literal example of the inability of the MIS to handle soft information. As Crozier describes it, the problem in these structures is that the power to formulate strategy rests at a different place from the information needed to do so.

The design of the Machine Bureaucracy also assumes that a strategy formulated in one place can later be implemented in another. That is a reasonable assumption under conditions of stability—as long as the world holds still (or at least undergoes predicted changes) while the plan unfolds. Unfortunately, all too often the world refuses to hold still; it insists on changing in unpredictable ways. This imposes the need to adapt, to alter the strategy as it is being implemented. **Under such fluid conditions, either the formulator must implement his own strategy so that he can reformulate it en route—which is what happens in the Simple Structure, which faces a simple, dynamic environment—or else the implementors must take responsibility for the formulation and do it adaptively—which is what happens in the Adhocracy, which decentralizes power for strategy making in the face of a complex, dynamic environment.**

We emerge from this discussion with two conclusions: First, **strategies must be formulated outside the machine bureaucratic structure if they are to be realistic.** Second, **the dichotomy between formulation and implementation ceases to have relevance in times of unpredictable change. Together these conclusions tell us that Machine Bureaucracies are fundamentally nonadaptive structures, ill-suited to changing their strategies.** But that should come as no surprise. After all, machines are designed for special purposes, not general ones. So, too, are Machine Bureaucracies.

These are, as Hunt noted, performance, not problem-solving organizations. Strategic diagnosis is simply not part of their repertoire of standard operating procedures. Machine Bureaucracies work best in stable environments because they have been designed for specific, predetermined missions. Efficiency is their forte, not innovation. An organization cannot put blinders on its personnel and then expect peripheral vision. The managers of the Machine Bureaucracy are rewarded for improving operating efficiency, reducing costs, finding better controls and standards; not for taking risks, testing new behaviors, encouraging innovation. Change makes a mess of the standard operating procedures. In the Machine Bureaucracy, everything is nicely coupled, carefully coordinated. Change a link, and the whole operating chain must be redesigned; change an element in an integrated strategy, and it disintegrates.

Thus, steel companies and post offices are not noted innovators, and the automobile of today is hardly different from that of Henry Ford's day. (Compare the generations of computers or airplanes of the last thirty years—products of very different structures, as we shall see—with the automobiles of the last fifty.)

When Machine Bureaucracies must change their strategies in important rather than cosmetic ways, their top managers tend to act idiosyncratically; they are not in the habit of making such changes, their MISs have obscured the kind of change that is needed, and their structures are ill-suited to receiving whatever change is eventually proposed. The top managers seem to succeed only when they are strong enough to cast aside their bureaucratic information and control systems and take matters into their own hands. In other words, ironically, **the top managers succeed in changing the Machine Bureaucracy only by reverting temporarily to the leaner, more flexible Simple Structure.**

To conclude, the Machine Bureaucracy is an inflexible configuration. As a machine, it is designed for one purpose only. It is efficient in its own limited domain but cannot easily adapt itself to any other. Above all, it cannot tolerate an environment that is either dynamic or complex. Nevertheless, the Machine Bureaucracy remains a dominant configuration—probably *the* dominant one in our specialized societies. As long as we demand standardized, inexpensive goods and services, and as long as people remain more efficient than automated machines at providing them—and remain willing to do so—the Machine Bureaucracy, with all its problems, will be with us.

10

THE PROFESSIONAL BUREAUCRACY

Prime Coordinating Mechanism:	Standardization of skills
Key Part of Organization:	Operating core
Main Design Parameters:	Training, horizontal job specialization, vertical and horizontal decentralization
Situational Factors:	Complex, stable environment; nonregulating, nonsophisticated technical system; fashionable

We have seen evidence at various points in this book that organizations can be bureaucratic without being centralized. Their operating work is stable, leading to "predetermined or predictable, in effect, standardized" behavior (our definition of bureaucracy in Chapter 2). But it is also complex, and so must be controlled directly by the operators who do it. Hence, the organization turns to the one coordinating mechanism that allows for standardization and decentralization at the same time—namely, the standardization of skills. This gives rise to a structural configuration sometimes called *Professional Bureaucracy*, common in universities, general hospitals, school systems, public accounting firms, social-work agencies, and craft production firms. All rely on the skills and knowledge of their operating professionals to function; all produce standard products or services.

The Basic Structure

The work of the operating core

Here again we have a tightly knit configuration of the design parameters. Most important, **the Professional Bureaucracy relies for coordination on the standardization of skills and its associated design parameter, training and indoctrination. It hires duly trained and indoctrinated specialists—professionals—for the operating core, and then gives them considerable control over their own work.** In effect, the work is highly specialized in the horizontal dimension, but enlarged in the vertical one.

Control over his own work means that the professional works relatively independently of his colleagues, but closely with the clients he serves. For example, "the teacher works alone within the classroom, relatively hidden from colleagues and superiors, so that he has a broad discretionary jurisdiction within the boundaries of the classroom" (Bidwell, 1965:976). Likewise, many doctors treat their own patients, and accountants maintain personal contact with the companies whose books they audit.

Most of the necessary coordination between the operating professionals is then handled by the standardization of skills and knowledge—in effect, by what they have learned to expect from their colleagues. During an operation as long and as complex as open-heart surgery, "very little needs to be said [between the anesthesiologist and the surgeon] preceding chest opening and during the procedure on the heart itself: lines, beats and lights on equipment are indicative of what everyone is expected to do and does—operations are performed in absolute silence, particularly following the chest-opening phase" (Gosselin, 1978). The point is perhaps best made in reverse, by the cartoon that shows six surgeons standing around a patient on an operating table with one saying, "Who opens?" Similarly, the policy and marketing courses of the management school may be integrated without the two professors involved having even met. As long as the courses are standard, each knows more or less what the other teaches.

Just how standardized complex professional work can be is illustrated in a paper read by Spencer (1976) before a meeting of the International Cardiovascular Society. Spencer noted that "becoming a skillful clinical surgeon requires a long period of training, probably five or more years" (p. 1178). An important feature of that training is "repetitive practice" to evoke "an automatic reflex" (p. 1179). So automatic, in fact, that Spencer keeps his series of surgical "cookbooks," in which he lists, even for "complex" operations, the essential steps as chains of thirty to forty symbols on a single sheet, to "be reviewed mentally in sixty to 120 seconds at some time during the day preceding the operation" (p. 1182). But no matter how standardized the knowledge and skills, their complexity ensures that considerable discretion remains in their application. No two professionals—no

190

two surgeons or teachers or social workers—ever apply them in exactly the same way. Many judgments are required.

Training and indoctrination are a complicated affair in the Professional Bureaucracy. The initial training typically takes place over a period of years in a university or special institution. Here the skills and knowledge of the profession are formally programmed into the would-be professional. But in many cases, that is only the first step, even if the most important one. There typically follows a long period of on-the-job training, such as internship in medicine and articling in accounting. Here the formal knowledge is applied and the practice of the skills perfected, under the close supervision of members of the profession. On-the-job training also completes the process of indoctrination, which began during the formal teaching. Once this process is completed, the professional association typically examines the trainee to determine whether he has the requisite knowledge, skills, and norms to enter the profession. That is not to say, however, that the person is "examined for the last time in his life, and is pronounced completely full," such that "after this, no new ideas can be imparted to him," as humorist and academic Stephen Leacock once commented about the Ph.D., the hurdle to entering the profession of university teaching. The entrance examination only tests the basic requirements at one point in time; the process of training continues. As new knowledge is generated and new skills develop, the professional upgrades his expertise. He reads the journals, attends the conferences, and perhaps also returns periodically for formal retraining.

The bureaucratic nature of the structure

All this training is geared to one goal—the internalization of standards that serve the client and coordinate the professional work. In other words, **the structure of these organizations is essentially bureaucratic, its coordination—like that of the Machine Bureaucracy—achieved by design, by standards that predetermine what is to be done.** Thus:

> . . . obstetrics and gynecology is a relatively routine department, which even has something resembling an assembly (or deassembly?) line wherein the mother moves from room to room and nurse to nurse during the predictable course of her labor. It is also one of the hospital units most often accused of impersonality and depersonalization. For the mother, the birth is unique, but not for the doctor and the rest of the staff who go through this many times a day. (Perrow, 1970:74)

But the two kinds of bureaucracies differ markedly in the source of their standardization. **Whereas the Machine Bureaucracy generates its own standards—its technostructure designing the work standards for its operators and its line managers enforcing them—the standards of the**

Professional Bureaucracy originate largely outside its own structure, in the self-governing associations its operators join with their colleagues from other Professional Bureaucracies. These associations set universal standards, which they make sure are taught by the universities and used by all the bureaucracies of the profession. **So whereas the Machine Bureaucracy relies on authority of a hierarchical nature—the power of office—the Professional Bureaucracy emphasizes authority of a professional nature—the power of expertise.**

The other forms of standardization are, in fact, difficult to rely on in the Professional Bureaucracy. The work processes themselves are too complex to be standardized directly by analysts. One need only try to imagine a work-study analyst following a cardiologist on his rounds or observing a teacher in a classroom in order to program the work. Similarly, the outputs of professional work cannot easily be measured and so do not lend themselves to standardization. Imagine a planner trying to define a cure in psychiatry, the amount of learning that takes place in the classroom, or the quality of an accountant's audit. Thus, Professional Bureaucracies cannot rely extensively on the formalization of professional work or on systems to plan and control it.

Much the same conclusion can be drawn for the two remaining coordinating mechanisms. Both direct supervision and mutual adjustment impede the professional's close relationships with his clients. That relationship is predicated on a high degree of professional autonomy—freedom from having not only to respond to managerial orders but also to consult extensively with peers. In any event, the use of the other four coordinating mechanisms is precluded by the capacity of the standardization of skills to achieve a good deal of the coordination necessary in the operating core.

The pigeonholing process

To understand how the Professional Bureaucracy functions in its operating core, it is helpful to think of it as a repertoire of standard programs— in effect, the set of skills the professionals stand ready to use—that are applied to predetermined situations, called contingencies, also standardized. As Weick (1976) notes of one case in point, "schools are in the business of building and maintaining categories" (p. 8). The process is sometimes known as *pigeonholing*. In this regard, **the professional has two basic tasks: (1) to categorize the client's need in terms of a contingency, which indicates which standard program to use, a task known as diagnosis; and (2) to apply, or execute, that program.** Pigeonholing simplifies matters enormously. "People are categorized and placed into pigeonholes because it would take enormous resources to treat every case as unique and requiring thorough analysis. Like stereotypes, categories allow us to move through the world without making continuous decisions at every moment" (Perrow, 1970:58). Thus, a psychiatrist examines the patient, declares him to be manic-depressive, and initiates psychotherapy. Similarly, a professor finds 100 students registered in his course and executes his lecture program; faced with twenty instead, he runs the class as a seminar. And the management consultant carries his own bag of standard acronymical tricks—MBO, MIS, LRP, PERT, OD. The client with project work gets PERT; the one with managerial conflicts, OD. Of course, clients often help out by categorizing themselves. As noted earlier, the person with an ingrown toenail does not visit a cardiologist; the student who wants to become a manager registers in the university's business school.

Simon captures the spirit of pigeonholing with his comment, "The pleasure that the good professional experiences in his work is not simply a pleasure in handling difficult matters; it is a pleasure in using skillfully a well-stocked kit of well-designed tools to handle problems that are comprehensible in their deep structure but unfamiliar in their detail" (1977:98).

It is this pigeonholing process that enables the Professional Bureaucracy to decouple its various operating tasks and assign them to individual, relatively autonomous professionals. Each can, instead of giving a great deal of attention to coordinating his work with his peers, focus on perfecting his skills. This is not to say that all uncertainty can be removed from the performance of the work, but only that attempts are made to contain whatever uncertainty does remain in the jobs of single professionals. Focusing the uncertainty in this way is one of the reasons the professional requires considerable discretion in his work.

In the pigeonholing process, we see fundamental differences among the Machine Bureaucracy, the Professional Bureaucracy, and the Adhocracy. The Machine Bureaucracy is a single-purpose structure; presented with a stimulus, it executes its one standard sequence of programs, just as we kick when tapped on the knee. No diagnosis is involved. In the Professional Bureaucracy, diagnosis is a fundamental task, but it is circumscribed. The organization seeks to match a predetermined contingency to a standard program. Fully open-ended diagnosis—that which seeks a creative solution to a unique problem—requires a third configuration, which we call Adhocracy. No standard contingencies or programs exist in that configuration.

It is an interesting characteristic of the Professional Bureaucracy that its pigeonholing process creates an equivalence in its structure between the functional and market bases for grouping. **Because clients are categorized, or categorize themselves, in terms of the functional specialists who serve them, the structure of the Professional Bureaucracy becomes at the same time both a functional and a market-based one.** Two illustrations help explain the point: A hospital gynecology department and a university chemistry department can be called functional because they group specialists according to the knowledge, skills, and work processes they use, or market-based because each unit deals with its own unique types of clients—women in the first case, chemistry students in the second. Thus, the distinction between functional and market bases for grouping breaks down in the special case of the Professional Bureaucracy.

Focus on the operating core

All the design parameters that we have discussed so far—the emphasis on the training of operators, their vertically enlarged jobs, the little use made of behavior formalization or planning and control systems—suggest that **the operating core is the key part of the Professional Bureaucracy. The only other part that is fully elaborated is the support staff, but that is focused very much on serving the operating core.** Given the high cost of the professionals, it makes sense to back them up with as much support as possible, to aid them and have others do whatever routine work can be formalized. Thus, universities have printing facilities, faculty clubs, alma mater funds, publishing houses, archives, athletics departments, libraries, computer facilities, and many, many other support units.

The technostructure and middle line of management are not highly elaborated in the Professional Bureaucracy. In other configurations (except Adhocracy), they coordinate the work of the operating core. But in the Professional Bureaucracy, they can do little to coordinate the operating work. Because the need for planning and the formalizing of the work of the professionals are very limited, there is little call for a technostructure (except, as we shall see, in the case of the nonprofessional support staff). In McGill University, for example, an institution with 17,000 students and 1,200 professors, the only units that could be identified by the author as technocratic were two small departments concerned with finance and budgeting, a small planning office, and a center to develop the professors' skills in pedagogy (the latter two fighting a continual uphill battle for acceptance). Likewise, the middle line in the Professional Bureaucracy is

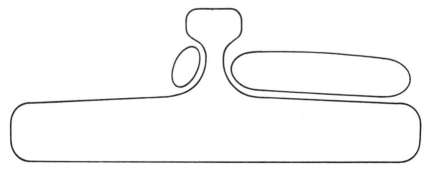

Figure 10-1. *The Professional Bureaucracy*

thin. With little need for direct supervision of the operators or mutual adjustment between them, the operating units can be very large, with few managers at the level of first-line supervisor, or, for that matter, above them. As noted earlier, the McGill Faculty of Management at the time of this writing functions effectively with sixty professors and a single manager, its dean.

Thus, Figure 10–1 shows the Professional Bureaucracy, in terms of our logo, as a flat structure with a thin middle line, a tiny technostructure, and a fully elaborated support staff. All these characteristics are reflected in the organigram of McGill University, shown in Figure 10–2.

Decentralization in the professional bureaucracy

Everything we have seen so far tells us that **the Professional Bureaucracy is a highly decentralized structure, in both the vertical and horizontal dimensions.** A great deal of the power over the operating work rests at the bottom of the structure, with the professionals of the operating core. Often, each works with his own clients, subject only to the collective control of his colleagues, who trained and indoctrinated him in the first place and thereafter reserve the right to censure him for malpractice.

The professional's power derives from the fact that not only is his work too complex to be supervised by managers or standardized by analysts, but also his services are typically in great demand. This gives the professional mobility, which enables him to insist on considerable autonomy in his work. When the professional does not get the autonomy he feels he requires, he is tempted to pick up his kit bag of skills and move on.

One is inclined to ask why professionals bother to join organizations in the first place. There are, in fact, a number of good reasons. For one thing, professionals can share resources, including support services, in a common organization. One surgeon cannot afford his own operating theater, so he shares it with others, just as professors share laboratories, lecture halls, libraries, and printing facilities. Organizing also brings the professionals together to learn from each other, and to train new recruits. Some professionals must join the organization to get clients. Although some physicians have their private patients, others receive them from the hospital emergency department or from in-patient referrals. Another reason professionals band together to form organizations is that the clients often need the services of more than one at the same time. An operation requires at least a surgeon, an anesthesiologist, and a nurse; an MBA program cannot be run with less than about a dozen different specialists. Finally, the bringing together of different types of professionals allows clients to be transferred between them when the initial diagnosis proves incorrect or the needs of the client change during execution. When the kidney patient develops heart trouble, that is no time to change hospitals

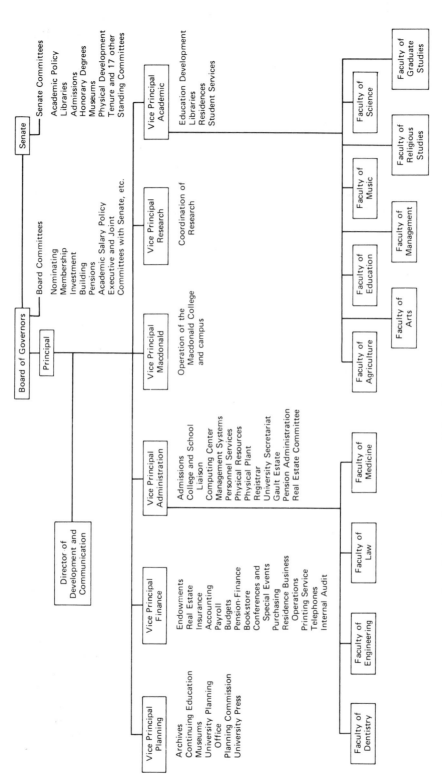

Note: This unofficial organigram was drawn by the author based upon University documents.

Figure 10-2. *Organigram of McGill University (circa 1978)*

in search of a cardiologist. Similarly, when an accountant finds his client needs tax advice, it is comforting to know that other departments in the same organization stand ready to provide the necessary service.

The administrative structure

What we have seen suggests that the Professional Bureaucracy is a highly democratic structure, at least for the professionals of the operating core. In fact, **not only do the professionals control their own work, but they also seek collective control of the administrative decisions that affect them—** decisions, for example, to hire colleagues, to promote them, and to distribute resources. Controlling these decisions requires control of the middle line of the organization, which professionals do by ensuring that it is staffed with "their own." Some of the administrative work the operating professionals do themselves. Every university professor, for example, serves on committees of one kind or another to ensure that he retains some control over the decisions that affect his work. Moreover, full-time administrators who wish to have any power at all in these structures must be certified members of the profession and preferably be elected by the professional operators, or at least appointed with their blessing. What emerges, therefore, is a rather democratic administrative structure.

This administrative structure itself relies largely on mutual adjustment for coordination. Thus, the liaison devices, although uncommon in the operating core, are important design parameters in the middle line. Task forces and especially standing committees abound, as indicated in Figure 10–2; a number of positions are designated to integrate the administrative efforts, as in the case of the ward manager in the hospital; and some Professional Bureaucracies even use matrix structure in administration.

Because of the power of their operators, Professional Bureaucracies are sometimes called "collegial" organizations. In fact, some professionals like to describe them as inverse pyramids, with the professional operators at the top and the administrators down below to serve them—to ensure that the surgical facilities are kept clean and the classrooms well supplied with chalk. Such a description underestimates the power of the *professional* administrator—a point we shall return to shortly—but it seems to be an accurate description of the nonprofessional one—namely, the administrator who manages the support units. For the support staff—often much larger than the professional one, but charged largely with doing nonprofessional work—there is no democracy in the Professional Bureaucracy, only the oligarchy of the professionals. Support units, such as housekeeping or kitchen in the hospital or printing in the university, are as likely as not to be managed tightly from the top. They exist, in effect, as machine bureaucratic constellations within the Professional Bureaucracy.

What frequently emerge in the Professional Bureaucracy are parallel administrative hierarchies, one democratic and bottom-up for the professionals, and a second machine bureaucratic and top-down for the support staff. In the professional hierarchy, power resides in expertise; one has influence by virtue of one's knowledge and skills. In other words, a good deal of power remains at the bottom of the hierarchy, with the professional operators themselves. That does not, of course, preclude a pecking order among them. But it does require the pecking order to mirror the professionals' experience and expertise. As they gain experience and reputation, academics move through the ranks of lecturer, and then assistant, associate, and full professor; and physicians enter the hospital as interns and move up to residents before they become members of the so-called medical staff. In fact, in many hospitals, this staff does not even report to the executive director—the chief executive officer—but reports directly to the board of trustees. (Indeed, Charns (1976) reports that 41 percent of the physicians he surveyed in academic medical centers claimed they were responsible to no one!) In the nonprofession hierarchy, in contrast, power and status reside in administrative office; one salutes the stripes, not the man. Unlike the case in the professional structure, here one must practice administration, not a specialized function of the organization, to attain status. But "research indicates that a professional orientation toward service and a bureaucratic orientation toward disciplined compliance with procedures are opposite approaches toward work and often create conflict in organizations" (Blau, 1967–68:456). Hence, these two parallel hierarchies are kept quite independent of each other, as shown in Figure 10–3.

The roles of the professional administrator

Where does all this leave the administrators of the professional hierarchy, the executive directors and chiefs of the hospitals and the presidents and deans of the universities? Are they powerless? Compared with their peers

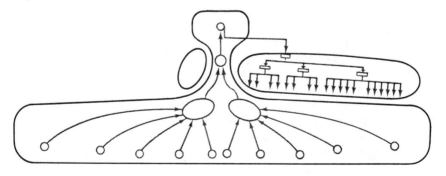

Figure 10-3. *Parallel Hierarchies in the Professional Bureaucracy*

in the Simple Structure and the Machine Bureaucracy, they certainly lack a good deal of power. But that is far from the whole story. The professional administrator may not be able to control the professionals directly, but he does perform a series of roles that gives him considerable indirect power in the structure.

First, **the professional administrator spends much time handling disturbances in the structure.** The pigeonholing process is an imperfect one at best, leading to all kinds of jurisdictional disputes between the professionals. Who should teach the statistics course in the MBA program—the mathematics department or the business school? Who should perform mastectomies in hospitals—surgeons who specialize in operations or gynecologists who specialize in women? Seldom, however, can a senior administrator impose a solution on the professionals or units involved in a dispute. Rather, the unit managers—chiefs, deans, or whoever—must sit down together and negotiate a solution on behalf of their constituencies. Coordination problems also arise frequently between the two parallel hierarchies, and it often falls to the professional administrators to resolve them.

Second, **the professional administrators—especially those at higher levels—serve key roles at the boundary of the organization, between the professionals inside and interested parties—governments, client associations, and so on—on the outside.** On the one hand, the administrators are expected to protect the professionals' autonomy, to "buffer" them from external pressures. On the other hand, the administrators are expected to woo these outsiders to support the organization, both morally and financially. Thus, the external roles of the manager—maintaining liaison contacts, acting as figurehead and spokesman in a public relations capacity, negotiating with outside agencies—emerge as primary ones in professional administration.

Some view the roles professional administrators are called upon to perform as signs of weakness. They see these people as the errand boys of the professionals, or else as pawns caught in various tugs of war—between one professional and another, between support staffer and professional, between outsider and professional. In fact, however, these roles are the very sources of administrator power. Power is, after all, gained at the locus of uncertainty. And that is exactly where the professional administrators sit. The administrator who succeeds in raising extra funds for his organization gains a say in how these are distributed. Similarly, the one who can reconcile conflicts in favor of his unit or who can effectively buffer the professionals from external influence becomes a valued—and therefore powerful—member of the organization.

Ironically, **the professional becomes dependent on the effective administrator.** The professional faces a fundamental dilemma. Frequently, he abhors administration, desiring only to be left alone to practice his profession. But that freedom is gained only at the price of administrative effort—raising funds, resolving conflicts, buffering the demands of outsiders. This leaves the professional two choices: to do the administrative work himself, in which case he has less time to practice his profession, or to leave it to administrators, in which case he must surrender some of his power over decision making. And that power must be surrendered, it should be added, to administrators who, by virtue of the fact that they do not wish to practice the profession, probably favor a different set of goals. Damned if he does and damned if he doesn't. Take the case of the university professor oriented to research. To ensure the fullest support for research in his department, he should involve himself in committees where questions of the commitment to teaching versus research are decided. But that takes time, specifically time away from research. What is the use of spending time protecting what one has no time left to do? So the professor is tempted to leave administration to full-time administrators, those who have expressed a lack of interest in research by virtue of seeking full-time administrative office.

We can conclude that **power in these structures does flow to those professionals who care to devote effort to doing administrative instead of professional work, especially to those who do it well. But that, it should be stressed, is not laissez-faire power: the professional administrator keeps his power only as long as the professionals perceive him to be serving their interests effectively.** The managers of the Professional Bureaucracy may be the weakest among those of the five configurations, but they are far from impotent. *Individually*, they are usually more powerful than individual professionals—the chief executive remaining the single most powerful member of the Professional Bureaucracy—even if that power can easily be overwhelmed by the *collective* power of the professionals.

Strategy formulation in the professional bureaucracy

A description of the strategy-formulation process in the Professional Bureaucracy perhaps best illustrates the two sides of the professional administrator's power. At the outset it should be noted that strategy takes on a very different form in these kinds of organizations. Since their outputs are difficult to measure, their goals cannot easily be agreed upon. So **the notion of a strategy—a single, integrated pattern of decisions common to the entire organization—loses a good deal of its meaning in the Professional Bureaucracy.**

Given the autonomy of each professional—his close working relationships with his clients, and his loose ones with his colleagues—it becomes logical to think in terms of a personal strategy for each professional. In many cases, each selects his own clients and his own methods of dealing with them—in effect, chooses his own product-market strategy. But professionals do not select their clients and methods at random. The professionals are significantly constrained by the professional standards and skills they have learned. That is, the professional associations and training institutions outside the organization play a major role in determining the strategies that the professionals pursue. Thus, to an important extent, all organizations in a given profession exhibit similar strategies, imposed on them from the outside. These strategies—concerning what clients to serve and how—are inculcated in the professionals during their formal training and are modified as new needs emerge and as the new methods developed to cope with them gain acceptance by the professional associations. This outside control of strategy can sometimes be very direct: in one of the McGill studies, a hospital that refused to adopt a new method of treatment was, in effect, censured when one of the associations of medical specialists passed a resolution declaring failure to use it tantamount to malpractice.

We can conclude, therefore, that **the strategies of the Professional Bureaucracy are largely ones of the individual professionals within the organization as well as of the professional associations on the outside.** Largely, but not completely. There are still degrees of freedom that allow each organization within the profession to adapt the basic strategies to its own needs and interests. There are, for example, mental hospitals, women's hospitals, and veterans' hospitals; all conform to standard medical practice, but each applies it to a different market that it has selected.

How do these organizational strategies develop? It would appear that **the Professional Bureaucracy's own strategies represent the cumulative effect over time of the projects, or strategic "initiatives," that its members are able to convince it to undertake**—to buy a new piece of equipment in a hospital, to establish a new degree program in a university, to develop a new specialty department in an accounting firm. Most of these initiatives are proposed by members of the operating core—by "professional entrepreneurs" willing to expend the efforts needed to negotiate the acceptance of new projects through the complex administrative structure (and if the method is new and controversial, through outside professional associations as well).

What is the role of the professional administrator in all this? Certainly far from passive. As noted earlier, administration is neither the forte nor the interest of the operating professional. So he depends on the full-time administrator to help him negotiate his project through the system. For one thing, the administrator has time to worry about such matters. After all, administration is his job; he no longer practices the profession. For another, the administrator has a full knowledge of the administrative committee system as well as many personal contacts within it, both of which are necessary to see a project through it. The administrator deals with the system every day; the professional entrepreneur may promote only one new project in his entire career. Finally, the administrator is more likely to have the requisite managerial skills—for example, those of negotiation and persuasion.

But the power of the effective administrator to influence strategy goes beyond helping the operating professionals. Every good manager seeks to change his organization in his own way, to alter its strategies to make it more effective. In the Professional Bureaucracy, this translates into a set of strategic initiatives that the administrator himself wishes to take. But in these structures—in principle, bottom-up—the administrator cannot impose his will on the professionals of the operating core. Instead, he must rely on his informal power, and apply it subtly. Knowing that the professionals want nothing more than to be left alone, the administrator moves carefully—in incremental steps, each one hardly discernible. In this way, he may achieve over time changes that the professionals would have rejected out of hand had they been proposed all at once.

Conditions of the Professional Bureaucracy

This third configuration appears wherever the operating core of an organization is dominated by skilled workers—professionals—who use procedures that are difficult to learn, yet are well defined. This means an environment that is both complex and stable—complex enough to require the use of difficult procedures that can be learned only in extensive formal training programs, yet stable enough to enable these skills to become well defined—in effect, standardized. Thus, the environment is the chief situational factor in the use of the Professional Bureaucracy.

In contrast, the factors of age and size are of less significance. Larger professional organizations may tend to be somewhat more formalized and to have more fully developed staff-support structures. But that does not preclude the existence of small Professional Bureaucracies, or, for that matter, of young ones as well. The Machine Bureaucracy has a lengthy start-up time because the standards need to be worked out within the organization. Thus, it passes through a period of Simple Structure before its procedures become routinized. In the Professional Bureaucracy, in contrast, the skilled employees bring the standards into the organization with them when they join, so there is little start-up time. Put a group of doctors in a new hospital or a group of lawyers in a new law office, and in no time they are functioning as if they had been there for years. Size would seem to be a relatively minor factor for the same reason, and also because the professionals to a large extent work independently. One accountant working on his own adheres to the same professional standards as 2,000 working in a giant firm. Thus, Professional Bureaucracies pass quickly through the stage of Simple Structure in their formative years.

Technical system is an important situational factor only for what it is not in the Professional Bureaucracy—neither highly regulating, sophisticated, nor automated. The professional operators of this configuration require considerable discretion in their work. It is they who serve the clients, usually directly and personally. So the technical system cannot be highly regulating, certainly not highly automated. The professional resists the rationalization of his skills—their division into simply executed steps— because that makes them programmable by the technostructure, destroys his basis of autonomy, and drives the structure to the machine bureaucratic form.

Nor can the technical system be sophisticated. The surgeon uses a scalpel, the accountant a pencil. Both must be sharp, but they are otherwise simple and commonplace instruments. Yet both allow their users to perform independently what can be exceedingly complex functions. More sophisticated instruments—such as the computer in the accounting firm or the coronary-care unit in the hospital—reduce the professional's autonomy by forcing him to work in multidisciplinary teams, as he does in the Adhocracy. These teams are concerned in large part with the design, modification, and maintenance of the equipment; its operation, because that tends to be regulating and often automated, impersonalizes the relationship between the professional and his clients. Thus, **in the pure form of the Professional Bureaucracy, the technology of the organization—its knowledge base—is sophisticated, but its technical system—the set of instruments it uses to apply that knowledge base—is not.**

Thus, the prime example of the Professional Bureaucracy is the *personal-service organization,* at least the one with complex, stable work. Schools and universities, consulting firms, law and accounting offices, and social-work agencies all rely on this configuration as long as they concentrate not on innovating in the solution of new problems, but on applying standard programs to well-defined problems. The same is true of hospitals, at least to the extent that their technical systems are simple. (In those areas that call for more sophisticated equipment—apparently a growing number, especially in teaching institutions—the hospital is driven toward a hybrid structure, with characteristics of the Adhocracy. But this tendency is mitigated by the hospital's overriding concern with safety. Only the tried and true can be used on regular patients. Institutions entrusted with the lives of their clients have a natural aversion to the looser, organic structures such as Adhocracy.) A good deal of the service sector of contemporary society, in fact, applies standard programs to well-defined problems. Hence, the Professional Bureaucracy tends to predominate there. And with the enormous growth of this sector in the last few decades, we find that this configuration has emerged as a major one.

So far, all our examples have come from the service sector. But Professional Bureaucracies can be found in manufacturing, too, notably where the environment demands work that is complex yet stable, and the technical system is neither regulating nor sophisticated. This is the case of the *craft enterprise*, an important variant of the Professional Bureaucracy. Here the organization relies on skilled craftsmen who use relatively simple instruments to produce standard outputs. The very term *craftsman* implies a kind of professional who learns traditional skills through long apprentice training and then is allowed to practice them free of direct supervision. Craft enterprises seem typically to have tiny administrations—no technostructures and few managers, many of whom, in any event, work alongside the craftsmen.

Many craftsmen were eliminated by the Industrial Revolution. Their jobs—for example, the making of shoes—were rationalized, and so control over them passed from the workers who did them to the analysts who designed them. Small craft enterprises metamorphosed into large Machine Bureaucracies. But some craft industries remain—for example, fine glasswork and handmade pottery, portrait photography, and gastronomic cuisine. In fact, as these examples indicate, the term *craft* has today come to be associated with functional art, handmade items that perform a function but are purchased for their aesthetic value. Evidence suggests that one major industry, construction, has also remained largely in the craft stage.

The markets of the Professional Bureaucracy are often diversified. As noted earlier, these organizations often bring together groups of professionals from different specialties who serve different types of clients. The hospital includes gynecologists to serve women, pediatricians to serve children, and so on; the university has its philosophy professors to teach those interested in general knowledge and its engineering professors for those in search of specific career skills. Hypothesis 11 would lead us to the conclusion that such market diversity encourages the use of the market basis for grouping the professionals. In fact, we have already seen this to be the case (although we also saw that the market basis for grouping turns out to be equivalent to the functional one in Professional Bureaucracies, as a result of the way in which professional services are selected).

Sometimes the markets of Professional Bureaucracies are diversified geographically, leading to a variant we call the *dispersed professional bureaucracy*. Here, the problem of maintaining loyalty to the organization becomes magnified, since the professionals do their autonomous work in remote locations, far from the administrative structure. The U.S. Forest Rangers, for example, are dispersed across the United States, each one on his own, as are CIA agents and certain consultants. As a result, their organizations must rely extensively on training and indoctrination, especially the latter. The employees are selected carefully, trained extensively, and indoctrinated heavily—often by the organization itself—before they are sent out to the remote areas to perform their work. Later, they are brought back to the central headquarters for fresh doses of indoctrination, and are often rotated in their jobs to ensure that their loyalty remains with the organization and does not shift to the geographical areas they serve.

The Professional Bureaucracy is also occasionally found as a hybrid structure. In our discussion of hospitals earlier, we alluded to a possible combination with characteristics of the Adhocracy that we can call the *professional bureau/adhocracy*. Another hybrid—the *simple professional bureaucracy*—occurs when highly trained professionals practicing standard skills nevertheless take their lead from a strong, sometimes even autocratic, leader, as in the Simple Structure. Consider, for example, the symphony orchestra, an organization staffed with highly skilled musicians who play standard repertoires. Some people have described it as a dictatorship of the conductor. In any event, there is no denying its need for strong leadership, based on direct supervision. In fact, after their revolution, the Russians tried a conductorless orchestra, but it lasted only a few years before conflicts among the musicians necessitated the reintroduction of a central leader.

Finally, we might note briefly the effects of the situational factors of power, notably fashion and the influence of the operators. *Professionalism* is a popular word among all kinds of identifiable specialists today. As a result, **Professional Bureaucracy is a highly fashionable structure**—and for good reason, since it is a rather democratic one. Thus, it is to the advantage of every operator to make his job more professional—to enhance the skills it requires, to keep the analysts of the technostructure from rationalizing those skills, and to establish associations that set industrywide standards to protect those skills. In these ways, the operator can achieve what always escapes him in the Machine Bureaucracy—control of his work and the decisions that affect it.

Some Issues Associated with Professional Bureaucracy

The Professional Bureaucracy is unique among the five configurations in answering two of the paramount needs of contemporary men and women. It is democratic, disseminating its power directly to its workers (at least those who are professional). And it provides them with extensive autonomy, freeing them even of the need to coordinate closely with their peers, and all the pressures and politics that entails. Thus, the professional has the best of both worlds: he is attached to an organization, yet is free to serve his clients in his own way, constrained only by the established standards of his profession.

As a result, professionals tend to emerge as responsible and highly motivated individuals, dedicated to their work and the clients they serve. Unlike the Machine Bureaucracy, which places barriers between the operator and the client, this configuration removes them, allowing a personal relationship to develop. Here the technical and social systems can function in complete harmony.

Moreover, **autonomy allows the professionals to perfect their skills, free of interference.** They repeat the same complex programs time after time, forever reducing the uncertainty until they get them just about perfect, like the Provençal potter who has spent his career perfecting the glazes he applies to identical pots. The professional's thought processes are "convergent"—vascular surgeon Spencer (1976) refers to them as deductive reasoning. He quotes approvingly the bridge aficionado who stood behind champion Charles Goren during a three-day tournament and concluded, "He didn't do anything I couldn't do, except he didn't make any mistakes" (p. 1181). That captures nicely the secure feelings of professionals and their clients in Professional Bureaucracies. The Provençal potter expects few surprises when he opens his kiln; so, too, do Dr. Spencer's patients when they climb onto his operating table. They know the program has been executed so many times—by this surgeon as well as by the many whose experiences he has read about in the journals—that the possibility of mistakes has been minimized. Hospitals do not even get to execute new programs on regular patients until those programs have been thoroughly tested and approved by the profession. So the client of the Professional Bureaucracy can take satisfaction in the knowledge that the professional about to serve him will draw on vast quantities of experience and skill, will apply them in a perfected, not an experimental procedure, and will probably be highly motivated in performing that procedure.

But in these same characteristics of democracy and autonomy lie the major problems of the Professional Bureaucracy. For **there is virtually no control of the work aside from that by the profession itself, no way to correct deficiencies that the professionals themselves choose to overlook.** What they tend to overlook are the major problems of coordination, of discretion, and of innovation that arise in these configurations.

Problems of coordination

The Professional Bureaucracy can coordinate effectively in its operating core only by the standardization of skills. Direct supervision and mutual adjustment are resisted as direct infringements on the professional's autonomy, in one case by administrators, in the other by colleagues. And standardization of work processes and of outputs are ineffective for the complex work with its ill-defined outputs. But **the standardization of skills is a loose coordinating mechanism at best, failing to cope with many of the needs that arise in the Professional Bureaucracy.**

There is, first of all, the need for coordination between the professionals and the support staff. To the professional, that is simply resolved: He gives the orders. But that only catches the support staffer between two systems of power pulling in different ways, the vertical power of line authority above him and the horizontal power of professional expertise to his side.

Perhaps more severe are the coordination problems among the professionals themselves. Unlike Machine Bureaucracies, Professional Bureaucracies are not integrated entities. They are collections of individuals who come together to draw on common resources and support services but otherwise want to be left alone. As long as the pigeonholing process works effectively, they can be. But that process can never be so good that client needs do not fall in the cracks between the standard programs. The world is a continuous intertwined system. Slicing it up, although necessary to comprehend it, inevitably distorts it (this book admittedly being no exception). Needs that fall at the margin or that overlap two categories tend to get forced—artificially—into one category or another. In contemporary medicine, for instance, the human body is treated less as one integrated system with interdependent parts than as a collection of loosely coupled organs that correspond to the different specialties. For the patient whose malady slots nicely into one of the specialties, problems of coordination do not arise. For others—the patient who falls between psychiatry and internal medicine, for instance—it means repeated transfers in search of the right department, a time-consuming process when time is critical. In universities, the pigeonholing process can be equally artificial, as in the case of the professor interested in the structure of production systems who fell between the operations and organizational behavior departments of his business school and so was denied tenure.

The pigeonholing process, in fact, emerges as the source of a great deal of the conflict of the Professional Bureaucracy. Much political blood is spilled in the continual reassessment of contingencies, imperfectly conceived, in terms of programs, artificially distinguished.

Problems of discretion

The assumption underlying the design of the Professional Bureaucracy is that the pigeonholing process contains all the uncertainties in single professional jobs. As we saw above, that assumption often proves false, to the detriment of the organization's performance. But even where it works, problems arise. For it focuses all the discretion in the hands of single professionals, whose complex skills, no matter how standardized, require the exercise of considerable judgment. Such discretion is, perhaps, appropriate for professionals who are competent and conscientious. Unfortunately, not all of them are. And **the Professional Bureaucracy cannot easily deal with professionals who are either incompetent or unconscientious.**

No two professionals are equally skilled. So the client who is forced to choose among them—to choose in ignorance, since he seeks professional help precisely because he lacks the specialized knowledge to help himself—is exposed to a kind of Russian Roulette, almost literally so in the case of medicine, where a single decision can mean life or death. But that is inevitable; little can be done aside from using the very best screening procedures for applicants to the training schools.

Of greater concern is the unconscientious professional—the one who refuses to update his skills after graduation, who cares more for his income than his clients, or who becomes so enamored with his skills that he forgets about the real needs of his clients. This last case represents a means–ends inversion common in Professional Bureaucracies, different from that found in Machine Bureaucracies but equally serious. In this case, the professional confuses the needs of his clients with the skills he has to offer them. He simply concentrates on the program that he favors to the exclusion of all the others—perhaps because he does it best or simply enjoys it most. This presents no problem as long as only those clients in need of that favorite program are directed his way. But should other clients slip in, trouble ensues. Thus, we have the psychiatrists who think that all patients (indeed, all people) need psychoanalysis; the consulting firms prepared to design the same planning system for all their clients, no matter how dynamic their environments; the professors who use the lecture method for classes of 500 students or five; the social workers who feel the compulsion to bring power to the people even when the people do not want it.

Dealing with this means–ends inversion is impeded by the difficulty of measuring the outputs of professional work. When psychiatrists cannot even define the words *cure* or *healthy*, how are they to prove that psychoanalysis is better for manic-depressives than chemical therapy would be? When no one has been able to measure the learning that takes place in the classroom, how can it be demonstrated with reliability that lectures are better or worse than seminars or, for that matter, than staying home and reading? That is one reason that the obvious solution to the problems of discretion—censure by the professional association—is seldom used. Another is that professionals are notoriously reluctant to act against their own—to wash their dirty linen in public, so to speak. In extreme cases, they will do so; certain behavior is too callous to ignore. But these instances are relatively rare. They do no more than expose the tip of the iceberg of misguided discretion.

Discretion not only enables some professionals to ignore the needs of their clients; it also encourages many of them to ignore the needs of the organization. Professionals in these structures do not generally consider themselves part of a team. To many, the organization is almost incidental, a convenient place to practice their skills. They are loyal to their profession, not to the place where they happen to practice it. But the organization has need for loyalty, too—to support its own strategies, to staff its administrative committees, to see it through conflicts with the professional association. Cooperation, as we saw earlier, is crucial to the functioning of the administrative structure. Yet, as we also saw, professionals resist it furiously. Professors hate to show up for curriculum meetings; they simply do not wish to be dependent on each other. One can say that they know each other only too well!

Problems of innovation

In these structures, major innovation also depends on cooperation. Existing programs can be perfected by individual specialists. But new ones usually cut across existing specialties—in essence, they require a rearrangement of the pigeonholes—and so call for interdisciplinary efforts. As a result, the reluctance of the professionals to work cooperatively with each other translates itself into problems of innovation.

Like the Machine Bureaucracy, the Professional Bureaucracy is an inflexible structure, well suited to producing its standard outputs but ill-suited to adapting to the production of new ones. All bureaucracies are geared to stable environments; they are performance structures designed to perfect programs for contingencies that can be predicted, not problem-solving ones designed to create new programs for needs that have never before been encountered.

The problems of innovation in the Professional Bureaucracy find their roots in convergent thinking, in the deductive reasoning of the professional who sees the specific situation in terms of the general concept. In the Professional Bureaucracy, this means that new problems are forced into old pigeonholes. The doctoral student in search of an interdisciplinary degree—for, after all, isn't the highest university degree meant to encourage the generation of new knowledge?—inevitably finds himself forced back into the old departmental mode. "It must be a D.B.A. or a D.Ed.; we don't offer educational administration here." Nowhere are the effects of this deductive reasoning better illustrated than in Spencer's (1976) comments, "All patients developing significant complications or death among our three hospitals . . . are reported to a central office with a narrative description of the sequence of events, with reports varying in length from a third to an entire page"; six to eight of these cases are discussed in the one-hour weekly "mortality-morbidity" conferences, including presentation of it by the surgeon and "questions and comments" by the audience (p. 1181). An "entire" page and ten minutes of discussion for cases with "significant complications"! Maybe enough to list the symptoms and slot them into pigeonholes; hardly enough even to begin to think about creative solutions. As Lucy once told Charlie Brown, great art cannot be done in half an hour; it takes at least forty-five minutes!

The fact is that great art and innovative problem solving require *inductive* reasoning—that is, the inference of new general concepts or programs from particular experiences. That kind of thinking is *divergent*—it breaks away from old routines or standards rather than perfecting existing ones. And that flies in the face of everything the Professional Bureaucracy is designed to do.

So it should come as no surprise that Professional Bureaucracies and the professional associations that control their procedures tend to be conservative bodies, hesitant to change their well-established ways. Whenever an entrepreneurial member takes up the torch of innovation, great political clashes inevitably ensue. Even in the Machine Bureaucracy, once the managers of the strategic apex finally recognize the need for change, they are able to force it down the hierarchy. In the Professional Bureaucracy, with operator autonomy and bottom-up decision making, and in the professional association with its own democratic procedures, power for strategic change is diffuse. Everybody, not just a few managers or professional representatives; must agree on the change. So change comes slowly and painfully, after much political intrigue and shrewd maneuvering by the professional and administrative entrepreneurs.

As long as the environment remains stable, the Professional Bureaucracy encounters no problem. It continues to perfect its skills and its given system of pigeonholes that slots them. But dynamic conditions call for change—new skills, new ways to slot them, and creative, cooperative efforts on the part of multidisciplinary teams of professionals. And that calls for another configuration, as we shall see in Chapter 12.

Dysfunctional responses

What responses do the problems of coordination, discretion, and innovation evoke? Most commonly, **those outside the profession—clients, nonprofessional administrators, members of the society at large and their representatives in government—see the problems as resulting from a lack of external control of the professional and of his profession. So they do the obvious: try to control the work with one of the other coordinating mechanisms. Specifically, they try to use direct supervision, standardization of work processes, or standardization of outputs.**

Direct supervision typically means imposing an intermediate level of supervision, preferably with a narrow "span of control"—in keeping with the tenets of the classical concepts of authority—to watch over the professionals. That may work in cases of gross negligence. The sloppy surgeon or the professor who misses too many classes can be "spoken to" or ultimately perhaps fired. But specific professional activities—complex in execution and vague in results—are difficult to control by anyone other than the professionals themselves. So the administrator detached from the work and bent on direct supervision is left nothing to do except engage in bothersome exercises. As in the case of certain district supervisors who sit between one Montreal school board and its schools and, according to the reports of a number of principals, spend time telephoning them at 4:59 on Friday afternoons to ensure that they have not left early for the weekend. The imposition of such intermediate levels of supervision stems from the assumption that professional work can be controlled, like any other, in a top-down manner, an assumption that has proven false again and again.

Likewise, the other forms of standardization, instead of achieving control of the professional work, often serve merely to impede and discourage the professionals. And for the same reasons—the complexity of the work and the vagueness of its outputs. Complex work processes cannot be formalized by rules and regulations, and vague outputs cannot be standardized by planning and control systems. Except in misguided ways, which program the wrong behaviors and measure the wrong outputs, forcing the professionals to play the Machine Bureaucratic game—satisfying the standards instead of serving the clients. Back to the old means–ends inversion. Like the policeman in Chicago who described to Studs Terkel the effects of various such standards on his work:

> My supervisor would say, "We need two policy arrests, so we can be equal with the other areas." So we go out and hunt for a policy operator. . . .
>
> So many points for a robbery, so many points for a man having a gun. When they go to the scene and the man with the gun has gone, they'll lock up somebody anyway, knowing he's not the one. The record says, "Locked up two people for UUW"—unlawful use of weapons. The report will say, "When we got there, we saw these guys and they looked suspicious." They'll get a point even if the case is thrown out of court. The arrest is all that counts. (1972:137, 139–40)

Graphic illustration of the futility of trying to control work that is essentially professional in nature. Similar things happen when accountants try to control the management-consulting arms of their firms—"obedience is stressed as an end in itself because the CPA as administrator is not able to judge the non-accountant expert on the basis of that expert's knowledge" (Montagna, 1968:144). And in school systems, when the government technostructure believes it can program the work of the teacher, as in that of East Germany described proudly to this author by a government planner, where each day every child in the country ostensibly opens the same book to the same page. The individual needs of the students—slow learners and fast, rural and urban—as well as the individual styles of the teachers have to be subordinated to the neatness of the system.

The fact is that complex work cannot be effectively performed unless it comes under the control of the operator who does it. Society may have to control the overall expenditures of its Professional Bureaucracies—

to keep the lid on them—and to legislate against the most callous kinds of professional behavior. But too much external control of the professional work itself leads, according to Hypothesis 14, to centralization and formalization of the structure, in effect driving the Professional Bureaucracy to Machine Bureaucracy. The decision-making power flows from the operators to the managers, and on to the analysts of the technostructure. The effect of this is to throw the baby out with the bathwater. Technocratic controls do not improve professional-type work, nor can they distinguish between responsible and irresponsible behavior—they constrain both equally. That may, of course, be appropriate for organizations in which responsible behavior is rare. But where it is not—presumably the majority of cases—**technocratic controls only serve to dampen professional conscientiousness.**

Controls also upset the delicate relationship between the professional and his client, a relationship predicated on unimpeded personal contact between the two. Thus, Cizanckas, a police chief, notes that the police officer at the bottom of the pecking order in the "paramilitary structure" is more than willing, in turn, "to vent his frustration on the lawbreaker" (paraphrased by Hatvany, 1976:73). The controls remove the responsibility for service from the professional and place it in the administrative structure, where it is of no use to the client. It is not the government that teaches the student, not even the school system or the school itself; it is not the hospital that delivers the baby, not the police force that apprehends the criminal, not the welfare department that helps the distraught family. These things are done by the individual professional. If that professional is incompetent, no plan or rule fashioned in the technostructure, no order from an administrator can ever make him competent. But such plans, rules, and orders can impede the competent professional from providing his service effectively. At least rationalization in the Machine Bureaucracy leaves the client with inexpensive outputs. In the case of professional work, it leaves him with impersonal, ineffective service.

Furthermore, **the incentive to perfect, even to innovate—the latter weak at the best of times in Professional Bureaucracy—can be reduced by external controls.** In losing control over their own work, the professionals become passive, like the operators of the Machine Bureaucracy. Even the job of professional administrator, never easy, becomes extremely difficult when there is a push for external control. In school systems, for example, the government looks top-down to the senior managers to implement its standards, and the professionals look bottom-up to them to resist the standards. The strategic apex gets caught between a government technostructure hungry for control and an operating core hanging on to its autonomy for dear life. No one gains in the process.

Are there then no solutions to a society concerned about its Professional Bureaucracies? Financial control of Professional Bureaucracies and legislation against irresponsible professional behavior are obviously necessary. But beyond that, must the professional be left with a blank check, free of public accountability? Solutions are available, but they grow from a recognition of professional work for what it is. **Change in the Professional Bureaucracy does not sweep in from new administrators taking office to announce major reforms, nor from government technostructures intent on bringing the professionals under their control. Rather, change seeps in by the slow process of changing the professionals—changing who can enter the profession, what they learn in its professional schools (norms as well as skills and knowledge), and thereafter how willing they are to upgrade their skills.** Where such changes are resisted, society may be best off to call on the professionals' sense of responsibility to serve the public, or, failing that, to bring pressures on the professional associations rather than on the Professional Bureaucracies.

11

THE DIVISIONALIZED FORM

Prime Coordinating Mechanism:	Standardization of outputs
Key Part of Organization:	Middle line
Main Design Parameters:	Market grouping, performance control system, limited vertical decentralization
Situational Factors:	Diversified markets (particularly products or services); old, large; power needs of middle managers; fashionable

Like the Professional Bureaucracy, the Divisionalized Form is not so much an integrated organization as a set of quasi-autonomous entities coupled together by a central administrative structure. But whereas those "loosely coupled" entities in the Professional Bureaucracy are individuals—professionals in the operating core—in the Divisionalized Form, they are units in the middle line. These units are generally called *divisions*, and the central administration, the *headquarters*. And here the flow of power is not bottom-up, but top-down.

The Divisionalized Form is most widely used in the private sector of the industrialized economy; the vast majority of the Fortune 500, America's largest corporations, use this structure or a variant of it. But it is also found in other sectors as well. The multiversity—the multiple campus institution, such as the University of California—uses a variant of this configuration, as does the hospital system comprising a number of specialized hospitals, and the socialist economy, where state enterprises serve as divisions and the economic agencies of the central government as the headquarters.

The Divisionalized Form differs from the other four configurations in one important respect. It does not constitute a complete structure from the strategic apex to the operating core, but rather a structure superimposed on others. That is, each division has its own structure. As we shall see, however, divisionalization has an effect on what that structure is—specifically, the divisions are drawn toward the Machine Bureaucracy configuration. But the Divisionalized Form configuration itself focuses on the structural relationship between the headquarters and the divisions; in effect, between the strategic apex and the top of the middle line. What happens beyond that is, ostensibly, inadvertent.

The Basic Structure

The design parameters

Most important, **the Divisionalized Form relies on the market basis for grouping units at the top of the middle line.** Divisions are created according to markets served and are then given control over the operating functions required to serve these markets. Thus, in Figure 11–1, a typical organigram for a divisionalized manufacturing firm, each division contains

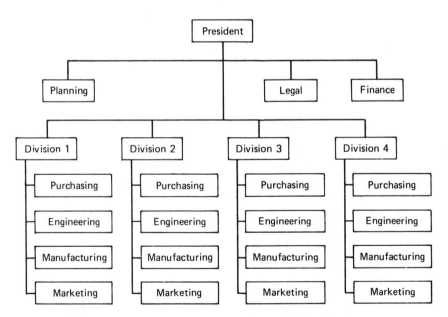

Figure 11-1. *Typical organigram for a divisionalized manufacturing firm*

its own purchasing, engineering, manufacturing, and marketing activities. **This dispersal (and duplication) of the operating functions minimizes the interdependence between divisions, so that each can operate as a quasi-autonomous entity, free of the need to coordinate with the others.** This, in turn, allows a large number of divisions to be grouped under the headquarters—in other words, **the span of control at the strategic apex of the Divisionalized Form can be rather wide.**

This structural arrangement naturally leads to pronounced decentralization from the headquarters: each division is delegated the powers needed to make the decisions concerning its own operations. But **the decentralization called for in the Divisionalized Form is highly circumscribed—not necessarily more than the delegation from the few managers at headquarters to the few more managers who run the divisions. In other words, the Divisionalized Form calls for decentralization of the parallel, limited vertical variety.** In fact, divisionalized structures can turn out to be rather *centralized* in nature. The division managers can hold the lion's share of the power, precluding further vertical decentralization (down the chain of authority) or horizontal decentralization (to staff specialists and operators). As the president of one conglomerate firm—an organization that inevitably uses the Divisionalized Form—commented:

> Our whole philosophy revolves around where profit responsibility is placed—the divisional general manager. I don't want anyone in this organization to have any doubts that the general manager is boss. This is where the entrepreneurial atmosphere begins. (quoted in Lorsch and Allen, 1973:55)

Of course, in theory, divisionalization does not preclude the further decentralization of power *within* the divisions. But as we shall soon see, other characteristics of this structure drive the divisions to centralize more power than they would if they were independent organizations.

Were the headquarters to delegate *all* its power to the division managers, it would cease to exist, and each division would, in effect, emerge as an independent organization. So some form of control or coordination is required between headquarters and the divisions. The question then becomes, How can the headquarters maintain control while allowing each division sufficient autonomy to manage its own operations? And the answer lies in one specific design parameter: the performance control system. **In general, the headquarters allows the divisions close to full autonomy to make their own decisions, and then monitors the results of these decisions.** This monitoring is done after the fact, in specific quantitative terms—in the case of the business corporations, by measures of profit, sales growth, and return on investment. As Ackerman notes, "Accounting reports are not immune to misinterpretation but they relieve the reviewer of the need to sift through and comprehend operating data from diverse businesses" (1975:49). So **the prime coordinating mechanism in the Divisionalized Form is the standardization of outputs, and a key design parameter is the performance control system.**

This coordinating mechanism and the three design parameters so far discussed determine the basic structure: market-based units at the top of the middle line; parallel, vertical decentralization to those units (but not necessarily within them); and reliance on standardization of the outputs of these units through the use of performance control systems to effect headquarters' control of the divisions. These form an ideal configuration. The market basis for grouping allows for autonomy of the divisions, which encourages decentralization to them and also allows for easy identification of their outputs, which can then be coordinated through performance control systems.

But other coordinating mechanisms and design parameters also have roles to play in this configuration, although they are not the primary ones.

The standardization of work processes is not used by headquarters as a coordinating mechanism because that would interfere with divisional autonomy. So little of the division's behavior is formalized by headquarters. Likewise, action planning is avoided because that, too, would impose decisions on the divisions that they need to make themselves. Mutual adjustment between the divisions, as well as the liaison devices that encourage it, are also precluded in this structure by the absence of interdependence between the divisions.

There is, however, a limited role for the two coordinating mechanisms that remain—standardization of skills and direct supervision. The Divisionalized Form is dependent for its success on the competence of the divisional managers, to whom much of the decision-making power is delegated. Whereas the managers at the top of the middle line of the other configurations tend to have functional orientations and limited freedom to act independently, those of the Divisionalized Form are "mini–general managers," who run their own operations. That is why the middle line emerges as the key part of this structure. But this characteristic puts the onus on the headquarters to train these division managers as well as it can (in effect, to standardize their managerial skills). Likewise, indoctrination is used to ensure that the division managers pursue the broader goals of the headquarters instead of the parochial goals of their divisions. Divisional managers are brought back to headquarters periodically for conferences and meetings with the central administrators, and they are sometimes rotated around the different divisions to develop a broad perspective of the organization. Direct supervision serves as a backup mechanism of coordination in the Divisionalized Form. When a division runs into trouble, the headquarters managers may have to step in, perhaps to replace the division manager. So some knowledge of the operations of the division is required, at least to know when to step in, as well as how. This need for direct supervision reduces the span of control of headquarters managers somewhat.

The structure of the divisions

Given an understanding of the means of control of the divisions by head-quarters—through performance controls backed up by management training, indoctrination, and direct supervision—we can return to the question of decentralization within the divisions. In theory, the Divisionalized Form can be superimposed on any of the other configurations. A multiversity or a national accounting firm with regional offices draws a set of Professional Bureaucracies into the Divisionalized Form; a newspaper chain does the same thing with a set of Adhocracies. And a venture capitalist with equity control of entrepreneurial firms may draw a set of Simple Structures into the Divisionalized Form. The divisions of any one organization may also exhibit a variety of structures, as, say, in the case of a municipal government with four "divisions"—a small Simple Structure antipoverty program, a Machine Bureaucracy sanitation service, a Professional Bureaucracy police force, and an Adhocracy urban development group.

But the Divisionalized Form works best with Machine Bureaucracy structures in its divisions and, moreover, drives these structures, no matter what their natural inclinations, toward the Machine Bureaucracy form. The explanation of this important point lies in the standardization of outputs, the key to the functioning of the divisionalized structure. The only way that headquarters can retain control yet protect divisional autonomy is by after-the-fact monitoring of divisional performance. That requires the establishment of clearly defined performance standards, the existence of which depends on two major assumptions. First, **each division must be treated as a single integrated system with a single, consistent set of goals.** In other words, although the divisions may be loosely coupled with each other, the assumption is that each is tightly coupled within.[1] Second, **those goals must be operational ones—in other words, lend themselves to quantitative measures of performance control.** In the organic configurations—Simple Structure and Adhocracy, which exist in dynamic environments—such performance standards are difficult to establish. In the Professional Bureaucracy, as noted in the last chapter, the complexity of the work precludes the establishment of such standards. Moreover, the Professional Bureaucracy is not one integrated system but a collection of individuals with a wide range of goals. That leaves only one configuration that satisfies the assumptions: the Machine Bureaucracy. In other words, the Division-

---

[1]Unless, of course, there is a second layer of divisions, as we shall see later, which simply takes this conclusion down another level in the hierarchy.

alized Form is best superimposed on the Machine Bureaucracy, the only structure that is integrated and has operational goals.

Now, what happens when the Divisionalized Form is superimposed on one of the other three configurations? To make that form work, the assumptions must be made to hold. That is, each division must be made to function as a single integrated system, on which one set of performance measures can be imposed. The division manager, to whom power is delegated from the headquarters, must be able to impose the measures on his division; in other words, he must treat it as a top-down, regulated system. For the Professional Bureaucracy and Adhocracy—in large part bottom-up and nonregulated—that amounts to a pressure to centralize. Moreover, when the division is organized on a functional basis—as it typically is in the Simple Structure, Machine Bureaucracy, and Adhocracy—the division manager is forced to use an action-planning system to ensure that division personnel pursue the performance goals. Action planning imposes ever more specific standards concerning decisions and actions on personnel down the line. That amounts to pressure to formalize (and bureaucratize) the structure of the division, especially the Simple Structure and Adhocracy, which are organic to begin with. So the Divisionalized Form drives the divisions to be more centralized and more formalized than they would be as independent organizations. (That is, of course, the effect predicted from Hypothesis 14, since the headquarters is a specific form of external control of the division.) And these are the two distinguishing characteristics of the Machine Bureaucracy. So we conclude that divisionalization drives the structure of the divisions, no matter what their natural inclinations, toward the Machine Bureaucracy form. The performance control system of the Divisionalized Form weakens the organic nature of the Simple Structure and the Adhocracy, and it upsets the notion of operator autonomy in the Professional Bureaucracy.[2] Only in the Machine Bureaucracy does divisionalization require no fundamental chance in structure.

Why, then, is "divisionalization" treated in so much of the literature as synonymous with "decentralization" (and implicitly with debureaucratization)? The answer seems to lie in the origins of the configuration. As

---

[2]Indeed, it could not be otherwise. If the divisions remained as Professional Bureaucracies, for example, the professional operators would retain their usual power, and so their control of the administrative structure would naturally extend beyond the divisions into the headquarters; as a result, the position of divisional manager would have no special relevance, and the entire organization would emerge as a single Professional Bureaucracy. What makes a structure divisionalized is *managerial* or *unit* autonomy, not professional autonomy. Alternatively, giving a great deal of power to department managers of a single Professional Bureaucracy drives the structure toward the Divisionalized Form. This apparently happened when deans and department heads assumed much power in the German universities early in this century, and apparently happens to a lesser extent in the British universities today for the same reason (Beyer and Lodahl, 1976:110).

certain Machine Bureaucracy corporations in America grew and diversified their markets early in this century, they became increasingly unwieldly—too centralized and too bureaucratic. The development of the Divisionalized Form—in du Pont in 1921—came as a godsend. Instead of one integrated functional structure, a set of them could be designed, one for each market. This eased the bottleneck at the strategic apex, allowing for less centralization and less formalization. So, compared with the Machine Bureaucracy structure—that is, with *one* overall Machine Bureaucracy for all markets—the Divisionalized Form, by creating many smaller and more focused Machine Bureaucracies, reduced the overall centralization of the structure.

But is the Divisionalized Form inherently decentralized, or, to be specific, more decentralized than the other configurations? Than the Simple Structure, with all power concentrated in a single office, certainly. Than the Machine Bureaucracy (operating in one market, as it is designed to do), not clear. Who is to say which structure distributes its power more widely—the one with limited *horizontal* decentralization, where the few analysts of the technostructure share power with the managers of the strategic apex, or the one with limited *vertical* decentralization, where the few managers at the top of the middle line share that power? And than the Professional Bureaucracy or Adhocracy, with their extensive decentralization deep into the line structure and out to a large number of operating or staff specialists, certainly not.

Moreover, there is another, more logical alternative to the Divisionalized Form: complete fragmentation of the organization. And that is also more decentralized. It is a rather small step from quasi-autonomous divisions controlled by one central headquarters to fully autonomous organizations, each controlled by its own board of directors. In fact, the Divisionalized Form often emerges not from the "decentralization" of a Machine Bureaucracy operating in many markets, but from the "centralization" of a set of independent organizations operating in different markets. They consolidate themselves into a single "federation" with a Divisionalized Form configuration, in the process surrendering some of their powers to a new central headquarters.

Ironically, this is what happened in the most famous example of divisionalization, the one most frequently touted as "decentralization"—Alfred P. Sloan's restructuring of General Motors in the 1920s. It was this example that set off the first waves of divisionalization among the Fortune 500. Yet no example better illustrates the fallacy of the "divisionalization means decentralization" relationship. For although Sloan may have divisionalized General Motors, by no stretch of the imagination did he decentralize it. As a well-known student of his actions commented, "If any *one* word is needed to describe the management *structure* of General Motors as it was recast by Sloan and the brilliant group around him, then that word is not decentralization, but *centralization"* (Harold Wolff, quoted in Perrow, 1974:38). As Chandler (1962) and even Sloan (1963) himself tell it, William C. Durant put General Motors together as a holding company, but failed to consolidate it into a single entity. Sloan was brought in to do that job. He instituted central controls, which reduced the power of the unit managers by subjecting their performance to headquarters control. In other words, Sloan consolidated the structure to the Divisionalized Form, and thereby centralized it. (Later in this chapter we shall see that this process of centralizing power in General Motors apparently continued throughout this century to the point where the current structure of the automotive component of the company can no longer be called divisionalized.)

The powers of the divisions and the headquarters

Both communication and decision flows in the Divisionalized Form reflect one central fact: **There is a sharp division of labor between the headquarters and the divisions. Communication between the two is circumscribed and largely formal, in good part restricted to the transmission of performance standards down to the divisions and of performance results back up. This is supplemented by personal interchanges between the managers at the two levels, but that is carefully limited. Too much detailed knowledge at the headquarters level can invite meddling in the decisions of the divisions, thereby defeating the very purpose of divisionalization—namely, divisional autonomy.**

In the Divisionalized Form, **the divisions are given the power to run their own businesses. They control the operations and determine the strategies for the markets that fall under their responsibility.** What powers then are retained by the headquarters? We shall discuss six in all. The first is the formation of the organization's overall product-market strategy. Whereas the divisions determine the strategies for given product markets, the headquarters decides which ones will be given. In effect, **the headquarters manages the strategic portfolio,** establishing, acquiring, selling, and closing down divisions in order to change its mix of products and markets. This, in fact, is one of the main reasons for using the Divisionalized Form and, according to studies of du Pont in the 1920s, explains why it evolved in the first place:

> Unencumbered by operating duties, the senior executives at the general office now had the time, information, and more of a psychological commitment to carry on the entrepreneurial activities and make the strategic decisions necessary to keep the over-all enterprise alive and growing and to coordinate, appraise, and plan for the work of the divisions. (Chandler, 1962:111)

Second, **headquarters allocates the overall financial resources.** Only pooled coupling exists among the divisions. That is, they do not pass their work back and forth but do share common financial resources. It is clearly the responsibility of the headquarters to manage these resources—to draw excess funds from the divisions that do not need them, to raise additional funds in the capital markets when necessary, and to allocate available funds among the divisions that do need them. Headquarters' power over resource allocation also includes the authorization of those divisional capital projects large enough to affect the overall capital budget of the organization. The need to seek such authorization may constitute some interference with the autonomy of the divisions, but that is an interference necessary to ensure the balanced allocation of funds. In general, however, the assessment by headquarters of divisional capital projects is purely financial in nature—concerned only with questions of risk and availability of funds, not with those of product-market strategy.

The key to the control of the divisions in this configuration is the performance control system. Hence, as its third major power, **the headquarters designs the performance control system.** The managers there, with the aid of their own technostructure, set up the system. They decide on performance measures and reporting periods, establish formats for plans and budgets, and design an MIS to feed performance results back to headquarters. They then operate the system, setting targets for each reporting period, perhaps jointly with the divisional managers, and reviewing the MIS results.

What happens when the MIS signals that a division has run into trouble, that it can no longer meet its performance targets? The management at headquarters must first decide whether the problem lies in conditions beyond the control of the division or in it. If the former—the problem being an economic downturn, the arrival of new competition, or whatever—headquarters basically has the choice of divesting itself of the division or carrying it financially to ride out the trouble. In other words, it acts in terms of one of its first two powers, the management of the strategic portfolio or the allocation of financial resources. But if the problem is perceived to lie in the division, then headquarters draws on its fourth major power. **The headquarters replaces and appoints the managers of the divisions.** This is a crucial power in the Divisionalized Form, because the structure precludes direct interference by the headquarters managers in the operating affairs of the divisions; the closest they can come is to determine who will run the divisions. To an important extent, therefore, success in the Divisionalized Form depends on this fourth power, on selecting the right people—general managers with the ability to run quasi-autonomous operations effectively, yet in accordance with the goals of the overall organization.

The performance control system may signal a problem in a division, but it is of little help in determining whether that problem is rooted in adverse conditions or incompetent management. Moreover, there are times when the performance control system fails to do a proper job of reporting problems. Being dependent on quantitative historical data, the MIS sometimes misses the nuances that signal imminent problems. The MIS can also be manipulated by the divisional management, as when an advertising or research budget is cut to show better short-term profit at the expense of long-run profitability. So, although the headquarters depends on the MIS to monitor divisional behavior, it cannot rely exclusively on that system. This leads to the fifth function. **The headquarters monitors divisional behavior on a personal basis.** Here coordination reverts partly back to direct supervision as a supplement to the standardization of outputs. Headquarters managers—sometimes called "group executives" and given charge of a number of divisions—visit the divisions periodically to "keep in touch," to get to know them well enough to be able to foresee problems. Such knowledge also enables the headquarters managers to assess requests by divisions for large capital expenditures, and it gives them knowledge of the people in the divisions when replacements must be made.

But, as noted earlier, too much direct supervision defeats the purpose of the Divisionalized Form—the provision of autonomy to the units in the middle line. So in normal times, the headquarters managers stand on a tightrope between being ignorant of division problems and becoming so familiar with them that they are tempted to interfere in their solution. Some divisionalized organizations try to achieve the right balance by restricting the size of the headquarters. In Textron in 1970, for example, with sales of more than $1.5 billion from thirty different divisions, the headquarters staff numbered only thirty executives and administrators, and the group vice-presidents had no assistants or private technocratic staff, just one secretary each.

As its sixth and final power, **the headquarters provides certain support services common to the divisions.** The location of support services—their concentration in headquarters or dispersal to the divisions—is a major design issue for the Divisionalized Form. Services that must be geared to the needs of single divisions, those that must be located in physically convenient places, and those that are relatively easy to duplicate—as in the cases of a marketing research group, a cafeteria, and a public relations unit, respectively—are typically dispersed to the divisions (and are sometimes duplicated at headquarters as well). But coordinated services that must be offered across the range of divisions, or those that must be provided at the common strategic apex, are concentrated in single units at headquarters. Thus, a central finance unit supports the headquarters role of resource allocation; looks after income tax, insurance, pension matters, and the like common to the different divisions; and may also house the technocratic staffers concerned with the performance control system. Again, however, any organization that wishes to be divisionalized must severely limit the number of support services it provides at headquarters. Each one imposes decisions on the divisions, thereby curtailing their autonomy.

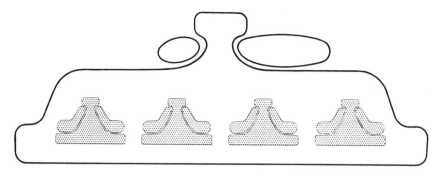

Figure 11-2. *The Divisionalized Form*

To conclude our discussion of the basic structure, Figure 11–2 shows the Divisionalized Form represented symbolically in terms of our logo. Headquarters is shown in three parts: a small strategic apex of top managers; a small technostructure to the left, concerned with the design and operation of the performance control system as well as some of the management-development programs; and a slightly larger staff support group to the right. Four divisions are shown below the headquarters, with a bulge put in at the level of division manager to indicate that the middle line is the key part of the organization. All four divisions are represented as Machine Bureaucracies to illustrate our point that divisionalization encourages the divisions to use this configuration.

Conditions of the Divisionalized Form

Market diversity

One situational factor above all drives the organization to use the Divisionalized Form—market diversity. The organization faced with a single integrated market simply cannot split itself into autonomous divisions; the one with distinct markets, however, has an incentive to create a unit to deal with each. This enables the organization to manage its strategic portfolio centrally, while giving each component of that portfolio the undivided attention of one unit.

This relationship between diversification and divisionalization has received a good deal of support in the literature. Research has demonstrated the spread of structural divisionalization as a direct response to product diversification. This has proceeded in waves, particularly since World War II, encompassing most of the Fortune 500 and then jumping across the Atlantic to large corporations in England, Germany, France, and Italy.

In our discussion of the conditions surrounding the other configurations, we noted that not only do the situational factors influence the choice

225

of the design parameters; the design parameters also influence the "choice" of the situational factors. In other words, the situational factors form a part of the configurations we are discussing. Here we have an excellent example of this. Chandler argued that structure follows strategy, that structural divisionalization results from strategic diversification. But the opposite relationship has held up in some research as well, that **divisionalization encourages further diversification.** The ease with which headquarters can add new divisions in this structure encourages it to do so; moreover, divisionalization generates a steady stream of general managers who look for more and larger divisions to run.

> . . . the divisional structure becomes a built-in "school of management," training middle level general managers in the problems and opportunities associated with economic responsibility. As a result, this form of organization provides a pool of trained talent from which to draw, a pool from which a new group may be formed in a few days or weeks to take over and manage a new activity. Both the structure and the internal "schooling" facilitate *rapid* and *profitable* exploitation of new ideas, a key element in the growth strategies of the [divisionalized] firms. (Scott, 1971:14)

This seems to explain why one study found that the more diversified American firms on the domestic scene were the ones most likely to develop international operations: when new products ran out at home, the aggressive young managers could be satisfied with foreign subsidiaries to manage.

In Chapter 3 we discussed three kinds of market diversity—product and service, client, and region. In theory, all three can lead to divisionalization. Physically dispersed markets, for example, create communication problems that give the organization an incentive to set up geographical divisions to deal with each region, as in retail chains, post offices, and railroads serving large areas. Add to this high transportation costs—as in the case of a cement manufacturer—and there is further incentive to divisionalize on a regional basis. Yet, **based on client or regional diversification in the absence of product or service diversification, divisionalization often turns out to be incomplete.** With identical products or services in each region or for each group of clients, the headquarters is encouraged to centralize a good deal of decision making and concentrate a good deal of support service at the center, to ensure common operating standards for all the divisions. This centralization and concentration of certain functions—some of them critical in formulating product-market strategies—seriously reduces divisional autonomy. In effect, the structure is driven toward integrated Machine Bureaucracy, but with one difference: Its operations are divided into distinct market-based units. Thus, one study found that insurance companies concentrate the critical function of investment, and retailers that of purchasing. The headquarters of the latter control sources of supply, product range, pricing, and volume terms, as well as site and property development and merchandising. Day-to-day operations of the retail stores are left to the store managers, who are supervised by a regional hierarchy.

We shall use the term *carbon-copy bureaucracy* for this hybrid of Divisionalized Form and Machine Bureaucracy, the structure that results when an organization sets up identical regional divisions and then concentrates certain critical functions at headquarters. Each division is a replica—a carbon copy—of all the others, performing the same activities in the same ways, unique only in its location. The carbon-copy bureaucracy is, in fact, found in all the examples given above of regional divisionalization, but it is probably most common in retailing—the supermarket chain with fifty identical stores, the post office with a duplicated facility in each city of the nation, the motel or fast-food franchise, where, once inside, customers can hardly tell whether they are in Driggs, Idaho, or Dublin, Ireland.

The carbon-copy bureaucracy can also be found in the manufacturing sector, where a simple and stable environment and standard products drive the structure toward Machine Bureaucracy, but dispersed markets coupled with either high transportation costs or perishable products encourage the organization to replicate its production facilities in different regions. Common examples are bakeries, breweries, cement producers, and soft-drink bottlers. They produce and market their products in each city of any size, subject to tight standards set and enforced by the central headquarters. (The recent introduction of a small oven in our local bread store—part of a chain operating exclusively in the Montreal area—suggests that manufacturing carbon-copy bureaucracies can exist on small scales indeed.)

The giant multinational enterprise with identical product lines in various national markets also tends to resemble the carbon-copy bureaucracy. A division or "subsidiary" is created in each market to manufacture and distribute the products subject to the dictates of headquarters. In other words, certain critical functions—most notably product development—are retained by the central administration. Of course, the more foreign the subsidiary, the more it needs the power to adapt the products and marketing techniques to its local conditions; in other words, the greater is the pull to pure divisionalization. But the multinational enterprise can avoid that pull by concentrating on products that can be standardized throughout the world (Coca-Cola being the classic example), and by avoiding very foreign markets. Thus, American corporations have typically expanded first into Canada—close, convenient, and minimally foreign—then into Europe, later perhaps beyond, but not frequently to the cultures most foreign to the West.

In Canada, in fact, the phenomenon of the headless subsidiary—one with no control over its main strategies—is so common that it has merited a special name: the *miniature replica effect*. It is set up in Canada to produce products designed in the United States according to American specifications on production lines engineered by the American technostructure. It is interesting how often these firms have reacted to attacks by Canadian nationalists with the claim that all their employees but one are Canadian nationals. That one is, of course, the president, placed on the shoulders of the subsidiary to receive the orders from its brain in New York.

Technical system

What of the role of the other situational factors—besides market diversity—in the Divisionalized Form? In one sense, technical system is a factor, specifically its economies of scale. **Divisionalization is possible only when the organization's technical system can be efficiently separated into segments, one for each division.** For example, whereas a geographically diversified cement company can duplicate its processing facilities many times across the face of the nation, a likewise diversified aluminum company with the same sales volume may be unable to if it cannot afford more than one smelter. And so the aluminum company retains a functional structure. (Even for the cement producer, divisionalization may be incomplete: Geographical diversification, as noted above, tends to encourage a functional-divisional hybrid, often the carbon-copy bureaucracy.) When it is the product lines rather than the geographical regions that are diversified, separation of the technical system usually takes place naturally, no matter what the economies of scale; different product lines require different technical systems to begin with.

There is, however, evidence of a more important, although indirect, relation between economies of scale and divisionalization. Organizations that must devote huge capital resources to very high fixed-cost technical systems—steel and aluminum producers, and other "heavies" of American industry—tend not to diversify in the first place, and so not to divisionalize. To be more precise, as a group they show little enthusiasm for "horizontal" diversification—into parallel or unrelated product lines. They do diversify "vertically," moving into the product lines at the two ends of their production chains, thereby becoming their own suppliers and customers. But as we shall see later in this chapter, the strong interdependences between product lines in the same production chain leads to an incomplete form of divisionalization.

Environment

In respect to the factors of environment, the Divisionalized Form differs funamentally from the other four configurations. Each of those has its own particular environment, specifically one of the four boxes of the static–dynamic, simple–complex matrix discussed in Chapter 6. In other words, whereas it is primarily the broad environmental dimensions of stability and complexity that position the other configurations, it is another, more restricted environmental dimension—market diversity, in particular, product diversity—that positions the Divisionalized Form.' This narrows its range of application considerably compared with the other four configurations.

Nevertheless, the Divisionalized Form does have a preferred environment, which it shares with the Machine Bureaucracy. That is because of another condition prerequisite to the use of the Divisionalized Form—outputs (specifically performance criteria) that can be standardized. As we saw in the last chapter, complex environments lead to outputs that cannot be measured or standardized. Likewise, in dynamic environments, outputs and performance standards cannot easily be pinned down. So **the Divisionalized Form works best in environments that are neither very complex nor very dynamic; in fact, the very same environments that favor the Machine Bureaucracy.** This leads to a rather precise specification of the conditions that most commonly accompany this configuration: **the Divisionalized Form is the structural response to a Machine Bureaucracy, operating in a simple, stable environment (typically without huge economies of scale), that has diversified its product or service lines horizontally.**

When an organization attempts to force divisionalization on units operating in other kinds of environments—complex or dynamic ones—where the outputs cannot be measured by performance controls, a hybrid structure normally results. In effect, the headquarters must rely on some mechanism other than the standardization of outputs to control the divisions. If it turns to rules and regulations—in effect, the imposition of standards that control decisions and work processes of the divisions directly—then a hybrid results with Machine Bureaucracy, similar to the carbon-copy bureaucracy. If, instead, the headquarters managers increase their personal surveillance (direct supervision) of the divisions through more frequent contact with their managers, then a hybrid with Simple Structure results, which we can call the *personalized divisionalized form.* Alternatively, should they seek to control the behavior of the divisions primarily through socialization—in effect, appointing only managers they can trust fully because these have been through an extensive program of indoctrination or for some other reason identify strongly with it—then a hybrid with some characteristics of Professional Bureaucracy emerges, which we can call the *socialized divisionalized form.*

Competition is another variable that has been suggested as an environmental determinant of the Divisionalized Form. In particular, Franko (1974) concluded in a study of European multinational firms that the absence of competition may delay the adaption of the Divisionalized Form despite product diversification. He found that European companies operating in cartels and the like tended to maintain their functional structures long after they diversified. Likewise, Scott (1973:141) found the most rapid spread of divisionalization in America during periods when competitive pressures were maintained by antitrust legislation and economic conditions, and in Europe when competitive pressures were generated by the Common Market and by supply catching up with demand in the 1960s.

This argument makes sense, but it is not unique to the Divisionalized Form. It is the need for efficiency that drives all organizations to make sure their structures match their situation. (That was the point of the congruence hypothesis presented in Chapter 6.) Structural change always lags situational change, the length of that lag affected by the pressures to be efficient. Competitive pressures figure prominently among these, not only forcing a shift to the Divisionalized Form soon after product diversification, but also presumably forcing a quick shift back to the functional form should the organization later consolidate its product lines.

Age and size

What about the factors of age and size? Although large size itself does not bring on divisionalization, surely it is not coincidental that most of America's largest corporations use some form of this structure. The fact is that **as organizations grow large, they become prone to diversify and then to divisionalize.** One reason is protection: Large manufacturing firms tend to be organized as Machine Bureaucracies, structures that, as we noted in Chapter 9, try to avoid risks. Diversification spreads the risk. Also, the larger a firm becomes vis-à-vis its competitors, the more it comes to dominate its traditional market. Eventually, it simply runs out of room for expansion (because there is no market share left or because its dominance has come to the attention of the antitrust regulators), and so it must find further growth opportunities elsewhere. Thus it diversifies, and later must divisionalize. Moreover, as noted earlier, divisionalization creates a cadre of aggressive general managers who push for further diversification and further growth. So we must conclude that there is, in fact, an important relationship between size and divisionalization, with diversification the intermediate variable. The giant corporations—with the few exceptions that remain in one business because of enormously high fixed-cost technical systems—not only require divisionalization but were able to reach their giant size only because of it.

In fact, many corporations have grown so large and diversified that the simple Divisionalized Form is not sufficient for them. They make use of a variant we call the *multiple-divisionalized form,* with divisions on top of divisions. For example, regional divisions may be superimposed on product divisions, or broad product divisions ("groups") may be superimposed on narrower ones, as in the case of General Electric, shown later in this chapter in Figure 11–5.

Like size, age is also associated with the Divisionalized Form. In larger organizations, the management runs out of places to expand in the traditional markets; in older ones, the managers sometimes get bored with the traditional markets and find diversion through diversification. In other cases, time brings new competitors into old market niches, forcing the management to look for new ones with better potential. Thus, with divisionalization most common among the largest and oldest corporations, the Divisionalized Form emerged in Chapter 6 as the third stage of structural development, following Maching Bureaucracy.

The Divisionalized Form need not, however, always follow other configurations at a late stage of development. Some organizations, in fact, begin their lives with it. They divisionalize from without, so to speak; that is, they agglomerate rather than diversify. Independent organizations that join together to form new alliances—perhaps to benefit from the sharing of financial resources or support services—but are intent on guarding as much of their previous autonomy as possible naturally prefer a variant of the Divisionalized Form. These alliances, generally known as associations or *federations,* occur when farmers create cooperatives to market their produce and when small construction firms do likewise to match the power of large unions or bigger competitors. Of course, not all agglomerations are voluntary: Stock-market operators take over corporations in proxy fights and force them into federations, as do governments when they nationalize firms to pool their resources for purposes of national planning or the development of the scale needed to meet foreign competition. When the units of the federated organization produce common products or services, strong pressures naturally arise to consolidate their activities into a tighter structure—specifically to concentrate critical functions at the administrative headquarters—and the divisionalized structure tends to be driven to an integrated Machine Bureaucracy one.

Power

These last points introduce our final set of situational factors, those related to power, which also play a role in the Divisionalized Form configuration. We have just seen that power can explain federation: Small organizations need to band together to match the power of the bigger ones, and governments or owners use their power to force unwilling partners to federate. We also saw earlier the role of power within the structure, that of the division managers who encourage growth, diversification, and divisionalization to enhance their own positions. Even in the functionally structured organization, the drive by the aggressive middle manager for more autonomy amounts to a pull to divisionalize at his level of the hierarchy. And in the case of the top manager, the Divisionalized Form is by far the most effective structure by which to increase the power of his overall organization, since it enables units to be added with relatively little effort and disruption. (Internally, the top manager must, of course, share much of that increased power with the divisional managers.) Indeed, the waves of conglomerate diversification in U.S. industry appear to represent a giant power game, with corporate chief executives vying with each other to see who can build the largest empire.

These same factors of power have hardly been absent in other spheres as well, helping to explain the growth in popularity of the Divisionalized Form in unions, school systems, universities, and especially governments. Thus, we have the story of the president of a multiversity—one public university among six in a Canadian province—who justified his attempt to take over the two smallest ones with the argument that it would be more "convenient" for the government to negotiate with four administrations instead of six. No mention of augmenting his power, no mention of the costs of his administration having to negotiate with two new campuses, no mention of the effects on those two small Professional Bureaucracies of the introduction of another, intermediate layer of supervision.

As government grows larger—itself often spurred on by similar "convenient" power grabs—it is forced more and more to revert to a kind of Divisionalized Form. That is, the central administrators, being unable to control all the agencies and departments (divisions) directly, settle for granting their managers considerable autonomy and then try to control their performance. One can, in fact, view the entire government as a giant Divisionalized Form (admittedly an oversimplification, since all kinds of interdependences exist among the departments), with its three main coordinative agencies corresponding to three main forms of control used by the headquarters of the divisionalized organization. The budgetary agency, technocratic in nature, concerns itself with performance control of the departments; the public service commission, also partly technocratic, concerns itself with the recruiting and training of government managers; and the executive (or Privy Council) office reviews the major proposals and initiatives of the departments. Perhaps this concept of the government as a giant Divisionalized Form is taken to its natural conclusion in the communist state, where public corporations and other agencies are tightly regulated by planning and control systems operated by a powerful central technostructure.

Finally, there is fashion, not an insignificant factor in the popularity of the Divisionalized Form. Our comments above suggest that this structural form is becoming increasingly popular in the public and institutional sectors. In the private sector, as noted, divisionalization became fashionable after the restructuring of du Pont and General Motors in the 1920s. Since that time, American corporations have undergone a number of waves of such structural change. Much of this was, as we have seen, stimulated by diversification. But not all. As one student of the Fortune 500 noted in looking at his data on divisionalization, structure also follows fashion (Rumelt, 1974:149). In recent years, some managements have re-organized "in response to normative theory rather than actual administrative pressure" (p. 77). In Europe, until recently, the Divisionalized Form was unfashionable, with many diversified corporations resisting its use. Now the pendulum has swung the other way, and no doubt some corporations with integrated markets have been carried along, to their eventual regret.

Stages in the Transition to the Divisionalized Form

We have a good deal of research on the transition of the corporation from the functional to the Divisionalized Form, much of it from the Harvard Business School, which has shown a special interest in the structure of the large corporation. Figure 11–3 and the discussion that follows borrow from these results to describe four stages of that transition.

We begin with the large corporation that produces all its products through one chain and so retains what we call the integrated form—a pure functional structure, a Machine Bureaucracy or perhaps an Adhocracy. As the corporation begins to market some of the intermediate products of its production processes, it makes the first shift toward divisionalization, called the by-product form. Further moves in the same direction, to the point where the by-products become more important than end products although a central theme remains in the product-market strategy, lead to a structure closer to the divisionalized one, which is called the related-product form. And finally, the complete breakdown of the production chain, to the point where the different products have no relationship with each other, takes the corporation to the conglomerate form, a pure divisional structure. Although some corporations may move through all these stages in sequence, we shall see that others stop at one stage along the way because of very high fixed-cost technical systems (typical in the case of the integrated form), operations based on a single raw material (typical in the case of the by-product form), or focus on a core technology or market theme (typical in the case of the related-product form).

The integrated form

At the top of Figure 11–3 is the pure functional form, used by the corporation whose production activities form one integrated, unbroken chain. Only the final output is sold to the customers. The tight interdependences of the different activities make it impossible for such corporations to use the Divisionalized Form—that is, to grant autonomy to units performing any of the steps in the chain—and so they organize themselves as func-

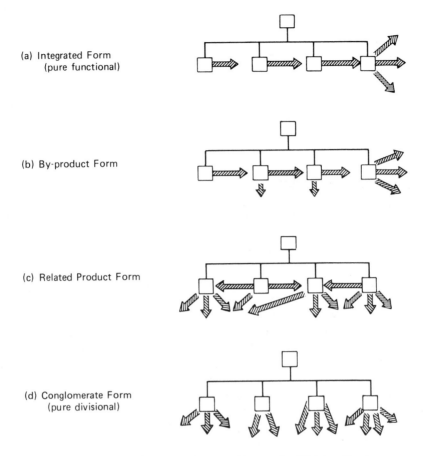

(a) Integrated Form
(pure functional)

(b) By-product Form

(c) Related Product Form

(d) Conglomerate Form
(pure divisional)

Figure 11-3. *Stages in the transition to the Divisionalized Form*

tional Machine Bureaucracies (or Adhocracies, if they face complex, dynamic environments). They typically product a single product line, or at least one line dominates. Large firms using this structure also tend to be vertically integrated and capital-intensive. Units responsible for different steps in the production chain are sometimes called "divisions," but since they have no choice but to buy from or sell to their sister units in the same corporation, they are essentially functional departments—means to the ultimate ends, or markets—and lack the autonomy of true divisions.

Ironically, despite its reputation as the very model of divisionalization, General Motors seems to fit best into this category. That is, aside from its nonautomotive activities, which are relatively small (under 10 percent of total sales), the corporation seems not to be truly divisionalized at all, despite its use of that term. Earlier we saw that Sloan consolidated the structure of General Motors in the 1920s, converted a holding company into a divisionalized one. In fact, he continued to consolidate it throughout his tenure as chief executive officer, as, apparently, did his successors right up to the present time. Thus, one study of General Motors (Wrigley, 1970) describes its automobile production process as one integrated "closed system," with neither the assembly operation nor Fisher Body permitted to sell its services to the open market, nor the automotive "divisions" (Chevrolet, Buick, and so on) to buy the services they need from that market. Central control of research, styling, engineering, plant construction, production scheduling, quality control, pricing, and labor and dealer relations renders the structure a virtual functional one, with the divisions in some ways resembling marketing departments (with circumscribed powers even over that function).

The by-product form

As the integrated firm seeks wider markets, it may choose to diversify its end-product lines and shift all the way over to the pure divisional structure. A less risky alternative, however, is to start by marketing its intermediate products on the open market. This introduces small breaks in its processing chain, which in turn call for a measure of divisionalization in its structure, what can be called the *by-product form*. Each link in the processing chain can now be given some autonomy in order to market its by-products, although it is understood that most of its outputs will be passed on internally to the next link in the chain. But because the processing chain remains more or less intact, headquarters retains considerable control over strategy formulation and some aspects of operations as well. Specifically, it relies on action planning to manage the interdependences between the divisions.

Many of the organizations that fall into this category are vertically integrated ones that base their operations on a single basic material, such as wood, oil, or aluminum, which they process to a variety of consumable end products. Figure 11–4 shows the 1969 processing chain for Alcoa, which earned 69 percent of its revenue from fabricated aluminum end products, such as cookware and auto parts, and 27 percent from intermediate by-products, including cargo space, chemicals, bauxite, and pit and ingot aluminum. (Real estate development—a horizontally diversified service—accounted for the remaining 4 percent.)

The related-product form

Some corporations continue to diversify their by-product markets, further breaking down their processing chain until what the divisions sell on the open market becomes more important than what they supply to each other. The organization then moves to the *related-product form*. For exam-

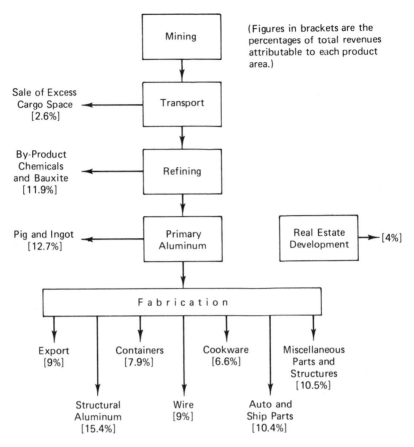

Figure 11-4. *By-product and end-product sales of Alcoa in 1969 (from Rumelt, 1974:21; prepared from data in company's annual reports)*

ple, a firm manufacturing washing machines may set up a division to produce the motors. Eventually, the motor division may become so successful on its own that the washing-machine division is no longer its dominant customer. A more serious form of divisionalization is then called for, to reflect the greater independence of the divisions.

What typically holds the divisions of these firms together is some common thread among their products, sometimes a core skill or technology, sometimes a central market theme. The divisions often sell to many of the same outside customers as well. In effect, the firm retains a semblance of an integrated product-market strategy.

Central planning at the headquarters in the related-product form must be less constraining than in the by-product form, more concerned with measuring performance than prescribing actions. A good deal of the control over the specific product-market strategies must revert to the divisions. But the interdependencies around the central product-market theme encourage the headquarters to retain functions common to the divisions— for example, research and development in the case of a core technology. These central functions are, of course, the "critical" ones for the corporation, so the functional/divisional hybrids—specifically, the ones with *product* or *service* divisions, such as insurance companies that centralize the critical function of investment—would fall into this grouping.

So too might a firm such as General Electric, whose organigram (circa 1975) is shown in Figure 11–5. As Wrigley described the firm in 1970, some products, such as artificial diamonds, were sold mainly to outside users, whereas others, such as small motors, were supplied both to inside and outside users. The structure was divisionalized—in fact, as can be seen, multiple-divisionalized—in a typical way, except that there were a greater number of support services at headquarters than we described earlier for the basic structure. Wrigley noted that these included labor relations (with line responsibility for major negotiations), market forecasting, engineering, and marketing (the last two providing consulting services), as well as the "spearhead" of the firm's massive research and development effort— one of its critical functions. He also noted that the division managers were given little control over management development or suppliers, two other functions apparently viewed as critical. Otherwise they had considerable freedom to run their own businesses and formulate their product-market strategies.

The conglomerate form

As the related-product firm expands into new markets or acquires other firms, with less and less regard for a central strategic theme, the organization moves to the *conglomerate form* and adopts a pure divisionalized structure, the one we described earlier in this chapter as the basic structure. Each division serves its own markets, producing product lines unrelated to those of the other divisions—thumbtacks in one, steam shovels in a second, funeral services in a third. In the conglomerate, there are no important interdependences among the divisions, save for the pooling of resources. As a result, the headquarters planning and control system becomes simply a vehicle for regulating performance, specifically financial performance. And the headquarters staff diminishes to almost nothing—a few general or group managers supported by some financial analysts and a minimum of other services. As a chief executive of Textron commented— where a central staff of thirty oversaw thirty divisions doing more than $1.5 billion of sales volume:

> A key concept is that we have a minimum of home staff. It consists almost entirely of line managers and clerical personnel, with virtually no staff helping the line managers. We have no R and D section or manufacturing section

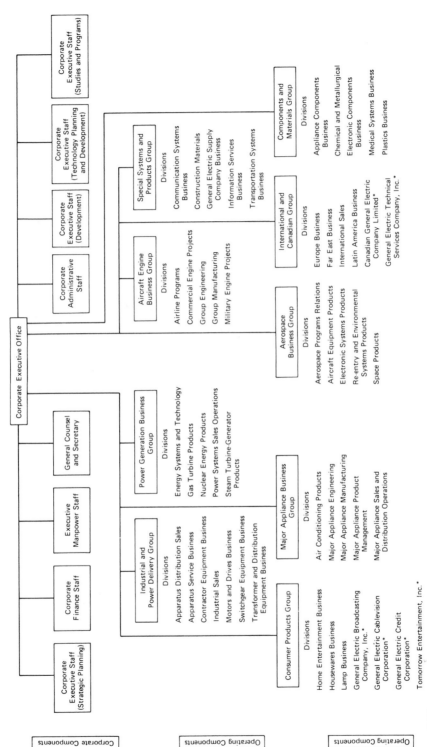

Figure 11-5. *Organigram of General Electric (circa 1975, used with permission)*

Corporate Components

Operating Components

Operating Components

Corporate Executive Office

Corporate Executive Staff (Strategic Planning)

Corporate Finance Staff

Executive Manpower Staff

General Counsel and Secretary

Corporate Administrative Staff

Corporate Executive Staff (Development)

Corporate Executive Staff (Technology Planning and Development)

Corporate Executive Staff (Studies and Programs)

Consumer Products Group

Divisions

Home Entertainment Business
Housewares Business
Lamp Business
General Electric Broadcasting Company, Inc.*
General Electric Cablevision Corporation*
General Electric Credit Corporation*
Tomorrow Entertainment, Inc.*

Industrial and Power Delivery Group

Divisions

Apparatus Distribution Sales
Apparatus Service Business
Contractor Equipment Business
Industrial Sales
Motors and Drives Business
Switchgear Equipment Business
Transformer and Distribution Equipment Business

Major Appliance Business Group

Divisions

Air Conditioning Products
Major Appliance Engineering
Major Appliance Manufacturing
Major Appliance Product Management
Major Appliance Sales and Distribution Operations

Power Generation Business Group

Divisions

Energy Systems and Technology
Gas Turbine Products
Nuclear Energy Products
Power Systems Sales Operations
Steam Turbine-Generator Products

Aerospace Business Group

Divisions

Aerospace Programs Relations
Aircraft Equipment Products
Electronic Systems Products
Re-entry and Environmental Systems Products
Space Products

Aircraft Engine Business Group

Divisions

Airline Programs
Commercial Engine Projects
Group Engineering
Group Manufacturing
Military Engine Projects

International and Canadian Group

Divisions

Europe Business
Far East Business
International Sales
Latin America Business
Canadian General Electric Company Limited*
General Electric Technical Services Company, Inc.*

Special Systems and Products Group

Divisions

Communication Systems Business
Construction Materials
General Electric Supply Company Business
Information Services Business
Transportation Systems Business

Components and Materials Group

Divisions

Appliance Components Business
Chemical and Metallurgical
Electronic Components Business
Medical Systems Business
Plastics Business

*Affiliate

or marketing section, for example. With our collection of businesses, what would they do? Neither do we have any corporate labour relations officer or staff. We want the unions to bargain separately in each of our divisions, and we will not send any corporate representatives to any labour negotiations. (quoted in Wrigley, 1970:V-76–77)

One thing that can, however, vary widely in the conglomerate form is the tightness of the performance control system, although it always remains financial. At one extreme is the highly managed system of ITT, which became increasingly fashionable in the 1970s, with tenth-of-the-month "flash" reports and the like. At the other extreme, although far less fashionable, is the holding company, a federation of businesses so loose that it is probably not even appropriate to think of it as one entity. The holding company typically has no central headquarters and no real control system, save for the occasional meeting of its different presidents. This is the logical finale to our discussion of the stages in the transition to the Divisionalized Form—fragmentation of structure to the point where we can no longer talk of a single organization.

Some Issues Associated with the Divisionalized Form

We begin our discussion of the issues associated with this configuration by enumerating some of the advantages traditionally claimed for the Divisionalized Form over the more integrated functional forms. Then, from society's perspective, we suggest that the Divisionalized Form should logically be compared with another alternative, that of the divisions constituted as independent organizations. In this context, we reassess its advantages. Both these discussions consider only the administrative and economic consequences of divisionalization. Next we turn to the social consequences, specifically the problems of Divisionalized Form poses for social responsibility and centralization of power in society. All these discussions focus on the conglomerate form in the private sector—conglomerate because it is the purest form of divisionalization, where the issues are most pronounced, and private sector because, as we shall see toward the end of our discussion, the pure Divisionalized Form turns out to be ill-suited to other sectors. We close our discussion of the issues with a description of the Divisionalized Forms as the most vulnerable of the five configurations, a structure symbolically on the edge of a cliff.

The economic advantages of divisionalization

The Divisionalized Form offers four basic advantages over the functional structure with integrated operations. First, the Divisionalized Form encourages efficient allocation of capital. Headquarters can choose where to put its money, and so can concentrate on its strongest markets, milking the surpluses of some divisions in favor of others. The functional structure has all its eggs in one strategic basket, so to speak. Second, by opening up opportunities to run individual businesses, the Divisionalized Form helps to train general managers. In contrast, the middle-line managers of functional structures are locked into dependent relationships with each other, which preclude individual responsibility and autonomy. Third, the Divisionalized Form spreads its risk across different markets. In contrast, one broken link in the operating chain of the functional structure brings the entire system to a grinding halt. Fourth, and perhaps most important, the Divisionalized Form is strategically responsive. The divisions can fine-tune their bureaucratic machines while the headquarters concentrates on its strategic portfolio. It can acquire new businesses and divest itself of older, ineffective ones.

But is the functional form the correct basis of comparison? Is it the real alternative to the Divisionalized Form? It is, if one wishes to compare diversified with nondiversified organizations. **Strategic diversification, because it leads to structural divisionalization, encourages the efficient allocation of capital within the organization; it trains general managers, reduces risks, and increases strategic responsiveness. In other words, it solves many of the economic problems that arise in the Machine Bureaucracy.** From the perspective of the organization itself, diversification followed by divisionalization offers a number of distinct advantages over remaining nondiversified.

But once an organization is diversified and then divisionalized, there is reason to change the basis of comparison. The real alternative, at least from society's perspective, becomes the taking of a further step along the same path, to the point of eliminating the headquarters and allowing the divisions to function as independent organizations. Textron, as described by Wrigley, had thirty divisions operating in as many different businesses; Beatrice Foods, described in a 1976 *Fortune* magazine article, had 397. The issue is whether either of these corporations was more efficient than thirty or 397 separate corporations. In effect, the perspective shifts from that of the organization to that of society. In this context, we can reconsider the four advantages discussed above.

In the divisionalized organization, headquarters allocates the capital resources among the thirty or 397 divisions. In the case of thirty or 397 independent corporations, the capital markets do the job instead. Which does it better? Two studies suggest that the answer is not a simple one.

Williamson (1975) argues that the Divisionalized Form does the better job. In fact, he describes it as the administrative response to inefficiencies in the capital markets—to idiosyncratic knowledge, opportunistic behaviors, and the like. By virtue of their elaborate performance control systems and their personal contacts, the headquarters managers are better able

than the investors to inform themselves of the potential of different businesses—at least, a limited number of businesses. Moreover, the headquarters managers are able to transfer capital between the divisions more quickly and flexibly than can be equivalent market mechanisms. So the
Divisionalized Form has "mitigated capital market failures by transferring
functions traditionally imputed to the capital market to the firm instead"
(p. 136).

Williamson's arguments may, in fact, explain why some conglomerate firms have been able to survive and prosper in the economic system.
But Moyer in a 1970 paper suggests that these advantages come at a price,
specifically that conglomeration—especially by acquisition, the most common way to achieve it—has proven more costly and, in some ways, *less*
flexible than the market mechanisms:

> An acquiring firm normally pays a 15% premium above the market price of
> the firm to be acquired in order to consummate a merger. Completely diversi-
> fied mutual funds can be purchased for a selling charge of 7–9% in the case of
> "load" funds. . . . Furthermore, an individual stockholder can diversify his
> own portfolio with brokerage costs averaging only 1.5% to 3.5% of the value
> of the stock purchased. . . .
>
> Because conglomerate firms have not been required in the past to pub-
> lish earnings for wholly owned divisions or subsidiaries . . . the stockholder
> is not in a position to make decisions as to whether subsidiaries which man-
> agement has seen fit to purchase are enhancing his earning power. An indi-
> vidually diversified portfolio has substantially more flexibility than a con-
> glomerate portfolio. The individual can buy and sell with a minimum of effort
> depending on the performance of individual stocks. It is a different and more
> involved matter for a conglomerate to decide to divest itself of one or more of
> its subsidiaries. (p. 22)

Moyer believes that conglomeration denies the shareholder one of his few
remaining prerogatives: the choice of an industry—and a risk level—in
which to put his capital. The choice among stocks of different conglomerate firms amounts to the choice among given portfolios—Beatrice Foods
instead of Dannon Yogurt.

On the issue of management development, the question becomes
whether the division managers receive better training and experience than
they would as company presidents. The Divisionalized Form is able to put
on training courses and to rotate its managers to vary their experiences; the
independent firm is limited in these respects. But if, as the proponents of
divisionalization claim, autonomy is the key to management development,
then presumably, the more autonomy the better. The division managers
have a headquarters to lean on—and to be leaned on by. In Textron, "The
price of autonomy is plan achievement. If a division cannot for one reason
or another meet its goals, it is subject to close and detailed supervision. . . ."

(Wrigley, 1970:V-91). In contrast, the company president is on his own, to make his own mistakes and learn from them.

On the third issue, of risk, the argument from the divisionalized perspective is that the independent organization is vulnerable during periods of internal crisis or economic slump; conglomeration provides it with the support to see it through such periods. The counterargument is that divisionalization may conceal bankruptcies, that ailing divisions are sometimes supported longer than necessary, whereas the market bankrupts the independent firm and is done with it. Another point, this one from the perspective of the organization itself, is that just as the Divisionalized Form spreads its risk, so too does it spread the consequences of that risk. A single division cannot go bankrupt; the whole organization is legally responsible for its debts. So a massive enough problem in one division—say, an enormous increase in the price of nuclear fuel a division has committed itself to buy in large quantities—can siphon off the resources of the healthy divisions and even bankrupt the whole organization. *Loose* coupling turns out to be riskier than *no* coupling!

Finally, there is the issue of strategic responsiveness. The loosely coupled Divisionalized Form may be more responsive than the tightly coupled functional form. But the question is, What price even loose coupling? In other words, what effect does conglomeration have on strategic responsiveness? The control system of the Divisionalized Form—which keeps that carrot just the right distance in front of the divisional managers—encourages them to strive for better and better financial performance. At the same time, however, it impedes their ability to innovate. "Textron's management has . . . learned that developing new inventions is not one of its strong points" (quoted in Wrigley, 1970:V-89). Bower explains why:

> . . . the risks to the division manager of a major innovation can be considerable if he is measured on short-run, year-to-year, earnings performance. The result is a tendency to avoid big risky bets, and the concomitant phenomenon that major new developments are, with few exceptions, made outside the major firms in the industry. Those exceptions tend to be single-product companies whose top managements are committed to true product leadership: Bell Laboratories, IBM, Xerox, and Polaroid. These are the top managements that can make major strategic moves for their whole company. Instead, the diversified companies give us a steady diet of small incremental change. (1970:194)

Innovation requires entrepreneurship, and entrepreneurship does not thrive under standardized external control. The entrepreneur takes his own risks to earn his own rewards. No control system managed from a headquarters can substitute for that kind of motivation. In fact, many entrepreneurs set up their own businesses to escape bureaucratic controls, the kind Textron's president described to Wrigley: "Anything out of routine must be analyzed and justified"; he and the chairman "are in more frequent contact with any division that has something especially big in the works" (p. V-90). Such procedures may avert risk, but they also avert the benefits of risk—true innovation as opposed to "small incremental change."

Thus, the independent firm appears to be more strategically responsive than the corporate divisions, although perhaps less motivated to achieve consistently high economic performance. Indeed, many divisionalized corporations depend on these firms for their strategic responsiveness, since they diversify not by innovating themselves but by acquiring the innovative results of independent entrepreneurs.

The contribution of headquarters

To assess the effectiveness of conglomeration, it is necessary to assess what actual contribution the headquarters makes to the divisions. Since the headquarters function of control is supposed to be performed by the board of directors of the independent firm, the question becomes, What does a headquarters offer to the division that an independent board of directors does not?

One thing that neither the headquarters managers nor the board of directors can offer is the management of the individual business. Both are involved with it only on a part-time basis.[3] The management of it is, therefore, logically left to its full-time managers—they have the required time and information. In fact, one issue that faces the Divisionalized Form more than an independent business, because of the closer links between headquarters and divisional managers, is the tendency to forget this point. **A strong set of forces encourages the headquarters managers to usurp divisional powers, to centralize certain product-market decisions at headquarters and so defeat the purpose of divisionalization.** Headquarters managers may believe they can do better; they may be tempted to eliminate duplication (one advertising department instead of 397); they may simply enjoy exercising the power that is potentially theirs; or they may be lured by new administrative techniques. An enthusiastic technostructure or consulting firm may oversell a sophisticated MIS or a system built on the principle that product-market decisions can be made according to data on market share or product life cycle.

The trouble with many of these systems is that they give the illusion of knowledge without giving the knowledge itself. As we noted earlier, a good deal of the information needed for formulating strategies is soft and speculative—bits and pieces of impression, rumor, and such that never get

---

[3]If the directors are full-time, they become, in effect, the management, and there is no formal external control of the firm.

documented or quantified. What the MIS carries back to headquarters are abstracted, aggregated generalizations. But no business can be understood solely from reports on market share, product life cycle, and the like. Such understanding requires soft information that inevitably remains behind in the divisions, whose managers are in personal touch with the specific situations. Even if the MIS could bring back the right information—or if the headquarters managers tried to use the telephone to get it verbally—they would lack the time to absorb it. Lack of time to understand many businesses is precisely the reason why organizations are divisionalized in the first place, to give each business the undivided attention of one manager and his unit. So the high-speed transmission lines only lure some headquarters managers into making decisions better left in the divisions. As one "disgruntled" British admiral commented after the Suez operation of 1956, "Nelson would never have won a single victory if there'd been a Telex" (quoted in Jay, 1970:79). Thus, one function of the headquarters managers of the conglomerate diversified corporation is *not* to manage the divisions. The wise ones know what they cannot know.

Among the functions headquarters managers *do* perform are the establishment of objectives for the divisions, the monitoring of their performance in terms of these objectives (an appropriate use for the MIS), the maintenance of limited personal contacts with division managers, and the approval of the major capital expenditures of the divisions. Interestingly, these are also the responsibilities of the board of directors, at least in theory. In practice, however, many boards—notably those of widely held corporations—do these things ineffectively, leaving management carte blanche to do what it likes. Here, then, we seem to have a major advantage of the the Divisionalized Form. It exists as an administrative arrangement to overcome another major weakness of the free-market system, the ineffective board. With the attention the headquarters pays to its formal and personal control systems, it induces divisional managers to strive for better and better financial results.

There is a catch in this argument, however, for conglomerate diversification often serves both to diffuse stock ownership and to render the corporation more difficult to understand and control by its board. For one thing, as we saw earlier, diversified corporations are typically large ones and so typically widely held and difficult to understand in any event. For another, the more businesses an organization operates, the harder it is for part-time directors to know what is going on. And finally, as Moyer notes, one common effect of conglomerate acquisition is to increase the number of shareholders, and so to make the corporation more widely held. Thus, the Divisionalized Form in some sense only resolves a problem of its own making. Had the corporation remained in one business, it may have been more narrowly held and easier to understand, and so its directors could have performed their functions more effectively. Diversification helped create the problem that divisionalization solved. Indeed, it is ironic that many a divisionalized corporation that does such an effective job of monitoring the performance of its own divisions is itself so poorly monitored by its board of directors.

A main purpose of this monitoring is to flag problems and correct them before they emerge as full-fledged crises. A well-known weakness of the independent corporation is that top management can pull the wool over the eyes of its directors, camouflaging serious problems. That is harder to do in the divisionalized corporation, with its persistent managers at headquarters. But camouflaging is hardly unknown in the Divisionalized Form either, and for the same reason—the detailed information rests with the full-time managers of each business, not with those who are supposed to control them on a part-time basis. The following story, told by an assistant controller at one headquarters, illustrates this clearly:

> Our top management likes to make all the major decisions. They think they do, but I've just seen one case where a division beat them.
>
> I received for editing a request from the division for a large chimney. I couldn't see what anyone could do with just a chimney, so I flew out for a visit. They've built and equipped a whole plant on plant expense orders. The chimney is the only indivisible item that exceeded the $50,000 limit we put on the expense orders.
>
> Apparently they learned informally that a new plant wouldn't be favorably received, so they built the damn thing. I don't know exactly what I'm going to say. (quoted in Bower, 1970:189)

What happens when a problem does get flagged? What can headquarters do about it that a board of directors could not? The chairman of Textron told a meeting of the New York Society of Security Analysts, in reference to the headquarters vice-presidents who oversee the divisions, that "it is not too difficult to coordinate five companies that are well run" (quoted in Wrigley, 1970:V-78). True enough. But what about five that are badly run? What can a staff of thirty administrators at headquarters really do to correct problems in thirty operating divisions? The natural tendency to tighten the control screws does not usually help once the problem has manifested itself, nor does exercising close surveillance. As noted earlier, the headquarters managers cannot manage the divisions. Essentially, that leaves them with two alternatives. They can replace the division manager, or they can divest the corporation of the division. Of course, the board of directors can also change the management. Indeed, that seems to be its only real prerogative; the management does everything else. So the question becomes, Who can better select the manager of a business, a headquarters or a board of directors? And the answer to that question is not clear. A headquarters can move faster, and it has a pool of managers from other divisions to draw from. But it has to be thinking about the managers of thirty or 397 divisions from time to time, whereas the board of directors need worry about only one. As for divestment, that merely puts the problem in somebody else's lap; from society's perspective, it does not solve it (unless, of course, conglomeration caused the problem in the first place!).

On balance, the case for one headquarters versus a set of separate boards of directors appears to be mixed. It should come as no surprise that one study found that corporations with "controlled diversity" had better profit than those with conglomerate diversity (Rumelt, 1974). Controlled diversity means interdependence among the divisions, which calls for an intermediate, or impure, form of divisionalization, with some critical functions concentrated at headquarters.

Pure divisionalization remedies certain inefficiencies in the capital market, but it introduces new ones of its own; it trains general managers, but then gives them less autonomy than does the independent business; it spreads its risks, but it also spreads the consequences of those risks; it protects vulnerable operations during economic slumps, including some that later prove not to have been worth protecting; its control systems encourage the steady improvement of financial performance yet discourage true entrepreneurial innovation; its headquarters does a better job of monitoring business performance than does the board of the widely held corporation, but its inherent diversification is one of the causes of corporations being widely held and boards being ill-informed in the first place; and in the final analysis, it can do little more than a board of directors to correct the fundamental problems in a business—ultimately, both are reduced to changing the management. Overall, the pure Divisionalized Form (that is, the conglomerate form) may offer some advantages over a weak system of boards of directors and inefficient capital markets; but most of those advantages would probably disappear if certain problems in capital markets and boards were rectified. And there is reason to argue that society would be better off trying to correct fundamental inefficiencies in its economic system rather than encouraging private administrative arrangements to circumvent them. In fact, as we now turn from the administrative and economic consequences of the Divisionalized Form to its social ones, we shall see two additional reasons to support this conclusion, one related to the social responsibility of the Divisionalized Form, the other to its tendency to concentrate power in society.

The social performance of the performance control system

The performance control system of the Divisionalized Form is one of its fundamental design parameters and the chief source of its economic efficiency. Yet this system also produces one of its most serious social consequences.

The Divisionalized Form requires that headquarters control the divisions primarily by quantitative performance criteria, and that typically means financial ones—profit, sales growth, return on investment, and the like. The problem is that these performance measures become virtual obsessions, driving out goals that cannot be measured—product quality, pride in work, customers well served, an environment protected or beautified. In effect, the economic goals drive out the social ones. "We, in Textron, worship the god of Net Worth" (quoted in Wrigley, 1970:V-86).

That would pose no problems if the social and economic consequences of decisions could easily be separated. Governments would look after the former, corporations the latter. But the fact is that the two are intertwined; **every strategic decision of the large corporation involves social as well as economic consequences.** As a result, **the control system of the Divisionalized Form drives it to act, at best socially unresponsively, at worst socially irresponsibly.** Forced to concentrate on the economic consequences of his decisions, the division manager comes to ignore their social consequences. And it should be remembered that the *specific* decisions of the divisionalized corporation—those with social impact—are controlled by the managers in the divisions, not those at headquarters. Thus, Bower finds that "the best record in the race relations area are those of single-product [nondivisionalized] companies whose strong top managements are deeply involved in the business" (1970:193).

Robert Ackerman (1975), in a study carried out at the Harvard Business School, tested the proposition that even though business leaders "would like to avoid doing what they believe to be irresponsible" (p. 4), the difficulty their firms "were having in satisfying their social critics might be precisely in the organizational innovations that had permitted them to cope effectively with diversification and competitive conditions" (p. vii). Ackerman found that the benefits of social responsiveness—such as "a rosier public image . . . pride among managers . . . an attractive posture for recruiting on campus" (p. 55)—cannot easily be measured. "From the accountant's point of view, they have unfortunate characteristics of being largely intangible, unassignable to the costs of organizational units creating them" (pp. 55–56). In other words, these criteria cannot be plugged into the performance control system. The result is that:

> . . . the financial reporting system may actually inhibit social responsiveness. By focusing on economic performance, even with appropriate safeguards to protect against sacrificing long-term benefits, such a system directs energy and resources to achieving results measured in financial terms. It is the only game in town, so to speak, at least the only one with an official scorecard. (p. 56)

Headquarters managers, concerned about public relations and corporate liability, are tempted to intervene directly in the divisions' responses to new social issues. But they are discouraged by the Divisionalized Form's strict division of labor; divisional autonomy requires no headquarters meddling in specific decisions. As long as the screws of the performance control system are not turned too tight, the division manager retains some discretion to consider the social consequences of his actions. But, as we saw earlier, the trend in the divisionalized corporation is the other way, to the imitation of the ITT system of tight controls. The manager who must send back a flash report to headquarters on the tenth day of every month can hardly worry about the results these reports do not measure. He keeps his attention firmly fixed on financial performance.

When the screws are turned really tight, the division manager intent on achieving the standards may have no choice but to act irresponsibly. Bower cites the well-known example of the General Electric price-fixing case of 1962:

> The corporate management of G.E. required its executives to sign the so-called "directive 20.5" which explicitly forbade price fixing or any other violation of the antitrust laws. But a very severely managed system of reward and punishment that demanded yearly improvements in earnings, return, and market share, applied indiscriminately to all divisions, yielded a situation which was—at the very least—conducive to collusion in the oligopolistic and mature electric equipment markets. (1970:193)

The headquarters managers may try to wash their hands of such divisional wrongdoing, proclaiming their ignorance of it, as did Ralph Cordiner, president of General Electric at the time. But they must accept responsibility for designing and exploiting the structure that evoked the behavior in question. Thus, we conclude, with Bower, that "while the planning process of the diversified [and divisionalized] firm may be highly efficient," at least in the strict economic sense, it may also tend to make the firm "socially irresponsible" (p. 193).

The problems of the concentration of power

Earlier we discussed the relationship between size and the Divisionalized Form, concluding that not only do large organizations tend to divisionalize but also that divisionalization encourages small organizations to grow large, and large organizations to grow larger. The Fortune 500 would count few billion-dollar corporations among its ranks if it were not for the development of the Divisionalized Form.

From society's point of view, we must ask, What price bigness? Clearly **there are potential economic costs to bigness, notably the threat to the competitive market.** In *The New Industrial State,* John Kenneth Galbraith (1967) develops the theme that giant corporations use their market power, coupled with their planning and marketing techniques, to subvert competitive conditions. Galbraith's points have been repeatedly attacked by the more conservative economists, but it seems difficult to deny that sheer size can affect competition—for example, through the ability to use massive advertising expenditure to restrict entry to markets. In the case of conglomerate diversification, there is the added danger of what is known as "reciprocity"—"I buy from you if you buy from me" deals between corporations.

But the social costs of bigness may be the most serious ones. For one thing, big means bureaucratic. As noted in Hypothesis 5, the larger an organization, the more formalized its behavior. Moreover, in the case of the Divisionalized Form, as noted earlier in this chapter, the performance control system drives the divisions to be more bureaucratic than they would be as independent corporations. The presence of a headquarters— an agency of external control—also makes them more centralized. So the Divisionalized Form becomes a force for formalization and centralization— in other words, for machine bureaucratization—in a society, as noted in Chapter 9, already burdened with too many such structures.

Moreover, there are forces in the Divisionalized Form that drive it to centralize power not only at the divisional level but also at the headquarters level. In the case of the giant corporation, this results in the concentrating of enormous amounts of power in very few hands.

One of these forces for headquarters centralization, discussed a few pages back, is the illusion that the MIS and other techniques give of providing the information needed to make effective business strategies. (Indeed, should that not prove an illusion, the danger of centralization would be far more serious.) Another force for centralization is the very fact that the divisions are coupled together in a single legal unit under a single name. As noted earlier, no single division can go bankrupt; nor can it keep its bad publicity to itself. It shares its mistakes with its sister divisions, in the name of the corporation. No matter how loosely coupled the system, the whole is liable for the errors of any of the parts. So there are pressures on the headquarters to involve itself in specific divisional decisions—for example, to review long-term contracts that could later drain corporate resources, and to oversee social behaviors that could lead to bad publicity. In fact, its control system, by encouraging socially unresponsive or irresponsible behavior, has brought the divisionalized corporation more and more bad publicity, which pushes it to centralize more and more power at headquarters in order to protect itself. In some sense, the giant corporation seems to have a choice between social irresponsibility and power centralization.

Another force for centralization is captured in Lord Acton's famous dictum, "Power tends to corrupt; absolute power corrupts absolutely." With strong chains of authority below and diffused shareholders above, the managers at the headquarters of the giant corporations have enormous amounts of potential power. This raises pressures to centralize for the sake of centralization. Market forces no doubt mitigate these tendencies, discouraging the use of overcentralized structures. But as noted earlier, the bigger the corporation, the less it tends to be subject to market forces.

So far we have seen that divisionalization encourages a concentration of power at the divisional and then at the headquarters level. Paradoxically, **the concentration of power within the corporation also leads to conglomeration, divisionalization, and the concentration of power in spheres outside the corporation. Unions federate and governments add agencies to establish countervailing powers—ones to match those of the corporation.** Government is, in fact, drawn to intervene directly in the affairs of the corporation because of the very issues we have been discussing—the concentration of too much power in too few hands; power exercised free of shareholder, societal, and sometimes even market control; and the tendency toward unresponsive or irresponsible social behavior. Citizens who question the legitimacy of the power base of the giant corporation naturally look to the government to intervene.

And it is the supreme irony that the very arguments used in favor of the Divisionalized Form suggest the way to government intervention. Consider Williamson's key point in this regard, that the administrative arrangements are efficient while the capital markets are not. Why should the government worry about interfering with markets that do not work efficiently? And if the administrative arrangements work as well as Williamson claims, why should government not use them too? If Beatrice Foods really can control 397 divisions, what is to stop Washington from believing that it can control 397 Beatrices? Using the same systems. With a public calling for more and more control of corporate behavior, and with Lord Acton's dictum ever present, what will stop government administrators from being lured by the illusion that an MIS can provide the information they need to control the corporation—whether through nationalization or national planning?

Of course, like the corporation, so too would governments be driven to favor economic goals over social ones, as a result of the nature of the control system they would have to use. This means that government control, while perhaps legitimizing the activities of the corporation, would not solve the fundamental social problems raised by divisionalization and would, in fact, aggravate that of the concentration of power in society.

In general, **the pure Divisionalized Form does not work effectively outside the private sector.** This despite widespread attempts to use it—in school systems, universities, hospitals, government corporations—indeed, in all of them together in one giant public-sector divisionalized monolith.

One problem is that government and sometimes other institutions cannot divest themselves of divisions, or at least, the realities of power are that they seldom do. So there is no vehicle for organizational renewal. Another problem in government is that its civil-service regulations on appointments interfere with the concept of managerial responsibility: "If a superior is to have complete confidence in his subordinates, he must have some measure of control over who his subordinates are. He must have a degree of freedom in their selection, their discipline, and if necessary their transfer or dismissal. The federal civil service system, however, places restrictions on such freedom" (Worthy, 1959:113).

But the most serious problem remains that of measurement: The goals governments and most institutions must plug into the performance control system—basically social goals—do not lend themselves to measurement. And without measurement, the pure Divisionalized Form cannot work. Nothing stops government and institutions from establishing market-based divisions. But lacking adequate performance measures, they must find other means to control these divisions (or force in artificial measures that fail to capture the spirit of the social goals or that ignore them entirely in favor of economic goals). One is socialization—the appointment of managers who believe in the social goals in question. But that can go only so far, and pressures arise to use other means of control. The obvious ones are direct supervision and standardization of work—the issuing of direct orders and general rules. But both damage divisional autonomy. **So the choices facing the government—and unions, multiversities, and other federated institutions that try to use the Divisionalized Form in the face of nonquantifiable goals—are to forget control beyond the appointment of socialized managers, to control machine bureaucratically, or to force in divisionalized control by the imposition of artificial performance standards.**

Examples abound of all three. The press regularly reports on government departments that have run out of control. Perhaps more common is the case of machine bureaucratic control, of government departments that lack the autonomy they need to act because of the plethora of blanket rules governments impose on all of their departments. And so, too, do examples get reported of artificial performance controls, perhaps the best one being Frank's (1958–59) description of the system used by the Soviet government to regulate the performance of its factories. Standards abounded: type, quantity, quality, and mix of production; amount of materials and labor used; wages paid; production norms for workers to achieve; special campaign goals; and many more. The standards were so tight and often contradictory that the managers on the receiving end had no choice but to act irresponsibly, just as do division managers in America who are overcontrolled. They lied about their factories' needs; they stockpiled materials; they complied with the letter but not the spirit of the standards—for example, by reducing product quality (which could not easily be measured); they hired the *tolkach*, the influence peddler, to make deals outside the control system.

In the final analysis, perhaps the best that can be done by governments and institutions intent on using some form of divisionalization is to appoint managers and other employees who believe in the social goals to be pursued and then to set up the mechanism for some kind of periodic personal review of their progress (requiring, in effect, the creation of some kind of independent board of directors).

In conclusion: a structure at the edge of a cliff

Our discussion has led to a "damned if you do, damned if you don't" conclusion. The pure (conglomerate) Divisionalized Form emerges as a configuration symbolically perched on the edge of the cliff, at the end of a long path. Ahead, it is one step away from *dis*integration—breaking up into separate organizations on the rocks below. Behind it is the way back to a more stable integration, perhaps a hybrid structure with Machine Bureaucracy at some intermediate spot along the path. And ever hovering above is the eagle, attracted by its position on the edge of the cliff and waiting for the chance to pull the Divisionalized Form up to more centralized social control, on another, perhaps more dangerous, cliff. The edge of the cliff is an uncomfortable place to be—maybe even a temporary one that must inevitably lead to disintegration on the rocks below, a trip to that cliff above, or a return to a safer resting place on the path behind.

In other words, **we conclude that the Divisionalized Form has the narrowest range of all the configurations. It has no real environment of its own; at best, it piggybacks on the Machine Bureaucracy in the simple, stable environment, and therefore always feels drawn back to that integrated structural form. The pure Divisionalized Form may prove inherently unstable, in a social context a legitimate tendency but not a legitimate structure. The economic advantages it offers over independent organizations reflect fundamental inefficiencies in capital markets and stockholder control systems that should themselves be corrected. And it creates fundamental social problems.** Perhaps there is justification only in its intermediate forms—by-product or related-product. It is, after all, the interdependencies among its activities that give an organization its justification, its reason to "organize." Perhaps the pure Divisionalized Form, with so few of these interdependencies, really is an "ideal type"—one to be approached but never reached.

12

THE ADHOCRACY

Prime Coordinating Mechanism:	Mutual adjustment
Key Part of Organization:	Support staff (in the Administrative Adhocracy; together with the operating core in the Operating Adhocracy)
Main Design Parameters:	Liaison devices, organic structure, selective decentralization, horizontal job specialization, training, functional and market grouping concurrently
Situational Factors:	Complex, dynamic, (sometimes disparate) environment; young (especially Operating Adhocracy); sophisticated and often automated technical system (in the Administrative Adhocracy); fashionable

None of the configurations so far discussed is capable of sophisticated innovation, the kind required of a space agency, an avant-garde film company, a factory manufacturing complex prototypes, an integrated petrochemicals company. The Simple Structure can certainly innovate, but only in relatively simple ways. Both the Machine and Professional Bureaucracies are performance, not problem-solving, structures. They are designed to perfect standard programs, not to invent new ones. And although the Divisionalized Form resolves the problem of strategic inflexibility in the Machine Bureaucracy, as noted in the last chapter, it, too, is not a true innovator. A focus on control by standardizing outputs does not encourage innovation.

Sophisticated innovation requires a fifth and very different configuration, one that is able to fuse experts drawn from different disciplines into smoothly functioning ad hoc project teams. To borrow the word Alvin Toffler popularized in *Future Shock*, these are the *Adhocracies* of our society. They appeared repeatedly in our review, in Lawrence and Lorsch's plastics companies, among Woodward's process producers, in NASA and the Boeing Company.

(Before beginning our discussion of the basic structure, we should note that Simple Structure, being almost nonstructure, generated a chapter that was short and simple. Machine and Professional Bureaucracy and the Divisionalized Form, being for the most part highly ordered structures, led to chapters that were highly ordered as well. Adhocracy, in contrast, is the most complex structure of the five, yet it is not highly ordered. Moreover, it is the newest of the five, the one about which we know the least. The reader is forewarned that the chapter cannot help reflecting the characteristics of the structure it describes.)

Description of the Basic Structure

The design parameters

In Adhocracy, we have a fifth distinct configuration: highly organic structure, with little formalization of behavior; high horizontal job specialization based on formal training; a tendency to group the specialists in functional units for housekeeping purposes but to deploy them in small, market-based project teams to do their work; a reliance on the liaison devices to encourage mutual adjustment, the key coordinating mechanism, within and between these teams; and selective decentralization to and within these teams, which are located at various places in the organization and involve various mixtures of line managers and staff and operating experts.

To innovate means to break away from established patterns. So the innovative organization cannot rely on any form of standardization for coordination. In other words, it must avoid all the trappings of bureaucratic structure, notably sharp divisions of labor, extensive unit differentiation, highly formalized behaviors, and an emphasis on planning and control systems. Above all, it must remain flexible. Thus Toffler (1970) notes that

Adhocracies "now change their internal shape with a frequency—and sometimes a rashness—that makes the head swim. . . . Vast organizational structures are taken apart, bolted together again in new forms, then rearranged again. Departments and divisions spring up overnight only to vanish in another, and yet another, reorganization" (p. 128). For example, the Manned Space Flight Center of NASA, America's most famous Adhocracy of the 1960s, changed its structure seventeen times in the first eight years of its existence (Litzinger et al., 1970:7). A search for organigrams to illustrate this chapter elicited the following response from one corporation well known for its Adhocracy structure: ". . . we would prefer not to supply an organization chart, since it would change too quickly to serve any useful purpose."

Of all the configurations, Adhocracy shows the least reverence for the classical principles of management, especially unity of command. The regulated system does not matter much either. In this configuration, information and decision processes flow flexibly and informally, wherever they must, to promote innovation. And that means overriding the chain of authority if need be.

The Simple Structure also retains an organic structure, and so is able to innovate as well. But that innovation is restricted to simple environments, ones that can be easily comprehended by a central leader. Innovation of the sophisticated variety takes place in environments not easily understood. So another kind of organic structure is required, one that relies on the application of sophisticated expertise. **The Adhocracy must hire and give power to experts—professionals whose knowledge and skills have been highly developed in training programs.** But unlike the Professional Bureaucracy, **the Adhocracy cannot rely on the standardized skills of these experts to achieve coordination,** because that would lead to standardization instead of innovation. Rather, it must treat existing knowledge and skills merely as bases on which to build new ones.

Moreover, the building of new knowledge and skills requires the combination of different bodies of existing ones. So rather than allowing the specialization of the expert or the differentiation of the functional unit to dominate its behavior, the Adhocracy must instead break through the boundaries of conventional specialization and differentiation. "An electrical specialist can spot a mechanical problem, perhaps in part because he does not know the conventional wisdom, and a bright engineer working in an apparently unrelated field can come up with a solution to a problem that has been frustrating the functional specialists" (Chandler and Sayles, 1971:202). Thus, whereas each professional of the Professional Bureaucracy can operate on his own, in the Adhocracy the professionals must amalgamate their efforts. "Traditional organizations can assume that they know all the problems and the methods. They therefore can assign expertise to a single specialist or compartmentalized, functional group" (p. 203). In sharp contrast, **in Adhocracies the different specialists must join forces in multidisciplinary teams, each formed around a specific project of innovation.**

How does the organization cope with the problem of "uprooting the professional yet allowing him to maintain his ties to his field of expertise" (Chandler and Sayles, p. 15)? The solution is obvious: **The Adhocracy tends to use the functional and market bases for grouping concurrently, in a matrix structure.** The experts are grouped in functional units for housekeeping purposes—for hiring, professional communication, and the like—but then are deployed in project teams to carry out their basic work of innovation.

And how is coordination effected in and between these project teams? As noted earlier, standardization is precluded as a major coordinating mechanism. The efforts must be innovative, not standardized. So, too, is direct supervision, because of the complexity of the work. Coordination must be effected by those with the knowledge, the experts who actually do the project work. That leaves mutual adjustment, the prime coordinating mechanism of the Adhocracy. And, of course, **with the concentration on mutual adjustment in the Adhocracy comes an emphasis on the design parameter meant to encourage it—namely, the set of liaison devices.** Integrating managers and liaison positions are established to coordinate the efforts among and between the functional units and project teams; the teams themselves are established as task forces; and, as noted above, matrix structure is favored to achieve concurrent functional and market grouping. As Sayles notes, matrix structure "*reuses* old organizations instead of creating new ones for new goals and problems. It forces organizations to keep changing themselves because of conflicting goals, values, and priorities and builds instability into the very structure of the organization" (1976:15).

Thus, **managers abound in the Adhocracy—functional managers, integrating managers, project managers.** The last-named are particularly numerous, since the project teams must be small to encourage mutual adjustment among their members, and each team needs a designated leader, a "manager." This results in narrow "spans of control" for the Adhocracy, by conventional measures. But that measure has nothing to do with the control; it merely reflects the small size of the work units. Most of the managers do not "manage" in the usual sense—that is, give orders by direct supervision. Instead, they spend a good deal of their time acting in a liaison and negotiating capacity, coordinating the work laterally among the different teams and between them and the functional units. Many of these managers are, in fact, experts, too, who take their place alongside the others on the project teams.

With its reliance on highly trained experts, the Adhocracy—like the Professional Bureaucracy—is decentralized. But not in the same way, because in the Adhocracy, the experts are distributed throughout the structure, notably in the support staff and managerial ranks as well as the operating core. So rather than a concentration of power in the operating core, there is a more even distribution of it in all the parts. **The decentralization of the Adhocracy is what we labeled** *selective* **in Chapter 5, in both the horizontal and vertical dimensions. Decision-making power is distributed among managers and nonmanagers at all the levels of the hierarchy, according to the nature of the different decisions to be made.** No one in the Adhocracy monopolizes the power to innovate.

To proceed with our discussion, and to elaborate on how the Adhocracy makes decisions, we must at this point divide it into two types—the Operating Adhocracy and the Administrative Adhocracy.

The operating adhocracy

The Operating Adhocracy innovates and solves problems directly on behalf of its clients. Its multidisciplinary teams of experts often work directly under contract, as in the think-tank consulting firm, creative advertising agency, or manufacturer of engineering prototypes. In some cases, however, there is no contract per se, as in the film-making agency or theater company.

In fact, **for every Operating Adhocracy, there is a corresponding Professional Bureaucracy, one that does similar work but with a narrower orientation.** Faced with a client problem, the Operating Adhocracy engages in creative effort to find a novel solution; the Professional Bureaucracy pigeonholes it into a known contingency to which it can apply a standard program. One engages in divergent thinking aimed at innovation; the other, in convergent thinking aimed at perfection. One management consulting firm treats each contract as a creative challenge; another interprets each as the need to divisionalize the client's structure or strengthen its planning system, or both. One theater company seeks out new avant-garde plays to perform; another perfects its performance of Shakespeare year after year. In effect, one is prepared to consider an infinite number of contingencies and solutions; the other restricts itself to a few. The missions are the same, but the outputs and the structures that produce them differ radically. Both decentralize power to their highly trained specialists. But because the Operating Adhocracy seeks to innovate, its specialists must interact informally by mutual adjustment in organically structured project teams; the Professional Bureaucracy, because it standardizes its services, structures itself as a bureaucracy in which each specialist can function on his own, his work automatically coordinated with the others by virtue of his standardized knowledge and skills.

A key feature of the Operating Adhocracy is that its administrative and operating work tend to blend into a single effort. That is, in ad hoc project work, it is difficult to differentiate the planning and design of the work from its execution. Both require the same specialized skills, on a project-by-project basis. As a result, the Operating Adhocracy may not even bother to distinguish its middle levels from its operating core. Managers of the middle line and members of what in other organizations would be called the support staff—typically a highly trained and important group in the Operating Adhocracy—may take their place right alongside the operating specialists on the project teams. And even when distinctions are made, a close rapport must develop between the administrative and operating levels, sometimes to the point where they are able to interchange their roles freely.

Figure 12–1 shows the organigram of the National Film Board of Canada, a classic Operating Adhocracy (even though it does produce an

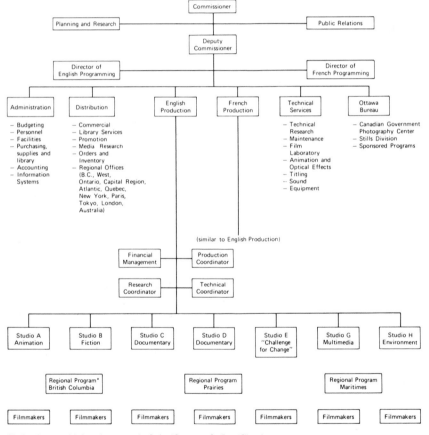

Figure 12-1. *The National Film Board of Canada: an Operating Adhocracy (circa 1975, used with permission)*

organigram—one that changes frequently, it might be added). The board is an agency of the Canadian federal government and produces mostly short films, many of them documentaries. The organigram shows a large number of support units as well as liaison positions (for example, research, technical, and production coordinators). The operating core can also be seen to include loose, concurrent functional and market groupings (the latter by region as well as type of film produced).

The administrative adhocracy

The second major type of Adhocracy also functions with project teams, but toward a different end. Whereas the Operating Adhocracy undertakes projects to serve its clients, **the Administrative Adhocracy undertakes its projects to serve itself. And in sharp contrast to the Operating Adhocracy, the Administrative Adhocracy makes a sharp distinction between its administrative component and operating core. The operating core is truncated—cut right off from the rest of the organization—so that the administrative component that remains can be structured as an Adhocracy.**

This truncation may take place in a number of ways. First, when an organization has a special need to be innovative, perhaps because of intense product competition or a very dynamic technology, but its operating core must be machine bureaucratic, the operating core may be established as a separate organization. As we saw in Chapter 9, the social tensions at the base of the Machine Bureaucracy overflow the operating core and permeate the administration. The whole organization becomes ridden with conflict and obsessed by control, too bureaucratic to innovate. By truncating the operating core—setting it up apart with its own administration that reports in at the strategic apex—the main administrative component of the organization can be structured organically for innovation.[1] **Second, the operating core may be done away with altogether—in effect, contracted out to other organizations.** This leaves the organization free to concentrate on development work. Thus, for the Apollo project, NASA conducted much of its own development work but contracted production out to independent manufacturing firms. **A third form of truncation arises when the operating core becomes automated.** This amounts to truncation because an automated operating core is able to run itself, largely free of the need for direct supervision or other direct control from the administrative component. The latter, because it need not give attention to routine operating matters, can structure itself as an Adhocracy, concerned with change and innovation, with projects to bring new operating facilities on line.

---

[1]The organization that truncates its bureaucratic operating core should not be confused with the one that gets up a venture team, a separate organic pocket for innovation. In that case, the innovative unit is cut off from the rest of the central administration, which remains bureaucratic.

Oil companies, because of the high automation of their production process, are in part at least drawn toward the Administrative Adhocracy configuration. Figure 12–2 shows the organigram for one oil company, reproduced exactly as presented by the company (except for modifications to mask its identity, made at the company's request). Note the domination of "Administration and Services," shown at the bottom of the chart; the operating functions, particularly "Production," are lost by comparison.

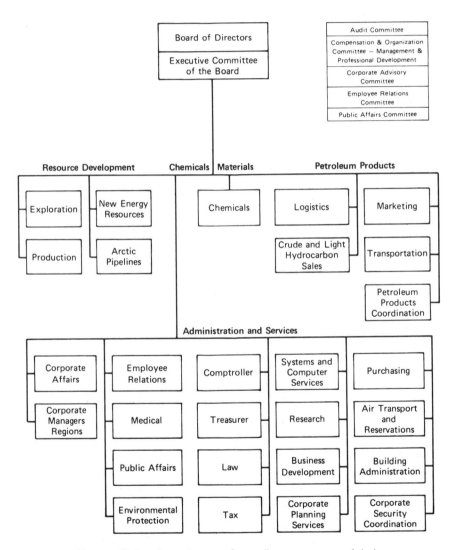

Figure 12-2. *Organigram of an oil company: an Administrative Adhocracy (circa 1976)*

Note also the description of the strategic apex in terms of standing committees instead of individual executives.

The administrative component of the adhocracies

The important conclusion to be drawn from this discussion is that in both types of Adhocracy, the relation between the operating core and the administrative component is unlike that of any other configuration. In the Administrative Adhocracy, the operating core is truncated and becomes a relatively unimportant part of the organization; in the Operating Adhocracy, the two merge into a single entity. In both cases, there is little need for line managers to exercise close direct supervision over the operators. Rather, **the managers become functioning members of the project teams, with special responsibility to effect coordination between them.** But in this capacity, they act more as peers than as supervisors, their influence deriving from their expertise and interpersonal skill rather than from their formal position. And, of course, to the extent that direct supervision and formal authority diminish in importance, **the distinction between line and staff blurs.** It no longer makes sense to distinguish those who have the formal power to decide from those who have only the informal right to advise. Power over decision making flows to anyone in the Adhocracy with expertise, regardless of position.

The support staff plays a key role in the Adhocracy. In fact, it is the key part of the Administrative Adhocracy, for that is where this configuration houses most of the experts on which it is so dependent. The Operating Adhocracy also depends on experts, but since it retains its operating core, it houses many of them there as well as in its support staff. But in both cases, as noted above, much of the support staff is not sharply differentiated from other parts of the organization, not off to one side, to speak only when spoken to, as in the bureaucratic configurations. Rather, the support staff, together with the line managers (and the operators, in the case of the Operating Adhocracy), form part of the central pool of expert talent from which the project personnel are drawn. (There are, of course, exceptions. Some support units must always remain bureaucratic, and apart. Even NASA needs cafeterias.)

Because the Adhocracy does not rely on standardization for coordination, it has little need for a technostructure to develop systems for regulation. The Administrative Adhocracy does employ analysts concerned with adaptation to its external environment, such as marketing researchers and economic forecasters. As we shall see later, it does do some action planning, although of a rather general kind. But these analysts do not design systems to control other people so much as take their place alongside the line managers and the support staffers as members of the project teams.

To summarize, **the administrative component of the Adhocracy**

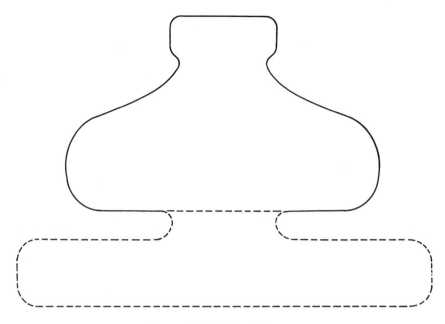

Figure 12-3. *The Adhocracy*

emerges as an organic mass of line managers and staff experts (with operators in the Operating Adhocracy), working together in ever-shifting relationships on ad hoc projects. Figure 12–3 shows the Adhocracy in terms of our logo, with its parts mingled together in one amorphous mass in the middle. In the Operating Adhocracy, this mass includes the middle line, support staff, technostructure, and operating core. The Administrative Adhocracy includes all of these except the operating core, which is kept apart in a truncated, bureaucratic structure, shown by the dotted section below the central mass. The reader will also note that the strategic apex of the figure is shown partly merged into the central mass as well. We shall see why in the discussion of strategy formation that follows.

Strategy formation in the adhocracy

In the Professional Bureaucracy, the strategy formulation process is controlled primarily by the professional associations outside the structure, secondarily by the professionals of the operating core themselves, and only after that by the administrators. In effect, the process is bottom-up, and outside-in. In all the other configurations so far discussed, the process is clearly top-down, controlled by the strategic apex (and in the Divisionalized Form, the strategic apexes of the divisions as well). In sharp contrast, **control of the strategy formulation process in the Adhocracy is not clearly placed, at the strategic apex or elsewhere.**

Moreover, the process is best thought of as strategy *formation*, because strategy in these structures is not so much formulated consciously by individuals as formed implicitly by the decisions they make, one at a time. The concept of the formulation–implementation dichotomy in strategy making—a pillar of the Machine Bureaucracy—loses its meaning in the Adhocracy. It is in the making of specific decisions within and about projects, what would normally be considered implementation, that strategies evolve—that is, are formed—in the Adhocracy. That is because when the central purpose of an organization is to innovate, the results of its efforts can never be predetermined. So it cannot specify a full strategy—a pattern or consistency in its stream of decisions—in advance, before it makes its decisions. Such patterns at best emerge after the fact, the results of specific decisions: "... goals continue to emerge as the task is pursued ... a single engine fighter plane may evolve into a twin-engine attack bomber; a funding program for exceptional children may become a strategy for integration; a construction project may become a training program for the unskilled" (Goodman and Goodman, 1976:496). That is why action planning cannot be extensively relied upon in the Adhocracy. Any process that separates conception from action—planning from execution, formalization from implementation—impedes the flexibility of the organization to respond creatively to its dynamic environment.[2]

Consider the case of the Operating Adhocracy, a structure never quite sure what it will do next. That depends on what projects come along, which in turn depends partly on how well it does in its current projects. So its strategy never really stabilizes, but changes continuously as projects change. To put this another way, when the strategy does stabilize, the structure ceases to be Adhocracy. A stable strategy means that the organization has determined which markets it will serve, and how; in other words, which contingencies it will respond to and with which standard programs. It has, in effect, restructured itself as a bureaucracy, machine if it concentrates on a single simple program, professional if it remains open to a few, complex ones. Now if strategy evolves continuously according to the projects being done, it stands to reason that strategy formation is controlled by whoever decides what projects are done and how. And in the Operating Adhocracy, that includes line managers, staff specialists, and operators—in other words, potentially everyone in the organization.

---

[2]The same dynamic conditions apply in the Simple Structure, with the same result—namely, that planning cannot be relied upon and that strategy formulation cannot be separated from strategy implementation. But because it innovates in simpler ways, the Simple Structure resolves the issue by focusing control for both at the strategic apex. The chief executive formulates a general vision of direction—a vague strategy—in his head and then implements it, continually reformulating his vision as he receives feedback on his actions. He does not make his strategy explicit, for that would announce it to others and so reduce his flexibility to change it at will.

Take the case of the National Film Board. Among its most important strategies are those related to the content of the one hundred or so mostly short documentary-type films that it makes each year—some about the geography of Canada and the sociology of its peoples, others on pure experimental themes, and so on. Were the board structured as a Machine Bureaucracy, the word on what films to make would come down from on high. There would be one stable film strategy, formulated at the strategic apex and implemented lower down. (If the Board were structured as the Divisionalized Form, the word would come down from the head of each film division.) If it were structured as a Professional Bureaucracy, each filmmaker would have his own standard repertoire of basic film scenarios, which he would repeat year after year, and the organization would have a series of stable film-content strategies coming up from the operating core.

In fact, because it is structured as an Operating Adhocracy, the Board follows none of these procedures. About one-third of its films are sponsored by agencies of the Canadian government. As long as interested filmmakers can be found, these are accepted, and clients can be thought to impose the strategy. The other two-thirds are proposed by the Board's own employees and are funded from its own general budget. Each proposal is submitted to a standing committee, which at the time of this writing consists of four members elected by the filmmakers, two appointed by the Distribution (marketing) Branch, and the Director of Production and the Director of Programming. The Commissioner—the chief executive—must approve the committee's choices. Thus, operators, middle-line managers, support staffers, and managers at the strategic apex all get involved in the choices of what films to make. But the vast majority of the proposals are initiated by the filmmakers and the executive producers. Each has his own general preferences, whether those be for animated or experimental films, documentaries, or whatever. But a glance at the Board's catalog invalidates any conclusion about standardization. Certain general themes do develop from time to time. But these also change frequently, according to styles and successes and so on. So although there is no stable film-content strategy, a dynamic one can be identified, one in a continual state of adaptation.

The Operating Adhocracy's strategy evolves continuously as hundreds of these kinds of decisions are made each year in complicated ways. Each project leaves its imprint on the strategy. And to return to the basic point being made, so many people at so many levels are involved in these projects—both in deciding which ones to carry out and then in actually carrying them out—that we cannot point a finger at any one part of the organization and say that is where the strategy is formulated. Everyone who gets involved—and that means top- and middle-level managers, staff specialists, and operators, all combined in various task forces and standing committees—has a hand in influencing the strategy that gets formed. That is why we concluded earlier that the Operating Adhocracy is decentralized selectively, in both the horizontal and vertical dimensions. The power for decision making is distributed widely, in the most complicated of ways, among managerial and nonmanagerial personnel, at all levels of the hierarchy.

Similar conclusions can be reached about the Administrative Adhocracy, although the strategy-making process is slightly neater there. That is because the Administrative Adhocracy tends to concentrate its attention on fewer projects, which involve more people in interdependent relationships. NASA's Apollo project involved most of its personnel for almost ten years; similarly, the bringing on line of a new processing plant can involve a good deal of the administrative staff of a petrochemical company for years. Moreover, since it carries out its projects only for itself, not for a range of outside clients, the Administrative Adhocracy tends to have a more concentrated product-market sphere of operations. Through the 1960s, for example, NASA focused on the single goal of landing an American on the moon before 1970.

Larger, more integrated projects and a more focused sphere of operations means that the efforts of the various specialists must be more carefully structured than in the Operating Adhocracy. As a result, **the Administrative Adhocracy structures itself as a system of work constellations, each located at the level of the hierarchy commensurate with the kinds of functional decisions it must make.** We saw a clear example of this in Chapter 5 (see Figure 5–2), with manufacturing, marketing, finance, and research constellations located at various levels of the hierarchy. Each constellation draws on line managers and staff specialists as necessary and distributes power to them according to the requirement for their expertise in the decisions that must be made. Hence, the Administrative Adhocracy is also decentralized selectively in the vertical and horizontal dimensions. And once again we cannot point to any one part of the organization as *the* place where strategy is formulated, although the existence of the work constellations does enable us to identify certain kinds of strategic decisions with certain parts of the organization.

The need to structure the efforts of the specialists also suggests a need for action planning in the Administrative Adhocracy. The problem with such planning, however, is that although the end or goal of the organization may be known, the means for reaching it are not. These must be worked out en route, by trial and error. So only a general kind of action planning can take place, one that sets out broad, flexible guidelines within which the work constellations can proceed to make their specific decisions. Again, therefore, it is only through the making of specific decisions— namely, those that determine which projects are undertaken and how these projects turn out—that strategies evolve. Even in the case of NASA, an organization thought to rely heavily on planning, that "turns out to be a dynamic, iterative process. This inevitably disperses authority, since a small group of expert, high-level 'planners' cannot define strategy" (Chandler and Sayles, 1971:7).

The roles of the strategic apex

The top managers of the strategic apex of the Adhocracy may not spend much time formulating explicit strategies, but they must spend a good deal of their time in the battles that ensue over strategic choices, and in handling the many other disturbances that arise all over these fluid structures. The Adhocracy combines organic working arrangements instead of bureaucratic ones, with expert power instead of formal authority. Together these conditions breed aggressiveness and conflict. But the job of the top managers is not to bottle up that aggressiveness, as in the Machine Bureaucracy—that would be impossible in any event—but to channel it to productive ends. Thus, the top managers of the Adhocracy (as well as those in its middle line) must be masters of human relations, able to use persuasion, negotiation, coalition, reputation, rapport, or whatever to fuse the individualistic experts into smoothly functioning multidisciplinary teams.

The top managers must also devote a good deal of time to monitoring the projects. Innovative project work is notoriously difficult to control. No MIS can be relied upon to send up complete, unambiguous results. So there must be careful, personal monitoring of projects to ensure that they are completed according to specifications, on schedule, and at the estimates projected (or, more exactly, not excessively late with too great cost overruns).

But perhaps the most important single role of the top management of Adhocracy (especially Operating Adhocracy) is that of liaison with the external environment. The other configurations tend to focus their attention on clearly defined markets, and are more or less assured of a steady flow of work. Not so in the Operating Adhocracy, which lives from project to project and disappears when it can find no more. Since each project is different, the Operating Adhocracy can never be sure where the next one will come from. Moreover, in the Professional Bureaucracy, it is frequently the operators who bring in their own clients. This is less common in the Operating Adhocracy, where the operators work in teams. So that responsibility often falls on the top managers. In the Operating Adhocracy, therefore, the managers of the strategic apex must devote a great deal of their time to ensuring a steady and balanced stream of incoming projects. That means developing liaison contacts with potential customers and negotiating contracts with them.

Nowhere is this more clearly illustrated than in the consulting business, particularly where the approach is innovative and the structure therefore Adhocracy in nature. An executive once commented to this author that "every consulting firm is three months away from bankruptcy."

In other words, three dry months could use up all the surplus funds, leaving none to pay the high professional salaries. And so when a consultant becomes a partner in one of these firms—in effect, moves into the strategic apex—he normally hangs up his calculator and becomes virtually a full-time salesperson. It is a distinguishing characteristic of many an Operating Adhocracy that the selling function literally takes place at the strategic apex.

Project work poses similar problems in the Administrative Adhocracy, with similar results. Reeser asked a group of managers in three aerospace companies, "What are some of the human problems of project management?" Among the common answers were two related to balancing the workload:

- The temporary nature of the organization often necessitates "make work" assignments for its displaced members after the organization has been disbanded, until productive jobs can be found for them. Sometimes the "make-work" assignments last so long that the individuals lose initiative.

- Members of the organization who are displaced because of the phasing out of the work upon which they are engaged may have to wait a long time before they get another assignment at as high a level of responsibility. (1969:463)

And so the top managers of the Administrative Adhocracy must also devote considerable attention to liaison and negotiation activities in order to ensure a steady stream of work. As Chandler and Sayles note in the case of NASA, dependent on government budgets and public support in general, "a good deal of the time of the key top managers was devoted to external relations with various units of the Executive Branch, with Congress, and with key public groups representing private business, universities, the scientific community, and various international interests" (1971:173).

Conditions of the Adhocracy

Basic environment

The conditions of the environment are the most important ones for this configuration; specifically, **the Adhocracy is clearly positioned in an environment that is both dynamic and complex.** According to Hypotheses 9 and 10, a dynamic environment calls for organic structure and a complex one calls for decentralized structure. And Adhocracy is the only configuration that is both organic and relatively decentralized. In effect, innovative work, being unpredictable, is associated with a dynamic environment; and the fact that the innovation must be sophisticated means that it is difficult to comprehend—in other words, associated with a complex environment. Thus, we find Adhocracies wherever the conditions of dynamism and complexity together prevail, in organizations ranging from guerrilla units to space agencies. There is no other way to fight a war in the jungle or put the first man on the moon.

As we have noted for all the configurations, organizations that prefer particular structures also try to "choose" environments appropriate to them. This is especially clear in the case of the Operating Adhocracy. As noted earlier, advertising agencies and consulting firms that prefer to structure themselves as Professional Bureaucracies seek out stable environments; those that prefer Adhocracy find environments that are dynamic, where the client needs are unpredictable.

Research-based organizations—whether laboratories that do nothing else, or corporations in high-technology industries that are heavily influenced by their research efforts—are drawn to the Adhocracy configuration because their work is by its very nature complex, unpredictable, and often competitive. Even hospitals and universities, described in Chapter 10 as closest to Professional Bureaucracy for their routine clinical and teaching work, are drawn to Adhocracy when they do truly innovative research. Their orientation to convergent, deductive thinking in their routine work precludes real innovation. So even though their professionals are often able to work alone when they apply their *standard* knowledge and skills, they must often join in organic multidisciplinary teams to create *new* knowledge and skills.

Disparate forces in the environment

Hypothesis 13 of Chapter 6 indicated that **disparities in an organization's environment encourage it to decentralize selectively to differentiated work constellations—in other words, to structure itself as an Administrative Adhocracy.** The organization must create different work constellations to deal with different aspects of its environment and then integrate all their efforts.

This seems to have happened recently in the case of a number of multinational firms. For years these firms have been predisposed to using the Divisionalized Form, grouping their major divisions either by region or by product line.[3] But recent changes in their environments have resulted in a near balance of the pressures to adopt each of these two bases of grouping, making the choice of one over the other an agonizing one. The choice of divisionalization by region denied the interdependencies that arose from marketing the same products in different places, resulting, for example, in

---

[3]Some used the multiple-divisionalized form, having both kinds of divisions, but with one over the other in the hierarchy.

the duplication of manufacturing faculties in each region. On the other hand, the choice of divisionalization by product line ignored the interdependences across product lines, requiring, for example, many different marketing units in the same region. Intent on maintaining the Division-' alized Form, these firms traded off one interdependence against the other. Or else they found themselves acting schizophrenically, changing their basis of grouping back and forth in a kind of perpetual game of Ping-Pong.

With the emergence of matrix structure, however, these firms were presented with a logical solution to their dilemma. They could establish regional *and* product divisions at the same level of the hierarchy, in a permanent matrix structure—as long, of course, as they were prepared to dispense with the principle of unity of command. A product manager in a given region could report to both an all-product regional division manager and an all-region (worldwide) product division manager. A hybrid structure could emerge, which we can call the *divisionalized adhocracy*, with characteristics of both the configurations from which it derives its name. Its markets are diversified, like all organizations that use the Divisionalized Form, but parts of its environment are more complex and dynamic (in essence, disparate) than others. There is evidence that some multinational firms have moved in this direction, but no evidence yet of a general trend. Nevertheless, **those multinational firms with interdependencies among their different product lines, and facing increasing complexity as well as dynamism in their environment, will feel drawn toward the divisionalized adhocracy hybrid.** For them at least, Adhocracy becomes a natural fourth stage of structural development, after Simple Structure, Machine Bureaucracy, and Divisionalized Form.

The divisionalized adhocracy may also have some relevance for noncommercial organizations that face similar conditions. In a thought-provoking study for UNICEF, the Scandinavian Institutes for Administrative Research (SIAR, 1975) propose such a structure for that United Nations agency. They describe the UNICEF structure at the time of their study as a regional Divisionalized Form but with a tendency toward too much headquarters control. That leads to the vicious circle of one-way communication: The headquarters staff tries to control the regional divisions, which ignore their policies because they are out of touch with the local needs, which leads to further efforts by headquarters to control the divisions, until it comes to dominate the communication channels. In the opinion of the SIAR group, UNICEF required a different structure because "the need for learning and adaptation throughout the organization is so extremely high" (p. 17). Essentially, UNICEF faced the same dilemma as the multinational corporations we just discussed: the concurrent needs to respect regional knowledge and to achieve interregional coordination. That can be resolved in the divisionalized organization not by more standardization and direct supervision from headquarters, which involves a shift of the entire structure toward Machine Bureaucracy, but by more mutual adjustment among divisions, which involves a shift toward Adhocracy. Thus, SIAR proposes what amounts to a divisionalized adhocracy for UNICEF: Considerable power should be delegated to the regions, according to their expertise; the headquarters staff should advise rather than supervise; and an interactive or team structure should be used in the field. The result would be a more organic structure, built around flexible projects carried out by work constellations.

The SIAR report proposes a list of measures to effect the proposed structural change—a list that may, in fact, be practical for any division-alized organization wishing to move toward Adhocracy. Among the rec-ommendations: the elimination of one tier in the divisionalized hierarchy (such as the group vice-president level in the multiple-divisionalized cor-poration) in order to reduce the emphasis on direct supervision; the inte-gration of the planning and programming functions at headquarters, which would work with new knowledge networks; the use of more team-work at headquarters; a reduction in the use of performance control tech-niques; in their place, occasional "extended visits" by a headquarters team, with a broad rather than a functional orientation and led by the chief executive; the institution of matrix structure; the encouragement of profes-sionalism in attitude, type of work, career pattern, and training; the re-orientation of the job of regional director to professional senior rather than administrative supervisor; and the reorientation of internal communication flows to emphasize dialogue, problem solving, and learning rather than reporting, controlling, and explaining.

Frequent product change

A number of organizations are drawn toward Adhocracy because of the dynamic conditions that result from very frequent product change. The extreme case is the *unit producer,* the manufacturing firm that custom-makes each of its products to order, as in the case of the engineering company that produces prototypes. Because each customer order con-stitutes a new project, the organization is encouraged to structure itself as an Operating Adhocracy. Woodward describes such a structure in the unit-production firms she studied—organic and rather decentralized, but with the middle-level development engineers having considerable power.

Similar to the unit producer is the small high-technology firm, such as those surrounding Boston on Route 128. For the most part, these firms do sophisticated project work—design and sometimes manufacturing—under direct contract to the U.S. government or to the larger corporations in industries such as defense, aerospace, and atomic energy. Their work being complex and their environments dynamic, these firms are depen-dent on highly trained experts who work in interdisciplinary project teams.

But these firms are also small and owned by individual entrepreneurs who maintain personal control. (They are able to do so, of course, only because they are as highly trained as their employees.) So the structure emerges as a hybrid between Operating Adhocracy and Simple Structure, which we call the *entrepreneurial adhocracy.*

Another variant of the unit producer is the newspaper or magazine. From the editorial point of view, every product—that is, every issue—is different. Moreover, the environment is typically very dynamic and often rather complex, especially in the case of daily newspapers and news-magazines, which must report a vast world of fast-breaking news with very short deadlines. Moreover, the efforts of all kinds of reporters, photographers, editors, and others must be integrated into a single product. So Adhocracy is called for in the editorial department. But from the point of view of the printing and distribution functions, there is great repetition—thousands, sometimes millions of copies of the same issue. And their environment is extremely stable—the tasks remain unchanged no matter what the content of the issue. So Machine Bureaucracy is called for in these functions. The need for two different structures is, of course, reconciled by truncation. The different functions are kept well separated, with standard outputs serving as the one interface. The Adhocracy editorial department completes its work and then converts it into standardized format—typed copy, page layouts, clipped photographs—which become the inputs to the bureaucratic production process.

Some manufacturers of consumer goods operate in markets so competitive that they must change their products almost continuously. Here again, dynamic conditions, when coupled with some complexity, drive the structure toward the Adhocracy form. An excellent example of what we shall call the *competitive adhocracy* is the pop recording company discussed earlier. Its dramatically short product life cycle and fluid supply of recording talent required extremely fast response based on a great deal of inside knowledge. As the student group that did the study noted, "The product life of a 45 rpm is three months. This is measured from the idea of releasing some song by an artist to the last sale of the single to stores. There is nothing quite so dead as yesterday's number one hit on the hit parade."[4] Other examples of competitive adhocracies are found in the cosmetics, pharmaceuticals, and plastics industries.

It should be noted that it is probably only product competition that leads to this kind of configuration. Competition based on price or marketing is simpler to understand and deal with, and so often can be handled in the Simple Structure or Machine Bureaucracy. In contrast, product competition requires more serious innovation and more complex decision mak-

[4]From a paper submitted to the author in Management Policy 276-661, November 1972, by Alain Berranger and Philip Feldman.

ing, often based on sophisticated research and development activity. So Adhocracy becomes the favored configuration, and of the administrative type. Finance and pricing decisions remain in the more senior work constellations, and product design, development, and marketing decisions are delegated to constellations lower down in the hierarchy (as was the case with the pop recording company).

Youth as a condition of the adhocracy

A number of nonenvironmental conditions are also associated with Adhocracy. One is age—or more exactly, youth—since Adhocracy is not a very stable configuration. It is difficult to keep any structure in that state for long periods of time—to keep behaviors from formalizing and to ensure a steady flow of truly innovative, ad hoc projects. **All kinds of forces drive the Adhocracy to bureaucratize itself as it ages.** On the other side of the coin, according to Hypothesis 1, young organizations tend to be structured organically, since they are still finding their way and also since they are typically eager for innovative, ad hoc projects on which to test themselves. So we can conclude that **the Adhocracy form tends to be associated with youth, with early stages in the development of organizational structures.**

The Operating Adhocracy is particularly prone to a short life. For one thing, it faces a risky market, which can quickly destroy it. Unlike the Professional Bureaucracy or Machine Bureaucracy, with their standardized outputs, the Operating Adhocracy can never be sure where its next project will come from. A downturn in the economy or the loss of a major contract can close it down literally overnight.

But if some Operating Adhocracies have short lives because they fail, others have short lives because they succeed. Success—and aging—encourage a metamorphosis in the Operating Adhocracy, driving it to more stable conditions and more bureaucratic structure. Over time, the successful organization develops a reputation for what it does best. That encourages it to repeat certain projects, in effect to focus its attention on specific contingencies and programs. And this tends to suit its employees, who, growing older themselves, welcome more stability in their work. So the Operating Adhocracy is driven over time toward the Professional Bureaucracy to concentrate on the programs it does best, sometimes even toward the Machine Bureaucracy to exploit a single program or invention. The organization survives, but the configuration dies.

Administrative Adhocracies typically live longer. They, too, feel the pressures to bureaucratize as they age. This leads many to try to stop innovating, or to innovate in stereotyped ways, and thereby to revert to more bureaucratic structure, notably of the machine type. But unlike the Operating Adhocracy, the Administrative Adhocracy typically cannot change its structure while remaining in the same industry. In choosing that industry, it chose a complex, dynamic environment. Stereotyped innovation will eventually destroy the organization. Newspapers and plastics and pharmaceuticals companies—at least those facing severe competition—may have no choice but to structure themselves as Adhocracies.

In recognition of the tendency for organizations to bureaucratize themselves as they age, a variant has emerged—"the organizational equivalent of paper dresses or throw-away tissues" (Toffler, 1970:133)—which might be called the *temporary adhocracy*. It draws together specialists from different organizations to carry out a project, and then it disbands. Temporary adhocracies are becoming common in a great many spheres of modern society: the production group that performs a single play, the election campaign committee that promotes a single candidate, the guerrilla group that overthrows a single government, the Olympic Committee that plans a single Games. A related variant is the *mammoth project adhocracy*, a giant temporary adhocracy that draws on thousands of experts for anywhere from a year to a decade to carry out a single task.

This last variant suggests that size is a less important condition than age for the Adhocracy. Administrative Adhocracies in particular can grow very large indeed. However, Operating Adhocracies tend to be small or middle-sized, constrained by the projects they do, by the number and size of the multidisciplinary teams they can organize, and by their desire to avoid the pressure to bureaucratize that comes from growing large.

Technical system as a condition of the adhocracy

Technical system is another important condition in certain cases of this configuration. Although Operating Adhocracies, like their sister Professional Bureaucracies, tend to have simple, nonregulating technical systems, the case for Administrative Adhocracies is frequently quite the opposite. **Many organizations use the Administrative Adhocracy because their technical systems are sophisticated and perhaps automated as well.**

As described in Hypothesis 7 of Chapter 6, when its technical system is sophisticated, the organization requires an elaborate, highly trained support staff to design or purchase, modify, and maintain it; the organization must give considerable power over its technical decisions to that support staff; and that staff, in turn, must use the liaison devices to coordinate its work. In other words, complex machinery requires specialists who have the knowledge, power, and flexible working arrangements to cope with it. The result is that support staffers emerge as powerful members of the organization, drawing power down from the strategic apex, up from the operating core, and over from the middle line. The organization is drawn to the Administrative Adhocracy configuration.

Automation of a sophisticated technical system evokes even stronger forces in the same direction. As we also saw in Chapter 6, the Machine

Bureaucracy that succeeds in automating its operating core undergoes a dramatic metamorphosis. The problem of motivating uninterested operators disappears, and with it goes the control mentality that permeates its structure; the distinction between line and staff blurs (machines being indifferent to who turns their knobs), which leads to another important reduction in conflict; the technostructure loses its influence, since control is built into the machinery itself by its designers rather than imposed on workers by the rules and standards of the analysts. Overall, the administrative structure becomes more decentralized and organic, emerging as the type we call the *automated adhocracy*.

Automation is common in the process industries, such as petrochemicals and cosmetics (another reason why firms in the latter industry would be drawn toward Adhocracy). That is presumably why Joan Woodward's description of the process producers fits Administrative Adhocracy to a T. But it should be noted that not all process firms use this configuration. Many are, in fact, far from fully automated, and therefore require large operating work forces that draw them toward Machine Bureaucracy. Steel companies, discussed in Chapter 9, are a case in point. Then there are the process producers that, although highly automated in production, exhibit strong Machine Bureaucracy as well as Administrative Adhocracy tendencies in some cases because they require large routine work forces for other operating functions (such as marketing in the oil company with many of its own retail outlets). Finally, there are the automated process producers with such simple environments and technical systems—for example, the small manufacturer of one line of hand creams—that the Simple Structure suffices instead of the Administrative Adhocracy.

Fashion as a condition of the adhocracy

We come now to the power factors. Power itself is not a major condition of the Adhocracy, except to the extent that the support staff of the Machine Bureaucracy is able to take control of certain technical decisions or the operators of the Professional Bureaucracy care to encourage innovation instead of standardization and thereby drive their structure toward Adhocracy. But **fashion most decidedly is a condition of Adhocracy.** Every characteristic of the Adhocracy is very much in vogue today: emphasis on expertise, organic structure, project teams and task forces, decentralization without a single concentration of power, matrix structure, sophisticated and automated technical systems, youth, and environments that are complex and dynamic. Ansoff's enthusiasm is typical of many of today's "future thinkers":

> . . . in the next ten years the concepts of structure and capability are due for a change as revolutionary as the transition from static trenches to mobile warfare. A vast majority of technology used in design or organizations today is based on a Maginot line concept of "permanent" or at best "semi-perma-

nent" structures. If the reasoning in this paper is only half-correct, the trend is toward the concept of flexible task-responsive "mobile warfare" capabilities. (1974:83)

If Simple Structure and Machine Bureaucracy were yesterday's structures, and Professional Bureaucracy and the Divisionalized Form are today's, then Adhocracy is clearly tomorrow's. This is the structure for a population growing ever better educated and more specialized, yet under constant exhortation to adopt the "systems" approach—to view the world as an integrated whole instead of a collection of loosely coupled parts. It is the structure for environments that are becoming more complex and demanding of innovation, and for technical systems becoming more sophisticated and highly automated. It is the only structure now available to those who believe organizations must become at the same time more democratic yet less bureaucratic.

Yet despite our current infatuation with it, Adhocracy is not the structure for all organizations. Like all the other configurations, it too has its place. And that place, as the examples of this chapter make clear, seems to be in the new industries of our age—aerospace, electronics, think-tank consulting, research, advertising, filmmaking, petrochemicals—virtually all the industries that grew up since World War II. Stinchcombe's descendants, should they choose sometime during the twenty-first century to verify his conclusion of 1965 that organizational structure reflects the age of founding of the industry, will no doubt identify Adhocracy as the configuration of the last half of the twentieth century.

Some Issues Associated with Adhocracy

There has been little exploration of the issues associated with Adhocracy, the newest of the five configurations. Simple Structure is so old that its advantages and disadvantages are by now taken for granted. The issues associated with Machine Bureaucracy have been discussed at great length in the literature, especially those concerning alienation and conflict. There has also been quite a bit of discussion of the issues associated with Professional Bureaucracy, and, more recently, of the Divisionalized Form as well. But all these configurations have been around for some time. In contrast, Adhocracy is new. And every new structure, because it solves problems the old ones could not, attracts a dedicated following—one enamored with its advantages and blind to its problems. With this kind of support, time is required to bring its issues into focus—time to live with the structure and learn about its weaknesses as well as its strengths, especially in the case of a configuration as complex as Adhocracy.

Nevertheless, some of the issues associated with Adhocracy are apparent, and three in particular merit attention here: its ambiguities and the reactions of people who must live with them, its inefficiencies, and its propensity to make inappropriate transitions to other configurations.

Human reactions to ambiguity

Many people, especially creative ones, dislike both structural rigidity and concentration of power. That leaves them only one configuration. Adhocracy is the one that is both organic and decentralized. Thus they find it a great place to work. In essence, **Adhocracy is the only configuration for those who believe in more democracy with less bureaucracy.**

But not every structure can be an Adhocracy. The organization's conditions must call for it. Forcing Adhocracy on, say, a simple, stable environment is as unnatural—and therefore as unpleasant for the participants—as forcing Machine Bureaucracy on a complex, dynamic one. Furthermore, not everyone shares the same vision of organizational utopia. As we saw in Chapter 9, there are those who prefer the life of Machine Bureaucracy, a life of stability and well-defined relationships. They, in fact, dislike the relationships of Adhocracy, viewing it as a nice place to visit but no place to spend a career. **Even dedicated members of the Adhocracies periodically exhibit the same low tolerance for its fluidity, confusion, and ambiguity.** "In these situations, all managers some of the time, and many managers all the time, yearn for more definition and structure" (Burns and Stalker, 1966:122–23).

Earlier we discussed two of the common responses Reeser (1969) received when he asked managers in three aerospace companies, "What are some of the human problems of project organization?" Of the other eight responses Reeser reports, six, in fact, relate to structural ambiguities: anxiety related to the eventual phaseout of the projects; confusion of members as to who their boss is, whom to impress to get promoted; low sense of member loyalty owing to frequent transfers between project organizations; a lack of clarity in job definitions, authority relationships, and lines of communication; random and unplanned personal development because of the short time under any one manager; and intense competition for resources, recognition, and rewards.

Reeser's last point raises another major problem of ambiguity, the politicization of the structure. **Coupling its ambiguities with its interdependencies, Adhocracy emerges as the most politicized of the five configurations.** No structure can be more Darwinian than the Adhocracy—more supportive of the fit, as long as they remain fit, and more destructive of the weak. Structures this fluid tend to be highly competitive and at times ruthless—breeding grounds for all kinds of political forces. The French have a graphic expression for this: *un panier de crabes*—a basket of crabs, all clawing at each other to get up, or out. Take, for example, matrix structure: as noted earlier, what it does is establish an adversary system, thereby institutionalizing organizational conflict.

There are conflicts that breed politics in the other configurations, too, as we have noted in each of the last four chapters. But these conflicts are always contained within well-defined ground rules. In the Simple Structure, the politics that do take place are directed at the chief executive. But his close, personal control precludes much of the political activity in the first place; those who do not like the structure simply get out. And in all the bureaucratic configurations, conflicts and politics are focused on well-defined issues—the power of line versus staff or professional versus non-professional, the resistance of workers to the control mentality, the biasing of information sent up to the central headquarters, the ambiguities of pigeonholing, and so on. In the Professional Bureaucracy, for example, highly trained experts with considerable power are naturally predisposed to do battle with each other, most often over territorial imperatives. But at least these battles are guided by professional norms and affiliations. And their incidence is sharply reduced by the fact that the professionals work largely on their own, often with their own clients. Not so in the Adhocracy, where specialists from different professions must work together on multi-disciplinary teams, and where, owing to the organic nature of the structure, the political games that result are played with few rules. Adhocracy requires the specialist to subordinate his individual goals and the standards of his profession to the needs of the group, in spite of the fact that he, like his colleague in the Professional Bureaucracy, remains—potentially at least—a strong individualist.

In bureaucracies—especially of the machine type—management must spend a good deal of time trying to bottle up the conflict. But in the Adhocracy, that must not be done—even if it could be. Such efforts only stifle creativity. **Conflict and aggressiveness are necessary elements in the Adhocracy; management's job is to channel them toward productive ends.**

Problems of efficiency

No structure is better suited to solving complex, ill-structured problems than that of Adhocracy. None can match it for sophisticated innovation. Or, unfortunately, for the costs of that innovation. Adhocracy is simply not an efficient structure. Although it is ideally suited for the one-of-a-kind project, **the Adhocracy is not competent at doing ordinary things.** It is designed for the *extra*ordinary. The bureaucracies are all mass producers; they gain efficiency through standardization. The Adhocracy is a custom producer, unable to standardize and so to be efficient.

The root of its inefficiency is the Adhocracy's high cost of communication. People talk a lot in these structures; that is how they combine their knowledge to develop new ideas. But that takes time, a great deal. Faced with the need to make a decision in the Machine Bureaucracy, someone up above gives an order and that is that. Not so in the Adhocracy. Everyone gets into the act. First are all the managers who must be consulted—functional managers, project managers, liaison managers. Then there are all the specialists who believe their point of view should be represented in the decision. A meeting is called, probably to schedule another meeting, eventually to decide who should participate in the decision. Then those people settle down to the decision process. The problem is defined and redefined, ideas for its solution are generated and debated, alliances build and fall around different solutions, and eventually everyone settles down to hard bargaining about the favored one. Finally, a decision emerges—that in itself is an accomplishment—although it is typically late and will probably be modified later. All this is the cost of having to find a creative solution to a complex, ill-structured problem.

It should be noted, however, that the heavy costs incurred in reaching a decision are partially recuperated in its execution. Widespread participation in decision making ensures widespread support for the decisions made. So the execution stage can be smoother in the Adhocracy than in the Machine Bureaucracy, where resistance by the operators, not party to the decision, is often encountered.

A further source of inefficiency in the Adhocracy is the unbalanced workloads, as mentioned earlier. It is almost impossible to keep the personnel of a project structure—high-priced personnel, it should be noted— busy on a steady basis. In January, the specialists are playing bridge for want of work; in March, they are working overtime with no hope of completing the new project on time.

The dangers of inappropriate transition

Of course, one solution to the problems of ambiguity and inefficiency is to change the structure. Employees no longer able to tolerate the ambiguity and customers fed up with the inefficiency try to drive the structure to a more stable, bureaucratic form.

That is relatively easily done in the Operating Adhocracy, as noted earlier. The organization simply selects the standard programs it does best and goes into the business of doing them. It becomes a Professional Bureaucracy. Or else it uses its creative talent one last time to find a single market niche, and then turns itself into a Machine Bureaucracy to mass-produce in that niche.

But **the transition from Operating Adhocracy into bureaucracy, however easily effected, is not always appropriate.** The organization came into being to solve problems imaginatively, not to apply standards indiscriminately. In many spheres, society has more mass producers than it needs; what it lacks are true problem solvers. It has little need for the laboratory that comes up with a modification of an old design when a new one is called for, the consulting firm ready with a standard technique when the client has a unique problem, the medical or university researcher who sees every new challenge in terms of an old theory. The standard output of bureaucracy will not do when the conditions call for the creativity of Adhocracy.

This seems to describe some of the problems of the television networks. Despite their need to be creative, the networks face one irresistible pressure to bureaucratize: the requirement that they produce on a routine basis, hour after hour, night after night, with never a break. One would think they would tend toward Professional Bureaucracy structures, but Jay's comments on his experiences as a producer for the BBC and other, comparable accounts in the literature suggest strong elements of Machine Bureaucracy. And the results are what one would expect of such structures: stereotyped programming, stale jokes supported by canned laughter, characters in serials that are interchangeable between channels, repetition of the old movies. Interestingly, the two bright spots on TV are the news and the specials, for reasons already suggested in our discussion of Adhocracy. The news department, like the newspaper, faces a truly dynamic environment. The networks can control and therefore stabilize the series, but never the news. Every day is different, and so, therefore, is every program. And the specials really are ad hoc—in this case, by the choice of the networks—and so lend themselves to the creative approach of Adhocracy. But elsewhere the pressures of the routine neutralize creativity, and the result is standardization.

Other organizations face these same dual pressures—to produce routinely yet also be creative. Universities and teaching hospitals must, for example, serve their regular clients yet also produce creative research. Universities sometimes set up research centers to differentiate the research function from teaching activities. These centers enable the professors with the greatest potential for research—often poor teachers—to do it without interruption. In the absence of such differentiation, the organization risks falling into a schizophrenic state, continually wavering between two kinds of structure, never clearly isolating either, to the detriment of both.

The Administrative Adhocracy runs into more serious difficulties when it succumbs to the pressures to bureaucratize. It exists to innovate for itself, in its own industry. The conditions of dynamism and complexity, requiring sophisticated innovation, typically cut across the entire industry. So unlike the Operating Adhocracy, the Administrative Adhocracy cannot often select new clients yet remain in the same industry. And so its conversion to Machine Bureaucracy—the natural transition for the Administrative Adhocracy tired of perpetual change—by destroying the organization's ability to innovate, can eventually destroy the organization itself.

To reiterate a central theme of our discussion throughout this book: **in general, there is no one best structure; in particular, there may be, as long as the design parameters are internally consistent and together with the situational factors form a coherent configuration.** We have delineated five such configurations in this last section of the book; their dimensions are summarized in Table 12–1.

TABLE 12-1. Dimensions of the Five Configurations*

	Simple Structure	Machine Bureaucracy	Professional Bureaucracy	Divisionalized Form	Adhocracy
Key coordinating mechanism	Direct supervision	Standardization of work	Standardization of skills	Standardization of outputs	Mutual adjustment
Key part of organization	Strategic apex	Technostructure	Operating core	Middle line	Support staff (with operating core in Op. Ad.)
Design parameters:					
Specialization of jobs	Little specialization	*Much horizontal and vertical specialization*	*Much horizontal specialization*	Some horizontal and vertical specialization (between divisions and HQ)	*Much horizontal specialization*
Training and indoctrination	Little training and indoctrination	Little training and indoctrination	*Much training and indoctrination*	Some training and indoctrination (of division managers)	Much training
Formalization of behavior, bureaucratic/organic	Little formalization, *organic*	*Much formalization, bureaucratic*	Little formalization, *bureaucratic*	Much formalization (within divisions), bureaucratic	Little formalization, *organic*
Grouping	Usually functional	*Usually functional*	Functional and market	*Market*	*Functional and market*
Unit size	Large	Large at bottom, small elsewhere	Large at bottom, small elsewhere	Large (at top)	*Small throughout*
Planning and control systems	Little planning and control	Action planning	Little planning and control	*Much performance control*	Limited action planning (esp. in Adm. Ad.)
Liaison devices	Few liaison devices	Few liaison devices	Liaison devices in administration	Few liaison devices	*Many liaison devices throughout*
Decentralization	*Centralization*	*Limited horizontal decentralization*	*Horizontal and vertical decentralization*	*Limited vertical decentralization*	*Selective decentralization*
Functioning:					
Strategic apex	All administrative work	Fine-tuning, coordination of functions, conflict resolution	External liaison, conflict resolution	Strategic portfolio, performance control	External liaison, conflict resolution, work balancing, project monitoring
Operating core	Informal work with little discretion	Routine, formalized work with little discretion	Skilled, standardized work with much individual autonomy	Tendency to formalize owing to divisionalization	Truncated (in Adm. Ad.) or merged with administration to do informal project work (in Op. Ad.)

Middle line	Insignificant	Elaborated and differentiated, conflict resolution, staff liaison, support of vertical flows	Controlled by professionals; much mutual adjustment	Formalization of division strategy, managing operations	Extensive but blurred with staff; involved in project work
Technostructure	None	Elaborated to formalize work	Little	Elaborated at HQ for performance control	Small and blurred within middle in project work
Support staff	Small	Often elaborated to reduce uncertainty	Elaborated to support professionals; Mach. Bur. structure	Split between HQ and divisions	Highly elaborated (esp. in Adm. Ad.) but blurred within middle in project work
Flow of authority	Significant from top	Significant throughout	Insignificant (except in support staff)	Significant throughout	Insignificant
Flow of regulated system	Insignificant	Significant throughout	Insignificant (except in support staff)	Significant throughout	Insignificant
Flow of informal communication	Significant	Discouraged	Significant in administration	Some between HQ and divisions	Significant throughout
Work constellations	None	Insignificant, esp. at lower levels	Some in administration	Insignificant	Significant throughout (esp. in Adm. Ad.)
Flow of decision making	Top-down	Top-down	Bottom-up	Differentiated between HQ and divisions	Mixed, all levels
Situational factors:					
Age and size	Typically young and small (first stage)	Typically old and large (second stage)	Varies	Typically old and very large (third stage)	Typically young (Op. Ad.)
Technical system	Simple, not regulating	Regulating but not automated, not sophisticated	Not regulating or sophisticated	Divisible, otherwise typically like Mach. Bur.	Very sophisticated, often automated (in Adm. Ad.); not regulating or sophisticated (in Op. Ad.)
Environment	Simple and dynamic; sometimes hostile	Simple and stable	Complex and stable	Relatively simple and stable; diversified markets (esp. products and services)	Complex and dynamic; sometimes disparate (in Adm. Ad.)
Power	Chief executive control; often owner-managed; not fashionable	Technocratic and sometimes external control; not fashionable	Professional operator control; fashionable	Middle-line control; fashionable (esp. in industry)	Expert control; very fashionable

*Italic type designates key design parameters.

13

BEYOND FIVE

In Chapter 1, I promised to return to the question, "Is five the magic number in the design of organizations?" Of course, by now the reader should have anticipated the answer: Certainly yes, and Certainly no. Five is magic if it enables the organization designer to build more effective organizations. But to believe that the world ends at five is clearly mythical—whether that be five planets, as we have already discovered, or five senses, as we shall no doubt soon find, any more than five configurations of organizational structure and situation.

Thus, I present a concluding chapter in which we go beyond five, in two directions. First we go back to one, and then we go on to six, maybe further. We go back to one by combining our configurations into a single integrated framework, or theory—a system unto themselves. And we go on to six by introducing another configuration, to suggest one last hypothesis on the effective designing of organizations.

The Five Configurations as One System

Do any of these configurations really exist? This is a strange question to raise after so many pages of discussion, filled with illustrations. But it is worth asking, in order to draw a tighter line between the five configurations and the reality they purport to describe.

In one sense, the configurations do not exist at all. After all, they are just words and pictures on pieces of paper, not reality itself. Real organizations are enormously complex, far more so than any of these five configurations on paper. What these constitute is a theory, and every theory necessarily simplifies and therefore distorts the reality. That was why the reader was warned at the outset to proceed under the assumption that every sentence in the last five chapters (including this one) was an overstatement.

But that should not lead to a rejection of the configurations. For the reader's choice is not between theory and reality so much as between alternative theories. No one carries reality around in his head; no head is that big. Rather, we carry around thoughts, impressions, and beliefs about reality, and measures of it we call facts. But all this is useless unless it is ordered in some way, just as a library of books is useless unless the books are catalogued. So, most important, we carry around in our heads comprehensible simplifications—concepts or models or theories—that enable us to catalogue our data and experience. The reader's choice then becomes one of alternative systems of cataloguing—that is, alternative theories.

The reader can trust the theories he builds himself, based on his own experiences, or else he can select from among those offered in books like this one, based on the experiences of the organizations reported in the research (as well as one author's own experiences). Or, more realistically, he selects from among them in building up his own models of reality. His choice of theories is normally based on two criteria: how rich the description is—that is, how powerfully it reflects the reality (or, alternatively, how little it distorts the reality)—and how simple it is to comprehend. The most useful theories are simple when stated yet powerful when applied, like $E = MC^2$.

And so in another sense—at least if I have done my job well—the configurations do indeed exist, in the reader's mind. The mind is where all knowledge exists. The classical principles of structure existed because people believed in them and so made them part of their reality. So, too, the concept of informal structure exists, and of the situational relationships. The five configurations will also exist if they prove to constitute a simple yet powerful theory, more useful in some ways than the others currently available.

To give the theory of the configurations a little push toward that end, this section discusses a number of possible applications of it. First, we discuss it as a set of five pulls acting on almost every organization; second, as a set of five pure types that reflect the structures and situations of many organizations; third, as the basis for describing hybrid structures; and fourth, as the basis for describing transitions from one structure and situation to another. Figure 13–1 seeks to capture the spirit of these four discussions. Symbolically, it shows the five configurations as forming a pentagon, bounding a reality within which real structures and situations can be found.

Each configuration sits at one of the nodes, pulling real organizations toward it. The Simple Structure, the first stage for many organizations, sits at the top. At the next level, on either side of it, are the two bureaucracies, Machine Bureaucracy on the left and Professional Bureaucracy on the right. Down at the third, bottom level are the two most elaborate configurations, the Divisionalized Form on the left and Adhocracy on the right. Some real organizations fall into position close to one node—one of the pure types—and others fall between two or more, as hybrids, perhaps in transition from one pure type to another.

The configurations as a set of basic pulls on the organization

To repeat a point made in Chapter 7, **the configurations represent a set of five forces that pull organizations in five different directions.** These pulls are shown in the pentagon and are listed below:

- First is the pull exercised by the strategic apex to centralize, to coordinate by direct supervision, and so to structure the organization as a Simple Structure.

- Second is the pull exercised by the technostructure, to coordinate by standardization—notably of work processes, the tightest kind—in order to increase its influence, and so to structure the organization as a Machine Bureaucracy.

- Third is the pull exercised by the operators to professionalize, to coordinate by the standardization of skills in order to maximize their autonomy, and so to structure the organization as a Professional Bureaucracy.

- Fourth is the pull exercised by the middle managers to Balkanize, to be given the autonomy to manage their own units, with coordination restricted to the standardization of outputs, and so to structure the organization as a Divisionalized Form.

- Fifth is the pull exercised by the support staff (and by the operators as well, in the Operating Adhocracy), for collaboration (and innovation) in decision making, to coordinate by mutual adjustment, and so to structure the organization as an Adhocracy.

Almost every organization experiences all five of these pulls. Take, for example, the case of the theater company, as described by Goodman and Goodman (1972:104). They note "the sense of ownership expressed by the directors," also their power "to a certain extent [to] shape a play into their own image," to choose the team to perform that play, and even to limit the creative contributions of members of that team. All these constitute pulls toward Simple Structure. Of course, put a number of such directors in the same organization and there emerges a pull toward the Divisionalized Form, where each can maximize his autonomy. One director kept "a detailed book which he made and used in the production of a large-scale musical comedy." That book, of course, constituted a pull toward Machine Bureaucracy. Sometimes, however—say, in experimental theater—the "ability to do detailed planning diminishes," the director being "less firm in knowing what he wants" and cuts and additions being

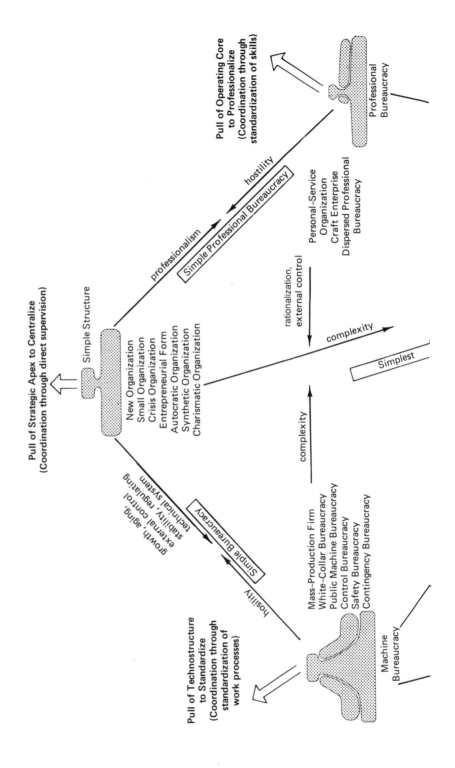

Pull of Strategic Apex to Centralize
(Coordination through direct supervision)

Simple Structure

New Organization
Small Organization
Crisis Organization
Entrepreneurial Form
Autocratic Organization
Synthetic Organization
Charismatic Organization

professionalism

hostility

Simple Professional Bureaucracy

Pull of Operating Core to Professionalize
(Coordination through standardization of skills)

Professional Bureaucracy

Personal–Service Organization
Craft Enterprise
Dispersed Professional Bureaucracy

rationalization, external control

complexity

Simplest

complexity

complexity

Mass–Production Firm
White–Collar Bureaucracy
Public Machine Bureaucracy
Control Bureaucracy
Safety Bureaucracy
Contingency Bureaucracy

Machine Bureaucracy

growth, aging,
external control,
stability, regulating
technical system

Simple Bureaucracy

hostility

Pull of Technostructure to Standardize
(Coordination through standardization of work processes)

286

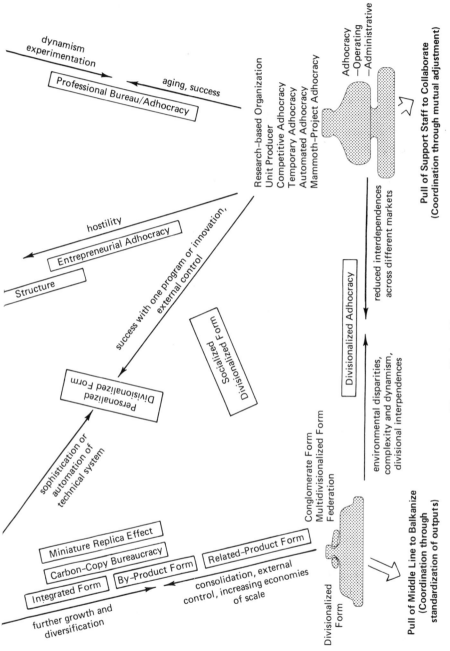

Figure 13-1. The pentagon

287

more frequent. The pull is toward Adhocracy. The members of theater companies are generally professional and work largely on their own: the "choreographer usually creates a dance sequence to fit music that has already been composed and to fit the space available given the existing set design. The three people need never see or speak to each other and are often working in separate locations. . . ." (p. 496). The pull is toward Professional Bureaucracy.

What structure the organization actually designs depends in good part on how strong each of the pulls turns out to be. As we shall see below, when one dominates, we expect the organization to emerge rather close to one of the pure types of configurations, close to one of the nodes on the pentagon. When two or more pulls coexist in relative balance, we expect a "hybrid" of our configurations to emerge. And as one pull displaces another as dominant, we should be able to describe the organization in a state of transition between two of the configurations.

The configurations as a set of pure types

In this second application of the system, **the set of configurations is treated as a framework, or typology of pure types, each one a description of a basic kind of organizational structure and its situation.**

Our examples throughout this section suggest that a great many organizations, being dominated by one of the five pulls, tend to design structures rather close to one of the configurations. No structure matches any one configuration perfectly, but some come remarkably close—like the small entrepreneurial firm controlled by its president in an almost pure Simple Structure, or the conglomerate corporation that fits virtually all the characteristics of the pure Divisionalized Form.

In the preceding five chapters, we have, in fact, labeled and discussed a number of examples and variants of each of the pure types. All these are listed on the pentagon of Figure 13–1, next to their own configurations. Their number gives some justification for treating the configurations as a typology of pure types.

Support for the notion of a pure type comes from the configuration hypothesis, which was introduced in Chapter 6: effective structuring requires an internal consistency among the design parameters. In other words, **the organization is often driven toward one of the configurations in its search for harmony in its structure.** It may experience pulls toward different configurations but it often exhibits a tendency to favor one of them. Better to be consistent and selective than comprehensive and half-hearted. In fact, we saw in the extended configuration hypothesis of Chapter 6, and in a good deal of evidence presented in the preceding five chapters, that this search for harmony and consistency extends to the situational factors as well. The organization with an integrated structure also favors an environment, a technical system, a size, even an age and a power system consistent with that structure.

Thus, we sometimes find that different organizations in the same industry prefer different configurations, depending on which pull (and segment of the industry) they decide to respond to. To return to the theater company, one may prefer Simple Structure because of a strong-willed director (or Divisionalized Form because of many of them), another Machine Bureaucracy because it chooses to produce musicals by the book, another Professional Bureaucracy in order to perfect its performance of Shakespeare year after year, and a fourth Adhocracy to produce experimental plays. Likewise, the restaurant can structure itself like a Simple Structure, Machine Bureaucracy, Divisionalized Form, or Professional Bureaucracy, depending on whether it wishes to remain a small "greasy spoon," grow larger through the serving of simple basic standards, such as steak and lobster, perhaps even through franchises, or develop the gourmet skills of its chefs through the offering of dishes difficult to prepare but highly standardized. (The restaurant structured as an Adhocracy in order to experiment with each dish it served would probably not attract enough clients to survive!)

The configurations as a system for describing structural hybrids

In this third application of the system, **the set of five configurations can be treated as the basis for describing structural hybrids.**

We have seen in our discussion that not all organizations choose to be consistent in designing their structures, at least not as we have described consistency. They use what we call hybrid structures, ones that exhibit characteristics of more than one configuration. **Some of the hybrids we have come across in our discussion seem to be dysfunctional,** indications of organizations that cannot make up their minds or, in wanting the best of more than one world, end up with the worst of many. Consider the organization that no sooner gives its middle managers autonomy subject to performance control, as in the Divisionalized Form, than it takes it away by the proliferation of rules and regulations, as in the Machine Bureaucracy. Or the highly regulated Machine Bureaucracy that believes it can give its workers job autonomy, as in the Professional Bureaucracy, through an overambitious quality-of-working-life program. The resulting confusion can render the organization less effective than the pure type of structure, despite its own inherent limitations.

In some cases, however, organizations have no choice: contradictory situational factors over which they have no control force them to adopt dysfunctional hybrids. We saw evidence of this in school systems, police forces, and other organizations with trained operators, that seem to require Professional Bureaucracy yet are driven by concentrated external control (usually governmental) to take on certain characteristics of Machine Bureaucracy, to the detriment of their performance.

But other hybrids seem perfectly logical, indications of the need to respond to more than one valid force at the same time—like the symphony orchestra, a simple professional bureaucracy, discussed in Chapter 10, that hires highly trained musicians and relies largely on their standardized skills to produce its music yet also requires a strong, sometimes autocratic leader to weld them into a tightly coordinated unit. Or the related-product corporation, discussed in Chapter 11, that needs to divisionalize yet also must coordinate certain critical functions near the strategic apex as in functional Machine Bureaucracy. Or the entrepreneurial adhocracy of Chapter 12, where the chief executive, an expert himself, is able to retain a semblance of central control despite the use of multidisciplinary project teams. All the hybrids discussed in the preceding five chapters are shown on the pentagon of Figure 13–1, each on a line between the two configurations from which it draws its characteristics.

The hybrids of Figure 13–1 all involve two configurations. But nothing precludes a combination of the characteristics of three or more configurations. Thus, one McGill student group described an effective church-run convalescent hospital as being tightly controlled by its chief executive—the students referred to her as the "top nun"—yet having a proliferation of its own work rules, and also being dependent on the skills of its medical staff. Here we have a Simple Structure–Machine Bureaucracy–Professional Bureaucracy hybrid. Another McGill group described a subsidiary of a Japanese trading company as "a divisionalized professional machine adhocracy." (Good thing it wasn't simple!)

Does the existence of such hybrids negate the theory? It is certainly true that the more common the hybrids, the more they should be called pure types and the configurations treated as the hybrids. But the presence of hybrids in a typology does not negate it. There is always gray between black and white. The theory remains useful as long as it helps us to describe a wide variety of structures, even hybrid ones. What matters is not that the theory always matches the reality, but that it helps us to understand the reality. That is its purpose. If we can better describe the Japanese trading company by using terms such as *adhocracy, machine, professional,* and *divisionalized,* then the theory has served us. By identifying its nodes, we are able to map the pentagon.

So far we have talked of the hybrid only as a combination throughout an organization of the design parameters of different configurations. But **there is another kind of hybrid as well, the one that uses different configurations in different parts of the organization.** In this way, there can be consistency in the structure of each part, if not in the overall organization. We saw an example of this in the case of the newspaper, with its editorial function structured like an Adhocracy and its printing function structured like a Machine Bureaucracy.

Is this notion of different structures in different parts of the organization inconsistent with the theme running through the preceding five chapters, that whole organizations can be described in terms of single configurations? Not necessarily. There are forces that drive a great many organizations to favor one configuration overall. But within these organizations, there are always forces that favor different structures in different places. (This point was noted in Chapters 2 to 5, in the concluding discussions of each of the design parameters by part of the organization.) Each part of the organization strives for the structure that is most appropriate to its own particular needs, in the face of pressures to conform to the most appropriate structure for the overall organization, and it ends up with some sort of compromise. NASA's cafeterias are, no doubt, run as bureaucracies, but they may prove to be more organic than most; likewise, General Motors' research laboratories no doubt favor Adhocracy structure, but they would probably prove to be more bureaucratic than those at NASA. And so, even though the theory may be a convenient tool to describe a whole organization in terms of a pure type, that description should always be recognized as a simplification, to be followed by deeper probes into the structure of each of its component parts.

In Chapter 10, for example, of the five configurations, we found that Professional Bureaucracy seemed best to describe the overall structure of the general hospital. But we also noted that the support staff tended to be structured along the lines of a Machine Bureaucracy. And then in Chapter 12, we noted that the research function might best be described as an Adhocracy. Professional Bureaucracy, in effect, really applied to the clinical mission, albeit the most critical one. But even when we look deeply within this mission, we find a range of interdependencies, with resulting variations in the use of the design parameters. Hospitals use incredibly complex structures; to understand them fully, we must look intensively at all their component parts—housekeeping and research and clinical medicine, and obstetrics and radiology and surgery, and plastic surgery and cardiovascular surgery and thoracic surgery.

Again, we conclude by emphasizing that the five configurations are meant to be treated not as five mutually exclusive systems, but as one, as an integrated frame of reference or theory—a pentagon—to guide us in trying to understand and to design complex real-world organizations.

The configurations as a system for describing structural transitions

The system of the configurations can also be used as a basis to help us to understand how and why organizations undertake transitions from one structure to another. Our discussion of the last five chapters has been laced with comments about such transitions—for example, from Simple Structure to Machine Bureaucracy as an organization ages and grows, or from Operating Adhocracy to Professional Bureaucracy as an organization tires of innovation and seeks to settle down. All the factors discussed in these chapters that cause a transition from one configuration to another are recorded on the pentagon, along arrows running between them.

Two major patterns have appeared among these transitions, both related to stages in the structural development of organizations. The first pattern applies to organizations that begin in simple environments; it flows around the left side of the pentagon starting at the top. Most organizations begin their lives with something close to the Simple Structure. As they age and grow, and perhaps come under external control, they tend to formalize their behaviors and eventually make a first transition toward Machine Bureaucracy. When these organizations continue to grow, they eventually tend to diversify and later may begin a second structural transition, toward the Divisionalized Form. They may stop along the way, with one of the intermediate, hybrid forms—such as the by-product or related-product form—or else go all the way to the pure Divisionalized Form. But as we noted in Chapter 11, this may prove to be an unstable structure, and pressures may arise for another transition. In the recognition of divisional interdependencies, the organization may consolidate back toward Machine Bureaucracy or else establish a new hybrid on the way to Adhocracy.

Of course, a number of other forces can intervene to change this sequence. Should the environment of the new organization become complex or its technical system sophisticated, it will find itself drawn toward Adhocracy instead of Machine Bureaucracy. Likewise, should the organization with a structure like Machine Bureaucracy find itself facing more complexity and less stability, perhaps owing to product competition or the need to use a more sophisticated or even automated technical system, it, too, will tend to shift toward Adhocracy. And should any of the later-stage organizations suddenly find themselves with a hostile environment, they will tend to revert back toward Simple Structure temporarily. Should external control instead become a strong force, the transition will be made back toward Machine Bureaucracy.

The second pattern among the transitions applies to organizations that are born in complex environments. This pattern begins at the bottom right side of the pentagon and then moves up and to the left. In this case, organizations adopt Adhocracy structures soon after birth, eager to develop innovative solutions to wide ranges of contingencies. Sometimes they remain there, perhaps locked in complex, dynamic environments. But many wish to escape, and some in fact are able to. As they age, these organizations become more conservative. In their search for stability, they begin a transition to bureaucracy. Some concentrate on a few contingencies at which they can become expert, and structure themselves like Professional Bureaucracies. Others focus on single, simple contingencies and shift toward Machine Bureaucracy.

Of course, some organizations also begin early with Professional Bureaucracy, imitating the structure of other established professional organizations. They often maintain these structures throughout their lives, unless rationalization of the professional tasks or external control eventually drives them toward Machine Bureaucracy, or the desire for more experimentation on the part of their professional operators, perhaps a reflection of a new dynamism in the environment, drives them toward Adhocracy.

It should be noted that **structural transitions often lag the new conditions that evoke them.** Structural change is always difficult, necessitating major rearrangements in established patterns of behavior. So there is a tendency to resist it. Such resistance, in fact, explains many of the dysfunctions found in structures—as in the case of the entrepreneur who hangs on to a Simple Structure even though his organization has grown too large for it, or the organization that continues to formalize even though its environment, having grown complex and dynamic, calls for a structure closer to Adhocracy. Their structures may be internally consistent, but they have outlived the conditions that supported them.

As the need for structural change is finally recognized, the organization begins its transition, perhaps gradually to soften the blow. We saw this in the case of the Machine Bureaucracy that diversifies in steps, passing through the by-product and related-product hybrids on its way to the pure Divisionalized Form. But some organizations never complete the transition; they remain in an intermediate, hybrid state because they experience contradictory forces—new ones calling for change, old ones for retention of the current structure. Thus, many corporations remain permanently in the by-product or related-product hybrid: they have diversified, but interdependencies remain among their product lines. But when the forces calling for change are unequivocal, the transition is probably best effected quickly and decisively. Wavering between two configurations—the old, established one no longer appropriate and the new, uncertain one now necessary—leads to a kind of organizational schizophrenia that may be the most damaging state of all.

To conclude, we have seen in this discussion a number of applications of our five configurations as a single system or theory. Together they help us to understand how organizations can be designed for effectiveness. But neither they nor the pentagon that represents them as a system completely bounds our reality—not only of possible organizational designs but also of the means toward organizational effectiveness.

To Six . . . and Beyond

Is there a sixth configuration? Well, the rainbow still has only five colors.[1] But the planets turned out to number more than five. We even seem to be

[1]In fact, various sources I consulted referred to five, six, and seven colors. I even tried to count, but there was considerable ambiguity in the sample of one I managed to collect. In any event, the rainbow almost certainly has the same number of colors it always did.

on the verge of recognizing that sixth sense. So why not a sixth configuration? As long, of course, as it maintains the harmony of our theory: it must have its own unique coordinating mechanism, and a new, sixth part of the organization must dominate it.

We do have a candidate for that sixth configuration—one, in fact, that appeared, like the others, repeatedly in this book. It came up in socialization and indoctrination in Chapter 2, then somehow got lost within Professional Bureaucracy in Chapter 10; it was passed over quickly in the mention in Chapter 5 of the democracy of the volunteer organization; it was hinted at in the mentions of loyalty and organizational identification in various places; one of its founding characteristics—charismatic leadership—was discussed under Simple Structure in Chapter 8. Moreover, its work is often simple and routine, as in Machine Bureaucracy, its members often function in quasi-autonomous cells or enclaves, as in the Divisionalized Form, and they are prepared to cooperate with each other like the members of the Adhocracy. A composite of all five configurations is obviously a signal to introduce a sixth.

The *Missionary* configuration has its own key coordinating mechanism—socialization, or, if you like, the *standardization of norms*—and a corresponding main design parameter, *indoctrination*, as well as a sixth and key part of the organization, *ideology*. Indeed, ideology is a living (if not technically animate) part of every organization, at least a part evident to those with that elusive sixth sense. The perceptive visitor "senses" it immediately. Ideology—here referring to the system of beliefs about the organization itself, not those of the society that surrounds it—represents a sixth important force on every organization, toward a sense of mission: the pull to evangelize on behalf of the organization. (Hence the ideology can be pictured as a halo that surrounds our entire logo, and the pull to evangelize as arrows emanating radially from this halo.) Usually this is one pull among many, in some cases strong enough to overlay missionary characteristics on what would otherwise have been something close to one of the other pure configurations. More often, perhaps, in today's organizations, the pull of ideology is lost in the stronger pulls to standardize, Balkanize, and so on. But the pull to evangelize can dominate too, giving rise to a relatively pure form of the Missionary configuration.

The pure Missionary is built around an inspiring mission—to change society in some way, or to change the organization's own members, or just to provide them with a unique experience—and an accompanying set of beliefs and norms. In this latter respect, the Missionary is a form of bureaucracy, since it coordinates based on the *standardization* of norms. In that sense, it too is inflexible and nonadaptive: the mission has to be distinctive and inspiring, but neither it nor the set of norms that surround it—"the word," so to speak—can be changed. Indeed, some Missionaries are intent on changing all organizations except themselves!

In other respects, however, the Missionary is very different from our other forms of bureaucracy. Above all, it is very loosely structured. Once its new members are duly socialized and indoctrinated, establishing their undivided loyalty, they can be trusted to perform their work free of all the controls of conventional bureaucracy. In other words, "normative" control is more than sufficient to achieve most of the needed coordination. Indeed, such loyalty can be maintained only by trusting all the members equally, which necessitates dispensing with these controls. This also requires a simple mission and a simple technical system, both free of the need for expert skills and all the status differences that accompany them.

From these basic features stem virtually all the other characteristics of the pure Missionary. A loose division of labor exists throughout, with job rotation in place of job specialization, and minimal or even no distinction between manager and operator or between line and staff. The organization achieves the purest form of decentralization, with no privileged group at all (making this the closest configuration to the democratic ideal, although strong, charismatic leadership—and Simple Structure—had to exist as a prior condition to create the ideology in the first place). Grouping is on the basis of market (that is, mission) in one relatively small unit. Should the organization grow larger, it will tend to keep dividing itself into small units (or *enclaves*), each autonomous except for its sharing of the common ideology. That is because personal contact is the only way to maintain the strong ideology.

Aside from these structural characteristics, the pure Missionary tends to exhibit an absence of others: hardly any direct supervision or standardization of work or outputs or skills, hence minimal hierarchy, no technostructure, barely any middle line, and a virtual absence of formalization, outside training, action planning, and performance control. Whatever mutual adjustment is needed to reinforce the standardization of norms can be achieved informally, with little need for the semiformal liaison devices. In other words, here we have a configuration of the design parameters (and of the situational factors) no less consistent than any of the others—and, in the literal sense, far more harmonious.[2]

We can obviously find something close to the pure Missionary configuration in volunteer organizations with strong systems of beliefs—traditional Israeli kibbutzim, ideological religious movements and sects, revolutionary political parties, groups such as Alcoholics Anonymous, and so on. But Missionary characteristics appear in more conventional organizations, too, when they develop their own powerful and unique ideologies—as in the highly idealistic small-town university, or the manufacturing firm

---

[2]The description of the Missionary configuration is developed more fully in my book, *Power In and Around Organizations* (Englewood Cliffs, N.J.: Prentice-Hall, 1983). So too is another configuration, the Political Arena. But that is another story.

whose employees thoroughly believe in its unique, carefully crafted products.

Indeed, the current interest in the organization of Japanese enterprise revolves around its essentially Missionary characteristics, which stand in sharp contrast to the Machine Bureaucracies of the West. The West has never had an era of the Missionary, in which that configuration was in fashion. But perhaps our descendants, in their wish to escape from instability and impersonal relationships in their "post-adhocratic" age, will turn increasingly toward ideology and the Missionary configuration in the structuring of their organizations.

One last point. Why introduce a sixth configuration at this point in our discussion? For its own sake, to be sure, since it is important in the effective structuring of organizations and seems destined to become increasingly so. Our pentagon should really be considered a hexagon. But for another reason, too: because the reader should be left to question one major premise of this book. Throughout, we have implied that the effective structuring of organizations is a kind of jigsaw puzzle. "Here are the pieces—five parts of the organization, five coordinating mechanisms, nine design parameters, four sets of situational factors. Now let's see how they fit together. Lo and behold, there turn out to be five ways. To design an effective organization, you should select one of these five images. Or at least put together a logical composite of the five of them. You define your situation and then slot right into the pigeonholes (just as the Professional Bureaucracy does with its clients)."

In fact, this makes good sense for many organizations (as it does for most of the clients of Professional Bureaucracies). But not all. Some need to break away from the standard solutions (as must the clients who have unique problems, and so had better find an Adhocracy instead). These organizations must, in other words, create their own configurations—play "Lego" with the pieces instead of jigsaw puzzle—building new, unthought-of, yet equally consistent structures. Thus, we offer a final hypothesis of organizational effectiveness, one that, while compatible with the calls of the others for congruence and consistency, transcends them. We call it the *creation* hypothesis: **effective structuring sometimes requires the creation of a new configuration, an original yet consistent combination of the design parameters and the situational factors.** Not every organization can create a whole new structural form. But some, to be truly effective, must. That is why those who possess real magic think beyond five.

And so it should be told that one day in her aging years, when Ms. Raku came down from her fifty-fifth story office to preside at the ground-breaking ceremony for Ceramico's largest-ever factory, she slipped on her shovel and fell in the mud. Her sense of revulsion at having dirtied her dress was suddenly replaced by one of profound nostalgia, for she realized that this was her first real contact with the earth since her days in the studio. There came the sudden revelation that making pots was more important than making money. And so the organization took on a new mission—the hand-making of beautiful yet functional pots—and it developed a new structure to reflect its new ideology. As her last act as president, Ms. Raku changed the name of the organization one last time—to Potters of the Earth.

BIBLIOGRAPHY[1]

ACKERMAN, R. W., *The Social Challenge to Business*. Cambridge, Mass.: Harvard University Press, 1975.

ANSOFF, H. I., *Corporate Structure: Present and Future*. Working paper, European Institute for Advanced Studies in Management. Brussels, Belgium, 1974.

BECKER, S. W., AND G. GORDON, "An Entrepreneurial Theory of Formal Organizations; Part I: Patterns of Formal Organizations," *Administrative Science Quarterly*, 1966–67, pp. 315–44.

BENNETT, R. C., *General Motors (F): Organizing a Corporate Purchase Agreement*. Case study, copyright by the President and Fellows of Harvard College. Cambridge, Mass.: Harvard Business School, 1977.

BENNIS, W. G., "The Coming Death of Bureaucracy," *Think Magazine*, November–December 1966, pp. 30–35.

———, AND P. L. SLATER, *The Temporary Society*. New York: Harper & Row, 1964.

BEYER, J. M., AND T. M. LODAHL, "A Comparative Study of Patterns of Influence in United States and English Universities," *Administrative Science Quarterly*, 1976, pp. 104–29.

BIDWELL, C. E., "The School as a Formal Organization," Chapter 23 in J. G. March, ed., *The Handbook of Organizations*. Chicago, Ill.: Rand McNally, 1965.

BLAU, P. M., "The Hierarchy of Authority in Organizations," *American Journal of Sociology*, 1967–68, pp. 453–67.

———, AND P. A. SCHOENHERR, *The Structure of Organizations*. New York: Basic Books, 1971.

BOWER, J. L., "Planning within the Firm," *The American Economic Review*, 1970, pp. 186–94.

BRAVERMAN, H., *Labor and Monopoly Capital: The Degradation of Work in the Twentieth Century*. New York: Monthly Review Press, 1974.

[1]This bibliography only contains works referenced in this book. A full bibliography on the subject may be found in *The Structuring of Organizations* by Henry Mintzberg (1979: Prentice-Hall).

BURNS, T., "Mechanistic and Organismic Structures," in D. S. Pugh, ed., *Organization Theory.* New York: Penguin, 1971.

_____, AND G. M. STALKER, *The Management of Innovation,* 2nd ed. London: Tavistock, 1966.

CHANDLER, A. D., *Strategy and Structure.* Cambridge, Mass.: The M.I.T. Press, 1962.

CHANDLER, M. K., AND L. R. SAYLES, *Managing Large Systems.* New York: Harper & Row, 1971.

CHARNS, M. P., "Breaking the Tradition Barrier: Managing Integration in Health Care Facilities," *Health Care Management Review,* Winter 1976, pp. 55–67.

CROZIER, M., *The Bureaucratic Phenomenon,* Eng. trans. Chicago: University of Chicago Press, 1964.

EMERY, F. E., "Democratization of the Work Place: A Historical Review of Studies," *International Studies of Management and Organization,* 1971, pp. 181–201.

FAYOL, H., *General and Industrial Management.* New York: Pitman, 1949. First published in French in 1916.

FELD, M. D., "Information and Authority: The Structure of Military Organization," *American Sociological Review,* 1959, pp. 15–22.

FIEDLER, F. E., "The Contingency Model: A Theory of Leadership Effectiveness," in H. Proshansky and B. Seidenberg, eds., *Basic Studies in Social Psychology.* New York: Holt, Rinehart & Winston, 1966.

FRANK, A. G., "Goal Ambiguity and Conflicting Standards: An Approach to the Study of Organization," *Human Organization,* Winter 1958–59, pp. 8–13.

FRANKO, L. G., "The Move toward a Multidivisional Structure in European Organizations," *Administrative Science Quarterly,* 1974, pp. 493–506.

GALBRAITH, J. K., *The New Industrial State.* Boston: Houghton Mifflin, 1967.

GALBRAITH, J. R., *Designing Complex Organizations.* Reading, Mass.: Addison-Wesley, 1973.

_____, "Matrix Organization Designs," *Business Horizons,* February 1971, pp. 29–40.

GERTH, H. H., AND C. W. MILLS, EDS., *From Max Weber: Essays in Sociology.* New York: Oxford University Press, 1958.

GOODMAN, L. P., AND R. A. GOODMAN, "Theater as a Temporary System," *Management Review,* Winter 1972, pp. 103–8.

GOODMAN, R. A., AND L. P. GOODMAN, "Some Management Issues in Temporary Systems: A Study of Professional Development and Manpower—Theater Case," *Administrative Science Quarterly,* 1976, pp. 494–501.

GOSSELIN, R., *A Study of the Interdependence of Medical Specialists in Quebec Teaching Hospitals.* Ph.D. thesis, Faculty of Management, McGill University, Montreal, 1978.

GUETZKOW, H., AND H. A. SIMON, "The Impact of Certain Communication Nets upon Organization and Performance in Task-Oriented Groups," *Management Science,* 1954–55, pp. 233–50.

HAIRE, M., *Psychology in Management.* New York: McGraw-Hill, 1964.

HATVANY, N. G., "Review of 'A Profile of Tomorrow's Police Officer and His Organization' by Victor Cizanckas," in A. M. Jaeger, ed., *Seminars on Organizations.* Stanford, Calif.: Stanford University, Winter and Spring 1976, pp. 72–74.

HERZBERG, F., "One More Time: How Do You Motivate Employees?" *Harvard Business Review,* January–Feburary 1968, pp. 53–62.

HICKSON, D. J., "A Convergence in Organization Theory," *Administrative Science Quarterly,* 1966–67, pp. 224–37.

HOLDEN, P. E., C. A. PEDERSON, AND G. E. GERMANE, *Top Management.* New York: McGraw-Hill, 1968.

HUNT, R. G., "Technology and Organization," *Academy of Management Journal,* 1970, pp. 235–52.

JAY, A., *Management and Machiavelli.* New York, Penguin Books, 1970.

KAUFMAN, H., AND D. SEIDMAN, "The Morphology of Organization," *Administrative Science Quarterly,* 1970, pp. 439–45.

KHANDWALLA, P. N., "Effect of Competition on the Structure of Top Management Control," *Academy of Management Journal,* 1973a, pp. 285–95.

———, "Mass Output Orientation of Operations Technology and Organizational Structure," *Administrative Science Quarterly,* 1974, pp. 74–97.

———, *Report on the Influence of the Techno-Economic Environment on Firms' Organization.* Report of research findings presented to participating corporations in a study of organizational structure, McGill University, Montreal, 1971.

———, "Viable and Effective Organizational Designs of Firms," *Academy of Management Journal,* 1973b, pp. 481–95.

KNIGHT, K., "Matrix Organization: A Review," *The Journal of Management Studies,* 1976, pp. 111–30.

KOCHEN, M., AND K. W. DEUTSCH, "Decentralization by Function and Location," *Management Science,* 1973, pp. 841–55.

KOVER, A. J., "Reorganization in an Advertising Agency: A Case Study of a Decrease in Integration," *Human Organization,* 1963–64, pp. 252–59.

LAWRENCE, P. R., AND J. W. LORSCH, *Organization and Environment.* Homewood, Ill.: Richard D. Irwin, 1967.

LITZINGER, W., A. MAYRINAC, AND J. WAGLE, "The Manned Spacecraft Center in Houston: The Practice of Matrix Management," *International Review of Administrative Sciences,* 1970, pp. 1–8.

LORSCH, J. W., AND S. A. ALLEN III, *Managing Diversity and Interdependence.* Cambridge, Mass.: Division of Research, Graduate School of Business Administration, Harvard University, 1973.

MASLOW, A. H., *Motivation and Personality.* New York: Harper & Row, 1954.

MELCHER, A. J., *Structure and Process of Organizations: A Systems Approach.* Englewood Cliffs, N.J.: Prentice-Hall, 1976.

MILLER, E. J., "Technology, Territory and Time: The Internal Differentiation of Complex Production Systems," *Human Relations*, 1959, pp. 243–72.

MINTZBERG, H., *The Nature of Managerial Work*. New York: Harper & Row, 1973a.

_____, "Strategy-Making in Three Modes," *California Management Review*, Winter 1973b, pp. 44–53.

_____, *The Structure of Organizations*. Englewood Cliffs, N.J.: Prentice-Hall, 1979.

MONTAGNA, P. D., "Professionalization and Bureaucratization in Large Professional Organizations," *The American Journal of Sociology*, 1968, pp. 138–45.

MOYER, R. C., "Berle and Means Revisited: The Conglomerate Merger," *Business and Society*, Spring 1970, pp. 20–29.

PATERSON, T. T., *Management Theory*. London: Business Publications Ltd., 1969.

PERROW, C., "Is Business Really Changing?" *Organizational Dynamics*, Summer 1974, pp. 31–44.

_____, *Organizational Analysis: A Sociological Review*. Belmont, Calif.: Wadsworth, 1970.

PFIFFNER, J. M., AND F. SHERWOOD, *Administrative Organization*. Englewood Cliffs, N.J.: Prentice-Hall, 1960.

PUGH, D. S., D. J. HICKSON, C. R. HININGS, K. M. MACDONALD, C. TURNER, AND T. LUPTON, "A Conceptual Scheme for Organizational Analysis," *Administrative Science Quarterly*, 1963–64, pp. 289–315.

REESER, C., "Some Potential Human Problems of the Project Form of Organization," *Academy of Management Journal*, 1969, pp. 459–67.

RUMELT, R. P., *Strategy, Structure, and Economic Performance*. Cambridge, Mass.: Division of Research, Graduate School of Business Administration, Harvard University, 1974.

SAYLES, L. R., "Matrix Organization: The Structure with a Future," *Organizational Dynamics*, Autumn 1976, pp. 2–17.

SCHEIN, E. H., "Organizational Socialization and the Profession of Management," *Industrial Management Review*, Winter 1968, pp. 1–16.

SCOTT, B. R., "The Industrial State: Old Myths and New Realities," *Harvard Business Review*, March–April 1973, pp. 133–48.

_____, *Stages of Corporate Development, Part I*. Working paper, Harvard Business School, 14-371-294; BP993, 1971.

SIAR, *Management Survey of UNICEF*. Stockholm: Scandinavian Institutes for Administrative Research, 1975.

SIMON, H. A., *Administrative Behavior*, 2nd ed. New York: Macmillan, 1957.

_____, "The Future of Information Processing Technology," *Management Science*, 1968, pp. 619–24.

_____, *The New Science of Management Decision*, rev. ed. Englewood Cliffs, N.J.: Prentice-Hall, 1977.

_____, *The Sciences of the Artificial*. Cambridge, Mass.: The M.I.T. Press, 1969.

SLOAN, A. P., *My Years at General Motors*. New York: Doubleday, 1963.

SMITH, A., *The Wealth of Nations*. London: Dent, 1910.

SPENCER, F. C., "Deductive Reasoning in the Lifelong Continuing Education of a Cardiovascular Surgeon," *Archives of Surgery*, 1976, pp. 1177–83.

STARBUCK, W. H., "Organizational Growth and Development," Chapter 11 in J. G. March, ed., *Handbook of Organizations*. Chicago, Ill.: Rand McNally, 1965.

STINCHCOMBE, A. L., "Social Structure and Organizations," Chapter 4 in J. G. March, ed., *Handbook of Organizations*. Chicago, Ill.: Rand McNally, 1965.

STRAUSS, G., "Tactics of Lateral Relationship: The Purchasing Agent," *Administrative Science Quarterly*, 1962–63, pp. 161–86.

_____, AND R. ROSENSTEIN, "Worker Participation: Critical View," *Industrial Relations*, 1970, pp. 197–214.

TAYLOR, F. W., *Scientific Management*. New York: Harper & Row, 1947. First published in 1911.

TERKEL, S., *Working*. New York: Pantheon, 1972, and Wildwood House, 1975.

THOMPSON, J. D., *Organizations in Action*. New York: McGraw-Hill, 1967.

THOMPSON, V. A., *Modern Organizations*. New York: Knopf, 1961.

TOFFLER, A., *Future Shock*. New York: Bantam Books, 1970.

TRIST, E. L., AND K. W. BAMFORTH, "Some Social and Psychological Consequences of the Long-Wall Method of Coal-Getting," *Human Relations*, 1951, pp. 3–38.

UDY, S. H., JR., *Organization of Work*. New Haven, Conn.: HRAF Press, 1959.

URWICK, L. F., "The Manager's Span of Control," *Harvard Business Reivew*, May–June 1956, pp. 39–47.

WEICK, K. E., "Educational Organizations as Loosely Coupled Systems," *Administrative Science Quarterly*, 1976, pp. 1–19.

WHISTLER, T., "Organizational Research and the Strategist." Speech presented at conference on "Strategy and Structure," Stanford University, December 1975.

WILENSKY, H. L., *Organizational Intelligence*. New York: Basic Books, 1967.

WILLIAMSON, O. E., *Markets and Hierarchies: Analysis and Antitrust Implications*. New York: Free Press, 1975.

WOODWARD, J., *Industrial Organization: Theory and Practice*. London: Oxford University Press, 1965.

WORTHY, J. C., *Big Business and Free Men*. New York: Harper & Row, 1959.

_____, "Organizational Structure and Employee Morale," *American Sociological Review*, 1950, pp. 169–79.

WRIGLEY, L., *Diversification and Divisional Autonomy*. D.B.A. thesis, Harvard Business School, 1970.

INDEX

309